Testing Business Ideas

Published by John Wiley & Sons, Inc., Hoboken, New Jersey.
Published simultaneously in Canada.

For general information on our other products and services or for technical support, please contact our Customer Care Department within the United States at (800) 762-2974, outside the United States at (317) 572-3993 or fax (317) 572-4002.

Wiley publishes in a variety of print and electronic formats and by print-on-demand. Some material included with standard print versions of this book may not be included in e-books or in print-on-demand. If this book refers to media such as a CD or DVD that is not included in the version you purchased, you may download this material at http://booksupport.wiley.com. For more information about Wiley products, visit www.wiley.com.

ISBN 9781119551447 (Paperback)
ISBN 9781119551423 (ePDF)
ISBN 9781119551416 (ePub)

Cover Design and Front Cover Illustration: © Alan Smith
Back Cover Illustrations by Owen D. Pomery

V10014284_092719

You're holding a field guide for rapid experimentation.
Use the 44 experiments inside to find your path to scale.
Systematically win big with small bets by...

Testing
Business
Ideas

strategyzer.com/test

WRITTEN BY

David J. Bland
Alex Osterwalder

DESIGNED BY

Alan Smith
Trish Papadakos

WILEY

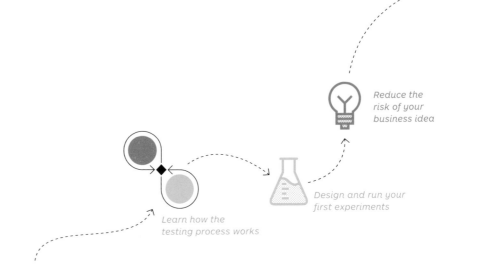

Reduce the
risk of your
business idea

Design and run your
first experiments

Learn how the
testing process works

This book will help you Start Testing Business Ideas

You are relatively new to the concept of Testing Business Ideas. Maybe you've read the leading books in the domain by Steve Blank and Eric Ries, maybe you haven't. However, you do know that you want to get started. You are eager to test your ideas.

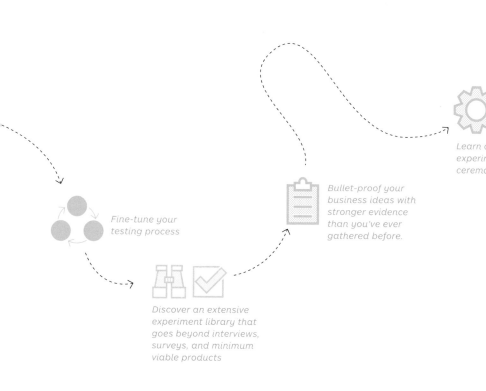

Fine-tune your testing process

Discover an extensive experiment library that goes beyond interviews, surveys, and minimum viable products

Bullet-proof your business ideas with stronger evidence than you've ever gathered before.

Learn about experimentation ceremonies.

Be able to share an extensive testing library with all your teams.

Reduce risk and uncertainty of new ideas across your organization.

Boost your Testing Skills

You are very familiar with the process of Testing Business Ideas. You have read all of the books that cover the topic. You have run several projects and built minimum viable products. Now you want to up your game and boost your testing skills.

Scale Testing in Your Organization

You are tasked with systematizing and scaling testing activities in your organization. You are experienced with the topic and are looking for state-of-the-art practical thinking to bring to teams throughout your organization.

This book was made for **Corporate Innovators**, **Startup Entrepreneurs**, and **Solopreneurs**.

Which best describes you?

☐ **Corporate Innovator** who is challenging the status quo and who is building new business ventures within the constraints of a large organization.

☐ **Startup Entrepreneur** who wants to test the building blocks of your business model to avoid wasting the time, energy, and money of the team, cofounders, and investors.

☐ **Solopreneur** who has a side hustle or an idea that isn't quite yet a business.

Which of the following resonates with you?

- ☐ I am seeking to find new ways to experiment, instead of always relying on focus groups, interviews, and surveys.

- ☐ I want to succeed at creating new growth but don't want to accidentally damage my company's brand in the testing process.

- ☐ I understand that to be truly disruptive, I need a dedicated team who owns the work and is capable of creating their own evidence.

- ☐ I know the perils of prematurely scaling a company that isn't quite ready yet, so I want to test my business model to produce evidence that shows I am on the right track.

- ☐ I know that I need to allocate limited resources wisely and make decisions based on strong evidence.

- ☐ I want to fall asleep at night knowing we've spent our frantic day working on the most important things that matter to our startup's success.

- ☐ I am mindful that we need to show evidence of progress to justify current and future investment rounds.

- ☐ I don't have the resources of a funded startup, let alone a corporation.

- ☐ I haven't necessarily tried any of this before, so I want to make these late nights and weekends worth it.

- ☐ I eventually want to devote all of my time to this idea, but it all seems so risky. In order to make the leap, I'll need the evidence that I'm onto something big.

- ☐ I have read a few books on entrepreneurship, but need guidance on how to test my ideas and what types of experiments to run.

How to Get from a Good Idea to a Validated Business

Too many entrepreneurs and innovators execute ideas prematurely because they look great in presentations, make excellent sense in the spreadsheet, and look irresistible in the business plan... only to learn later that their vision turned out to be a hallucination.

Don't make the mistake of executing business ideas without evidence: test your ideas thoroughly, regardless of how great they may seem in theory.

Idea

Search & Testing

Execution

Business

Navigate the Experiment Library in This Book to Make Your Ideas Bulletproof

Testing is the activity of reducing the risk of pursuing ideas that look good in theory, but won't work in reality. You test ideas by conducting rapid experiments that allow you to learn and adapt.

This book outlines the most extensive testing library on the market to help you make your ideas bulletproof with evidence. Test extensively to avoid wasting time, energy, and resources on ideas that won't work.

The entrepreneur's and innovator's #1 task is to reduce risk and uncertainty.

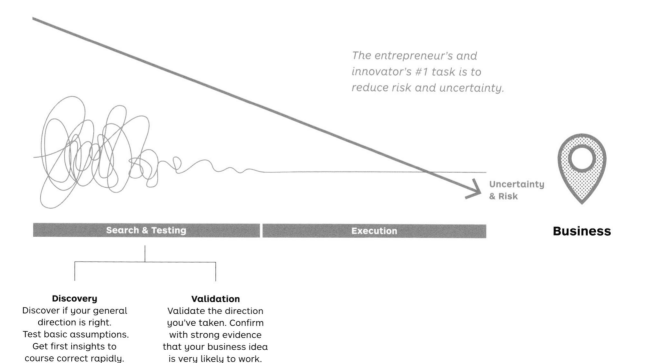

Idea

Search & Testing

Execution

Uncertainty & Risk

Business

Discovery
Discover if your general direction is right. Test basic assumptions. Get first insights to course correct rapidly.

Validation
Validate the direction you've taken. Confirm with strong evidence that your business idea is very likely to work.

The Iterative Process

Business Concept Design

Design is the activity of turning vague ideas, market insights, and evidence into concrete value propositions and solid business models. Good design involves the use of strong business model patterns to maximize returns and compete beyond product, price, and technology.

The risk is that a business can't get access to key resources (technology, IP, brand, etc.), can't develop capabilities to perform key activities, or can't find key partners to build and scale the value proposition.

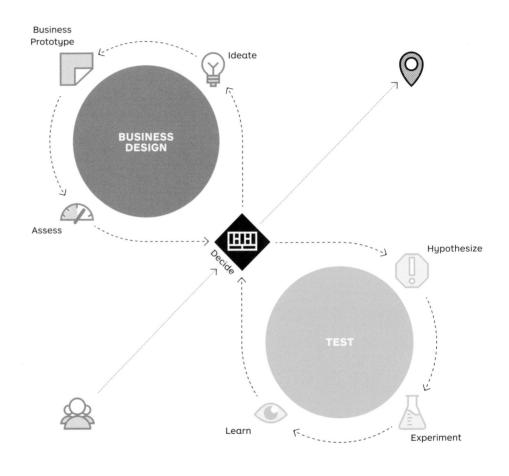

Business Prototype

Ideate

BUSINESS DESIGN

Assess

Decide

Hypothesize

TEST

Learn

Experiment

 Idea  **Business Model** 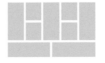 **Value Proposition**

Testing and reducing risk

To test a big business idea you break it down into smaller chunks of testable hypotheses. These hypotheses cover three types of risk. First, that customers aren't interested in your idea (desirability).

Second, that you can't build and deliver your idea (feasibility). Third, that you can't earn enough money from your idea (viability).

You test your most important hypotheses with appropriate experiments. Each experiment generates evidence and insights that allow you to learn and decide. Based on the evidence and your insights you either adapt your idea, if you learn you were on the wrong path, or continue testing other aspects of your idea, if the evidence supports your direction.

 Key Hypotheses   **Experiments**   **Key Insights** **=** Reducing Uncertainty & Risk

Desirability risk
Customers aren't interested

The risk is that the market a business is targeting is too small; that too few customers want the value proposition; or that the company can't reach, acquire, and retain targeted customers.

Feasibility risk
We can't build and deliver

The risk is that a business can't get access to key resources (technology, IP, brand, etc.), can't develop capabilities to perform key activities, or can't find key partners to build and scale the value proposition.

Viability risk
We can't earn enough money

The risk is that a business can't generate successful revenue streams, that customers are unwilling to pay (enough), or that the costs are too high to make a sustainable profit.

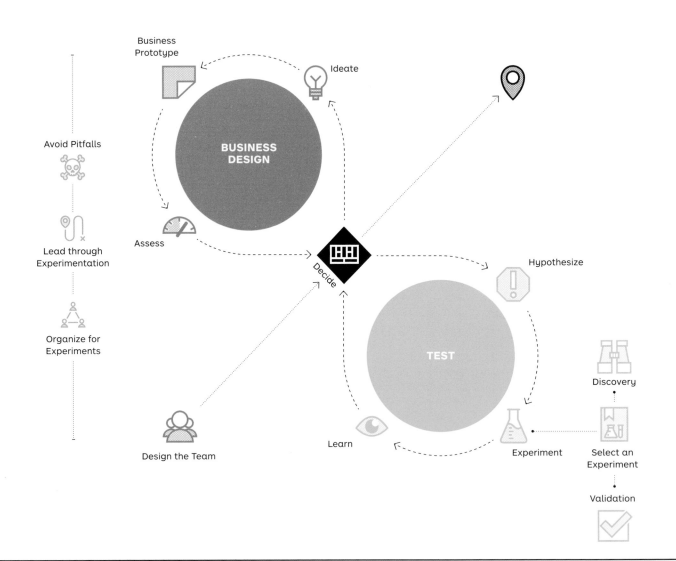

Avoid Pitfalls

Lead through Experimentation

Organize for Experiments

Business Prototype

Ideate

BUSINESS DESIGN

Assess

Decide

Design the Team

TEST

Hypothesize

Learn

Experiment

Discovery

Select an Experiment

Validation

Des

sign

"The strength of the team
is each individual member.
The strength of each member
is the team."

———

Phil Jackson
Former NBA Coach

1.1 — DESIGN THE TEAM

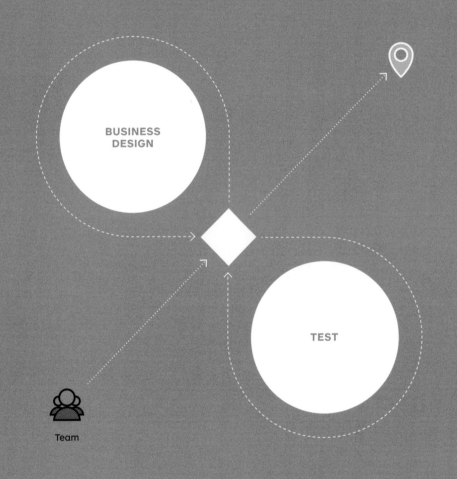

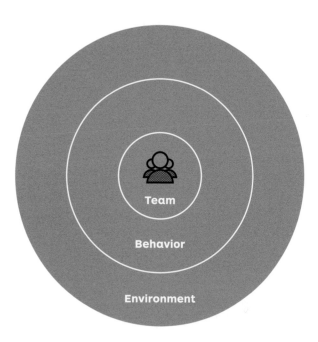

Team Design

What kind of team do we need to create our business?

Having worked with teams all around the world, we have learned that behind every successful new venture is a great team. If you are at a startup, the founding team is the glue that holds it all together. If you are in a corporation, you'll still need a solid team to create a new business venture. If you are a solopreneur, the team you eventually bring in will make or break your business.

Commonly Required Skills to Test Business Ideas

 Design   Sales

 Product   Marketing

 Tech   Research

 Legal   Finance

Data

Cross-Functional Skillset

A cross-functional team has all the core abilities needed to ship the product and learn from customers. A common basic example of a cross-functional team consists of design, product, and engineering.

Adapted from Jeff Patton.

Access to Missing Skillsets

If you do not have all of the skills needed or are unable to partner with external team members, then evaluate technological tools to fill the void.

Testing Tools

There are new tools coming on to the market every day that allow you to:

- Create landing pages
- Design logos
- Run online ads
- And more...

All with little or no expertise needed.

Entrepreneurial Experience

It's not a coincidence that successful businesses benefit from those who already have entrepreneurial experience.

Many entrepreneurs needed several attempts before finding success. Rovio's hit game, Angry Birds, was preceded by six years and 51 failed games.

Diversity

Team member diversity means they vary in aspects such as race, ethnicity, gender, age, experience, and thought. Now, more than ever, new businesses have real world impact on people and society. If the people who make up your team all have similar life experiences, thoughts, and appearance, then it can make it very difficult to navigate uncertainty.

A lack of diverse experiences and perspectives on a team will result in baking your biases right into the business.

When forming your team, keep diversity top of mind, rather than as an afterthought. Lead by example, by having a diverse leadership team. The issues that arise from having a homogeneous team are very difficult to rectify later.

SYNOPSIS

Team Behavior

How does our team need to act?

Team design is necessary, but not sufficient. You can have entrepreneurial experience, but how you interact with your team needs to exhibit entrepreneurial characteristics as well. Team behavior can be unpacked into six categories that are leading indicators of team success.

Successful Teams Exhibit Six Behaviors

1. Data Influenced

You do not have to be data driven, but you need to be data influenced. Teams no longer have the luxury of burning down a product backlog of features. The insights generated from data shape the backlog and strategy.

2. Experiment Driven

Teams are willing to be wrong and experiment. They are not only focused on the delivery of features, but also craft experiments to learn about their riskiest assumptions. Match experiments to what you are trying to learn over time.

3. Customer Centric

To create new businesses today, teams have to know "the why" behind the work. This begins with being constantly connected to the customer. This should not be limited to the new customer experience, and expands to both inside and outside of the product.

4. Entrepreneurial

Move fast and validate things. Teams have a sense of urgency and create momentum toward a viable outcome. This includes creative problem-solving at speed.

5. Iterative Approach

Teams aim for a desired result by means of a repeated cycle of operations. The iterative approach assumes you may not know the solution, so you iterate through different tactics to achieve the outcome.

6. Question Assumptions

Teams have to be willing to challenge the status quo and business as usual. They aren't afraid to test out a disruptive business model that will lead to big results, as compared to always playing it safe.

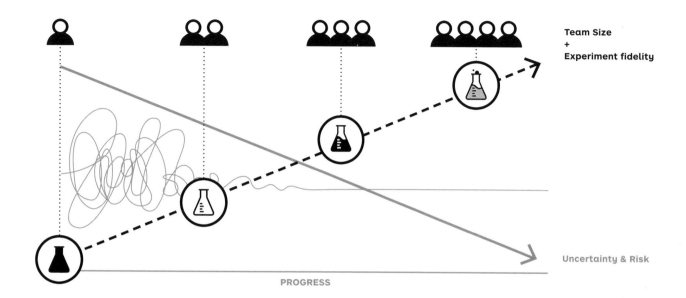

Team Size + Experiment fidelity

Uncertainty & Risk

PROGRESS

Growing the Team

You can begin this journey without a team, but as experiments get more complicated over time, chances are you'll be adding to your team. Expect to grow and evolve your team configuration over time, as you eventually find product/market fit, build the right way, and scale.

SYNOPSIS

Team Environment

How can you design an environment for your team to thrive?

Teams need a supportive environment to explore new business opportunities. They cannot be held to a standard where failure is not an option. Failure will occur, but failure isn't the goal. The goal is to learn faster than the competition and put that learning into action. Leaders need to intentionally design an environment where this can occur, otherwise even an ideal team configuration with the right behaviors will eventually stall out and give up.

The Team Needs to be...

Dedicated

Teams need an environment in which they can be dedicated to the work. Multitasking across several projects will silently kill any progress. Small teams who are dedicated to the work make more progress than large teams who are not dedicated.

Funded

It's unrealistic to expect these teams to function without a budget or funding. Experiments cost money. Incrementally fund the teams using a venture-capital style approach, based on the learnings they share during stakeholder reviews.

Autonomous

Teams need to be given space to own the work. Do not micromanage them to the extent where it slows down their progress. Instead, give them space to give an accounting of how they are making progress toward the goal.

The Company Needs to Provide...

Support

Leadership
Teams need an environment that has the right type of leadership support. A facilitative leadership style is ideal here because you do not know the solution. Lead with questions, not answers, and be mindful that the bottleneck is always at the top of the bottle.

Coaching
Teams need coaching, especially if this is their first journey together. Coaches, either internal or external, can help guide the teams when they are stuck trying to find the next experiment to run. Teams that have only used interviews and surveys can benefit from coaches who've seen a wide range of experiments.

Access

Customers
Teams need access to customers. The trend over the years has been to isolate teams from the customer, but in order to solve customer problems, this can no longer be the case. If teams keep getting pushback on customer access, they'll eventually just guess and build it anyway.

Resources
Teams need access to resources in order to be successful. Constraints are good, but starving a team will not yield results. They need enough resources to make progress and generate evidence. Resources can be physical or digital in nature, depending on the new business idea.

Direction

Strategy
Teams need a direction and strategy, or it'll be very difficult to make informed pivot, persevere, or kill decisions on the new business idea. Without a clear coherent strategy, you'll mistake being busy with making progress.

Guidance
Teams need constraints to focus their experimentation. Whether it's an adjacent market or creating a new one, to unlock new revenue teams need direction on where they will play.

KPIs
Teams need key performance indicators (KPIs) to help everyone understand whether they are making progress toward a goal. Without signposts along the way, it may be challenging to know if you should invest in the new business.

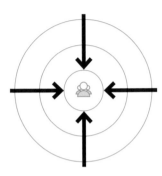

SYNOPSIS

Team Alignment

How can you ensure your team members are aligned?

Teams often lack a shared goal, context, and language when being formed. This can be devastating later on, if not resolved during the team formation and kickoff.

The Team Alignment Map, created by Stefano Mastrogiacomo, is a visual tool that allows participants to prepare for action: hold more productive meetings and structure the content of their conversations. It can help teams have more productive kickoffs, with better engagement and increased business success.

Each building block illustrates essential information to be discussed with your team. Identifying perception gaps early on can prevent you from being misaligned without even knowing it.

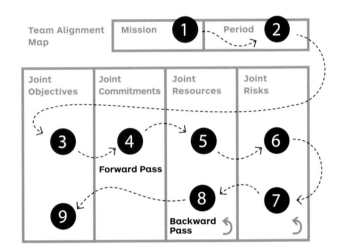

1. Define the mission.

2. Define the time box for the agreement.

3. Create joint team objectives.
   Joint Objectives
   What do we intend to achieve together?

4. Identify commitment levels for team members.
   Joint Commitments
   Who does what?

5. Document joint resources needed to succeed.
   Joint Resources
   What resources do we need?

6. Write down the biggest risks that could arise.
   Joint Risks
   What can prevent us from succeeding?

7. Describe how to address the biggest risks by creating new objectives and commitments.

8. Describe how to address resource constraints.

9. Set joint dates and validate.

To learn more about the Team Map visit www.teamalignment.co.

Team Alignment Map

Mission: Period:

Joint Objectives ◉

What do we intend to achieve together?

Joint Commitments 🤝

Who does what?

Joint Resources 🔋

What resources do we need?

Joint Risks 👁

What can prevent us from succeeding?

teamalignment.co

"Generating ideas
is not a problem."

———————

Rita McGrath
Professor of Management
Columbia Business School

SECTION 1 — DESIGN

1.2 — SHAPE THE IDEA

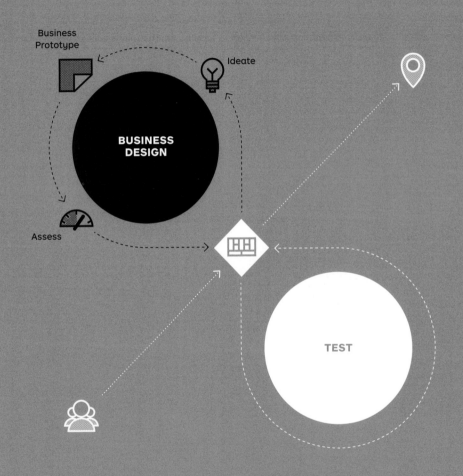

Business
Prototype

Ideate

BUSINESS
DESIGN

Assess

TEST

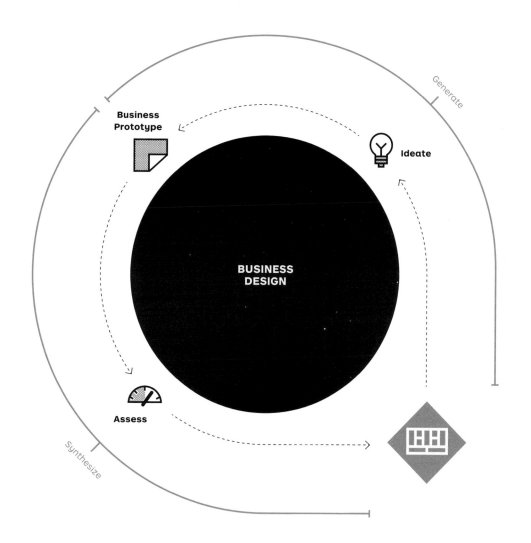

Business Design

In the design loop you shape and reshape your business idea to turn it into the best possible value proposition and business model. Your first iterations are based on your intuition and starting point (product idea, technology, market opportunity, etc.). Subsequent iterations are based on evidence and insights from the testing loop.

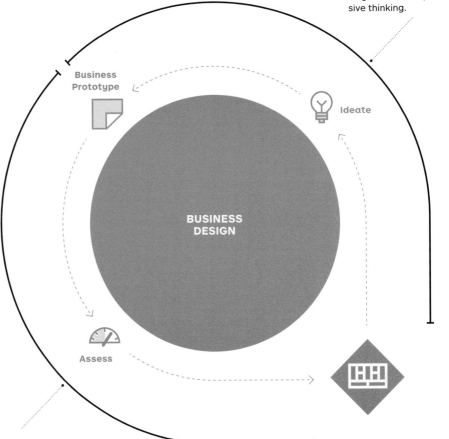

Generate

The first phase of the design loop is about generating as many possibilities and ideas as you can. It requires expansive thinking.

Business Prototype

Ideate

BUSINESS DESIGN

Assess

Synthesize

The second phase of the design loop is about synthesizing possibilities and narrowing the options down to the most promising opportunity.

The design loop has three steps.

1. Ideate

In this first step you try to come up with as many alternative ways as possible to use your initial intuition or insights from testing to turn your idea into a strong business. Don't fall in love with your first ideas.

2. Business Prototype

In this second step you narrow down the alternatives from ideation with business prototypes. When you start out you might use rough prototypes like napkin sketches. Subsequently, use the Value Proposition Canvas and Business Model Canvas to make your ideas clear and tangible. In this book we use these two tools to break ideas into smaller testable chunks. You will constantly improve your business prototypes with insights from testing in future iterations.

3. Assess

In this last step of the design loop you assess the design of your business proto-types. You ask questions like "Is this the best way to address our customers' jobs, pains, and gains?," or, "Is this the best way to monetize our idea?," or, "Does this best take into account what we have learned from testing?" Once you are satisfied with the design of your business prototypes you start testing in the field or go back to testing, if you are working on subsequent iterations.

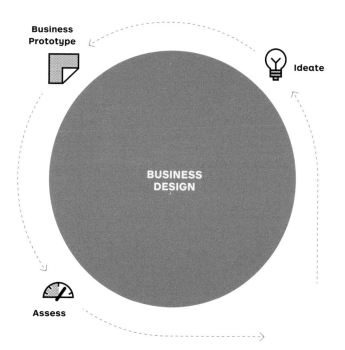

Caveat

This book focuses on Testing Business Ideas and provides you with a library of experiments to test your ideas and business prototypes. If you want to learn more about business design, we suggest you read *Business Model Generation* (Wiley, 2010) and *Value Proposition Design* (Wiley, 2014) or download the free online material.

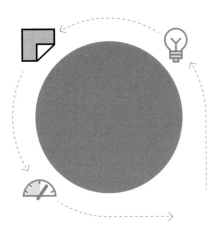

SYNOPSIS

The Business Model Canvas

You don't have to be a master of the Business Model Canvas to use this book, but you can use it to shape ideas into a business model so you can define, test, and manage risk. In this book, we use the Business Model Canvas to define the desirability, feasibility, and viability of an idea. If you'd like to go deeper than the synopsis of the Business Model Canvas, we recommend reading *Business Model Generation* or go online to learn more.

Customer Segments

Describe the different groups of people or organizations you aim to reach and serve.

Value Propositions

Describe the bundle of products and services that create value for a specific customer segment.

Channels

Describe how a company communicates with and reaches its customer segments to deliver a value proposition.

Customer Relationships

Describe the types of relationships a company establishes with specific customer segments.

Revenue Streams

Describe the cash a company generates from each customer segment.

Key Resources

Describe the most important assets required to make a business model work.

Key Activities

Describe the most important things a company must do to make its business model work.

Key Partners

Describe the network of suppliers and partners that make the business model work.

Cost Structure

Describe all costs incurred to operate a business model.

To learn more about the Business Model Canvas visit strategyzer.com/books/business-model-generation.

The Business Model Canvas

Designed for: Designed by: Date: Version:

Key Partners	Key Activities	Value Propositions	Customer Relationships	Customer Segments
	Key Resources		**Channels**	

Cost Structure

Revenue Streams

Strategyzer
strategyzer.com

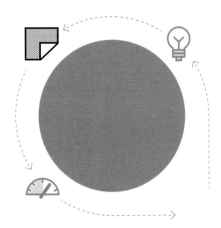

The Value Proposition Canvas

Much like the Business Model Canvas, the same goes for the Value Proposition Canvas. You'll get value from this book without having a proficiency in using it, but we do reference it for framing your experimentation, especially with regard to understanding the customer and how your products and services create value. If you'd like to go deeper than the synopsis of the Value Proposition Canvas, we recommend reading *Value Proposition Design* or go online to learn more.

Value Map

Describes the features of a specific value proposition in your business model in a structured and detailed way.

Customer Profile

Describes a specific customer segment in your business in a structured and detailed way.

Products and Services

List the products and services your value proposition is built around.

Customer Jobs

Describe what customers are trying to get done in their work and in their lives.

Gain Creators

Describe how your products and services create customer gains.

Gains

Describe the outcomes customers want to achieve or the concrete benefits they are seeking.

Pain Relievers

Describe how your products and services alleviate customer pains.

Pains

Describe the bad outcomes, risk, and obstacles related to customer jobs.

To learn more about the Value Proposition Canvas visit strategyzer.com/books/value-proposition-design.

The Value Proposition Canvas

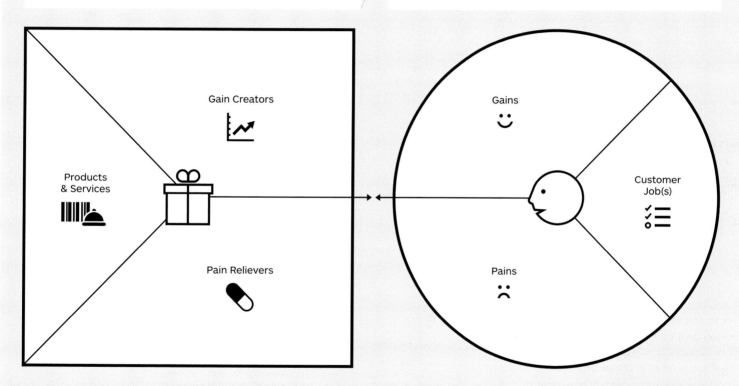

Value Proposition

Customer Segment

Gain Creators

Products & Services

Pain Relievers

Gains

Customer Job(s)

Pains

⊚Strategyzer

strategyzer.com

st

"A founding vision for a startup
is similar to a scientific hypothesis."

————

Rashmi Sinha
Founder, Slideshare

2.1 — HYPOTHESIZE

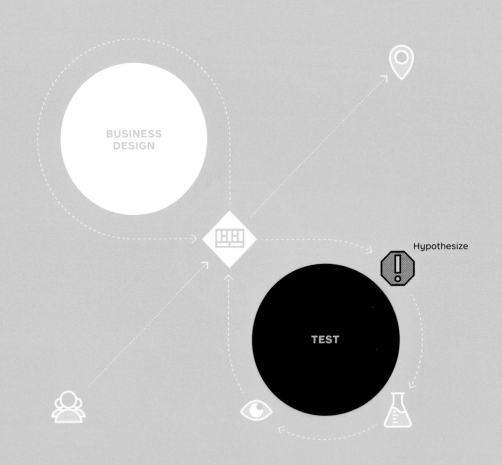

BUSINESS
DESIGN

TEST

Hypothesize

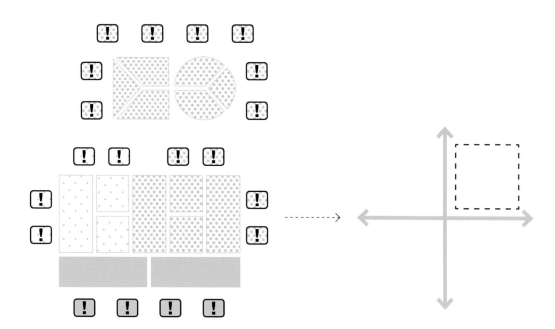

1. **Identify the Hypotheses Underlying Your Idea**
   To test a business idea you first have to make explicit all the risks that your idea won't work. You need to turn the assumptions underlying your idea into clear hypotheses that you can test.

2. **Prioritize Most Important Hypotheses**
   To identify the most important hypotheses to test first, you need to ask two questions. First, "What is the most important hypothesis that needs to be true for my idea to work?" Second, "For which hypotheses do I lack concrete evidence from the field?"

Hypothesis

The hypothesis has its roots in ancient civilization. The English word "hypothesis" comes from the Greek word hupothesis *which means "to suppose." Some even refer to a hypothesis as an educated guess. Hypotheses are instruments you use to prove or refute your assumptions.*

For the purposes of Testing Business Ideas, we focus on your business hypothesis, which is defined as:

- an assumption that your value proposition, business model, or strategy builds on.
- what you need to learn about to understand if your business idea might work.

Creating a good business hypothesis

When creating hypotheses you believe to be true for your business idea, begin by writing the phrase "We believe that..."

"We believe that millennial parents will subscribe to monthly educational science projects for their kids."

Be mindful that if you create all of your hypotheses in the "We believe that..." format, you can fall into a confirmation bias trap. You'll be constantly trying to prove what you believe, instead of trying to refute it. In order to prevent this from occurring create a few hypotheses that try to disprove your assumptions.

"We believe that millennial parents won't subscribe to monthly educational science projects for their kids."

You can even test these competing hypotheses at the same time. This is especially helpful when team members cannot agree on which hypothesis to test.

Characteristics of a good hypothesis

A well-formed business hypothesis describes
a testable, precise, and discrete thing you
want to investigate. With that in mind,
we can continue to refine and unpack our
hypotheses about the science project
subscription business.

	✗	✓
Testable Your hypothesis is testable when it can be shown true (validated) or false (invalidated), based on evidence (and guided by experience).	– *We believe millennial parents prefer craft projects.*	☐ *We believe millennial parents prefer curated science projects that match their kids' education level.*
Precise Your hypothesis is precise when you know what success looks like. Ideally, it describes the precise what, who, and when of your assumptions.	– *We believe millennials will spend a lot on science projects.*	☐ *We believe millennial parents with kids ages 5–9 will pay $15 a month for curated science projects that match their kids' education level.*
Discrete Your hypothesis is discrete when it describes only one distinct, testable, and precise thing you want to investigate.	– *We believe we can buy and ship science project boxes at a profit.*	☐ *We believe we can purchase science project materials at wholesale for less than $3 a box.* ☐ *We believe we can ship science project materials domestically for less than $5 a box.*

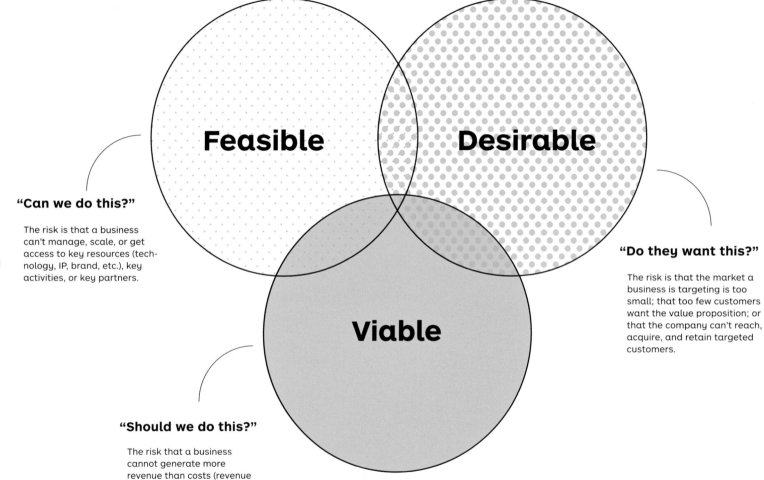

"Can we do this?"

The risk is that a business can't manage, scale, or get access to key resources (technology, IP, brand, etc.), key activities, or key partners.

"Do they want this?"

The risk is that the market a business is targeting is too small; that too few customers want the value proposition; or that the company can't reach, acquire, and retain targeted customers.

"Should we do this?"

The risk that a business cannot generate more revenue than costs (revenue stream and cost structure).

Types of Hypotheses

Adapted from Larry Keeley, Doblin Group and IDEO.

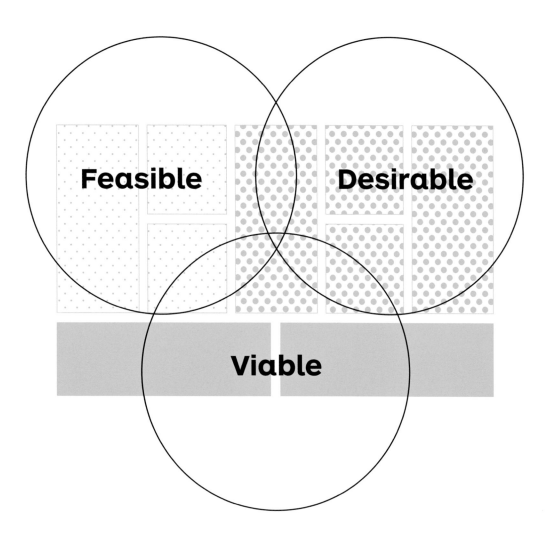

Types of Hypotheses on the Business Model Canvas

Desirability Hypotheses
Explore first

The Value Proposition Canvas contains market risk in both the Value Map and Customer Profile. Identify the desirability hypotheses you are making in:

The Business Model Canvas contains market risk in the value proposition, customer segment, channel, and customer relationship components. Identify the desirability hypotheses you are making in:

TEST

Customer Profile
We believe that we...

- are addressing jobs that really matter to customers.

- are focused on pains that really matter to customers.

- are focused on gains that really matter to customers.

Value Map
We believe...

- our products and services really solve for high-value customer jobs.

- our products and services relieve top customer pains.

- our products and services create important customer gains.

Customer Segments
We believe...

- we are targeting the right customer segments.

- the segments we are targeting actually exist.

- the segments we are targeting are big enough.

Value Propositions
We believe...

- we have the right value propositions for the customer segments we are targeting.

- our value proposition is unique enough to replicate.

Channels
We believe...

- we have the right channels to reach and acquire our customers.

- we can master the channels to deliver value.

Customer Relationships
We believe...

- we can build the right relationships with customers.

- it is difficult for customers to switch to a competitor's product.

- we can retain customers.

Feasibility Hypotheses
Explore second

The Business Model Canvas contains infrastructure risk in the key partners, key activities, and key resources components. Identify the feasibility hypotheses you are making in:

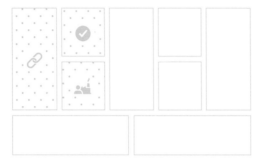

Key Activities
We believe that we...

- can perform all activities (at scale) and at the right quality level that is required to build our business model.

Key Resources
We believe that we...

- can secure and manage all technologies and resources (at scale) that are required to build our business model, including intellectual property and human, financial, and other resources.

Key Partners
We believe that we...

- can create the partnerships required to build our business.

Viability Hypotheses
Explore third

The Business Model Canvas contains financial risk in the revenue stream and cost structure. Identify the viability hypotheses you are making in:

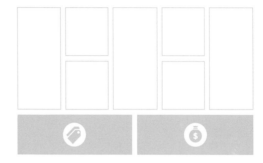

Revenue Streams
We believe that we...

- can get customers to pay a specific price for our value propositions.
- can generate sufficient revenues.

Cost Structure
We believe that we...

- can manage costs from our infrastacture and keep them under control.

Profit
We believe that we...

- can generate more revenues than costs in order to make a profit.

DEFINITION

Assumptions Mapping

A team exercise where desirability, viability, and feasibility hypotheses are made explicit and prioritized in terms of importance and evidence.

Every radically new idea, product, service, value proposition, business model, or strategy requires a leap of faith. If proven false, these important and yet unproven aspects of your idea can make or break your business. The Assumptions Mapping exercise is designed to help you make all risks explicit in the form of hypotheses, so you can prioritize them and focus your near-term experimentation.

Adapted from Gothelf & Seiden, Lean UX

How to Facilitate

Core team

The core team consists of individuals who are going to be dedicated to making this new business endeavor a success. They are cross-functional. This means they have product, design, and technology skills needed to ship and learn rapidly in the market with real customers. At a minimum, the core team needs to be present when mapping out the assumptions from your Business Model Canvas.

Supporting team

The supporting team consists of individuals who are not necessarily dedicated to the business endeavor but who are needed for it to be a success. People from legal, safety, compliance, marketing, and user research will be required for testing assumptions where the core team lacks the domain knowledge and know-how.

Without a strong supporting team, the core members may lack evidence and make uninformed decisions about what's important.

Identify Hypotheses
Step 1

Use a sticky note to write down each:

- desirability hypothesis and put it on your canvases.
- feasibility hypothesis and put it on your canvases.
- viability hypothesis and put it on your canvases.

Best Practices

- Use different color sticky notes for desirability, feasibility, and viability hypotheses.
- Your hypotheses should be as specific as possible, to the best of your knowledge, based on what you know today.
- Every hypothesis should be a single sticky note. Don't use bullet points; that makes it easier to prioritize your hypotheses.
- Keep your hypotheses short and precise. No blah blah blah.
- Discuss and agree as a team when writing.

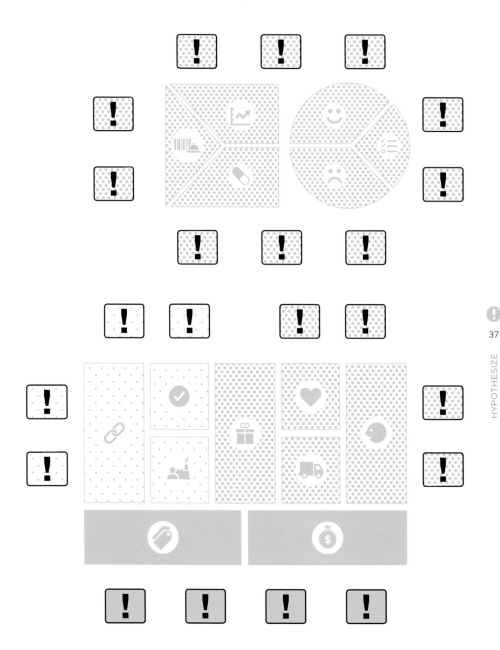

Prioritize Hypotheses
Step 2

Use the Assumptions Map to prioritize all your hypotheses in terms of importance and existence or absence of evidence that supports different types of hypotheses.

x-Axis: Evidence
On the x-axis you place all your hypotheses positioned to show how much evidence you have or don't have to support or refute a specific hypothesis. You place a hypothesis on the left if you are able to produce relevant, observable, and recent evidence to support a hypothesis. You place a hypothesis on the right if you do not have evidence and therefore will need to generate it.

y-Axis: Importance
On the y-axis you place all your hypotheses in terms of importance. Position a hypothesis at the top if it is absolutely critical for your business idea to succeed. In other words, if that hypothesis is proven wrong, your business idea will fail and all other hypotheses become irrelevant. You place a hypothesis at the bottom if it is not one of the first things you'd go out and test.

Top Left

Share

Check the top left quadrant against your evidence and share it with the team. Do these hypotheses really have observable evidence to back them up? Challenge the evidence to make sure it's good enough. Keep track of these hypotheses in your plan going forward.

Top Right

Experiment

Focus on the top right quadrant to identify which hypotheses to test first. This defines your near-term experimentation. Create experiments to address these high-risk themes in your business.

TEST

Identify and Prioritize Riskiest Hypotheses

Step 3

For the purposes of this book, the major focus will be on how to test the top right quadrant of your Assumptions Map: experiments with important hypotheses and with light evidence. These assumptions, if proven false, will cause your business to fail.

Prioritize Desirability Hypotheses

As a team, pull over each desirability hypothesis and place it on the Assumptions Map.

Prioritize Feasibility Hypotheses

Next, pull over each feasibility hypothesis and place it on the Assumptions Map.

Prioritize Viability Hypotheses

Then pull over each viability hypothesis and place it on the Assumptions Map.

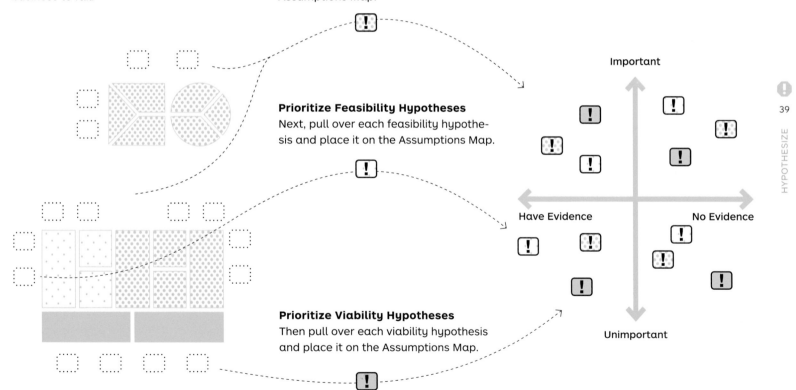

Important

Have Evidence   No Evidence

Unimportant

"It doesn't matter how beautiful
your theory is, it doesn't matter
how smart you are. If it doesn't
agree with experiment, it's wrong."

———

Richard Feynman
American theoretical physicist

2.2 — EXPERIMENT

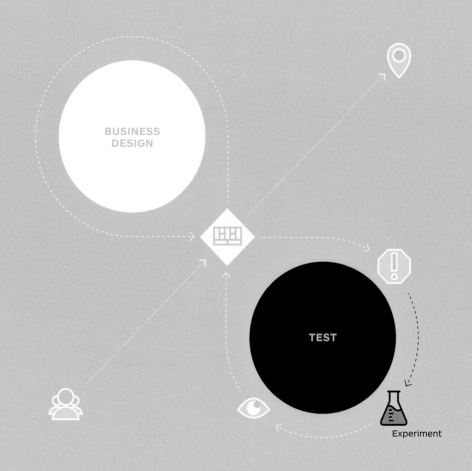

BUSINESS
DESIGN

TEST

Experiment

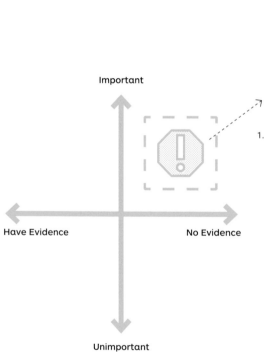

Important

Have Evidence ← → No Evidence

Unimportant

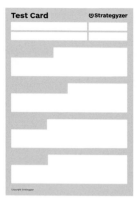

Test Card   ⊕ Strategyzer

1. **Design Experiment**

To get started with testing your business idea, you turn your most important hypotheses into experiments. You should start with cheap and fast experiments to learn quickly. Every experiment will reduce the risk that you'll spend time, energy, and money on ideas that won't work.

2. **Run Experiment**

Every experiment has a specific run time to generate sufficient evidence that you can learn from. Make sure you run your experiments almost like a scientist, so that your evidence is clean and not misleading.

Experiment

Experiments are the means to reduce the risk and uncertainty of your business idea.

The experiment is at the core of scientific method. Like the hypothesis, it can be traced back through history to everything from how the vision works with the eye to measuring time.

What has remained consistent over time is that the scientific method is a valuable method for generating insights.

Children naturally experiment and iterate their way through problems. Once they begin to progress through traditional schooling, experimentation gradually becomes less and less of a practice outside of science class. The way students are graded, judged, and tested means they have to find the single right answer. In life, as it is in business, there is rarely a single right answer. So over time people optimize for being right, instead of making progress, because they're accustomed to being penalized for being wrong.

It's no surprise that children raised in this style of educational system become adults who often struggle with the idea of being wrong. The culture of rewarding who is right and penalizing who is wrong extends into their businesses. They've been conditioned to look for that one right answer.

As you read this book and learn how to test your business ideas, you will find there is often not one path forward, but many.

As you experiment, think back to what it felt like to be in kindergarten and preschool: when you were allowed to try to fit the square peg into the round hole. Experimentation is about structured creativity. Tap into that energy within yourself and with your teams.

For the purposes of Testing Business Ideas, the focus is on business experiments, which:

- are procedures to reduce the risk and uncertainty of a business idea.
- produce weak or strong evidence that supports or refutes a hypothesis.
- can be fast/slow and cheap/expensive to conduct.

What is a good experiment?

A good experiment is precise enough so that team members can replicate it and generate usable and comparable data.

- Defines the "who" precisely (test subject)
- Defines the "where" precisely (test context)
- Defines the "what" precisely (test elements)

What are the components of an experiment?

A well-formed business experiment is made up of four components:

1. Hypothesis
The most critical hypothesis from the top right quadrant of your Assumptions Map.

2. Experiment
The description of the experiment you will run to support or refute the hypothesis.

3. Metrics
The data you will measure as part of the experiment.

4. Criteria
The success criteria for your experiment metrics.

Call-to-Action Experiment

A specific type of experiment that prompts a test subject to perform an observable action. Used in an experiment in order to test one or more hypotheses.

Test Card   **Strategyzer**

Test Name

Deadline

Assigned to

Duration

STEP 1: HYPOTHESIS

We believe that

Critical:

STEP 2: TEST

To verify that, we will

Test Cost: Data Reliability:

STEP 3: METRIC

And measure

Time Required:

STEP 4: CRITERIA

We are right if

Copyright Strategyzer AG   *The makers of Business Model Generation and Strategyzer*

Create multiple experiments for your hypothesis

We've yet to work with a team who created just one experiment, had a major break-through, and then went on to create a multibillion dollar business from it. In reality, it takes a series of experiments to generate the possibility of a successful business. Use the Test Cards and the experiment library to create well-formed experiments to test your business hypotheses.

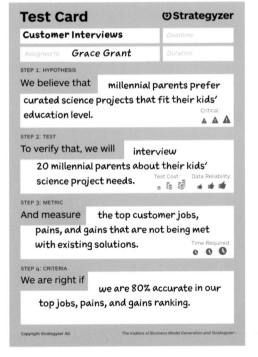

Test Card — ⓦ **Strategyzer**

Customer Interviews — *Deadline*

Assigned to **Grace Grant** — *Duration*

STEP 1: HYPOTHESIS
We believe that **millennial parents prefer curated science projects that fit their kids' education level.** Critical: ▲ ▲ ⚠

STEP 2: TEST
To verify that, we will **interview** **20 millennial parents about their kids' science project needs.** Test Cost: Data Reliability:

STEP 3: METRIC
And measure **the top customer jobs, pains, and gains that are not being met with existing solutions.** Time Required:

STEP 4: CRITERIA
We are right if **we are 80% accurate in our top jobs, pains, and gains ranking.**

Copyright Strategyzer AG — *The makers of Business Model Generation and Strategyzer*

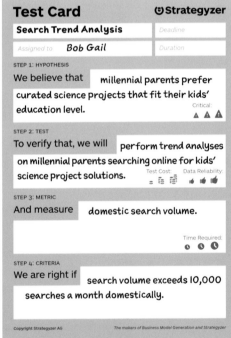

Test Card — ⓦ **Strategyzer**

Search Trend Analysis — *Deadline*

Assigned to **Bob Gail** — *Duration*

STEP 1: HYPOTHESIS
We believe that **millennial parents prefer curated science projects that fit their kids' education level.** Critical: ▲ ▲ ⚠

STEP 2: TEST
To verify that, we will **perform trend analyses on millennial parents searching online for kids' science project solutions.** Test Cost: Data Reliability:

STEP 3: METRIC
And measure **domestic search volume.** Time Required:

STEP 4: CRITERIA
We are right if **search volume exceeds 10,000 searches a month domestically.**

Copyright Strategyzer AG — *The makers of Business Model Generation and Strategyzer*

Test Card — ⓦ **Strategyzer**

Concierge — *Deadline*

Assigned to **Claire McCain** — *Duration*

STEP 1: HYPOTHESIS
We believe that **millennial parents prefer curated science projects that fit their kids' education level.** Critical: ▲ ▲ ⚠

STEP 2: TEST
To verify that, we will **manually curate science project kits for 20 children of millennial parents.** Test Cost: Data Reliability:

STEP 3: METRIC
And measure **time to create, cost to create, cost to ship, and customer satisfaction.** Time Required:

STEP 4: CRITERIA
We are right if **the customer satisfaction score is "partially satisfied" to "very satisfied" for 16 of the 20 parents.**

Copyright Strategyzer AG — *The makers of Business Model Generation and Strategyzer*

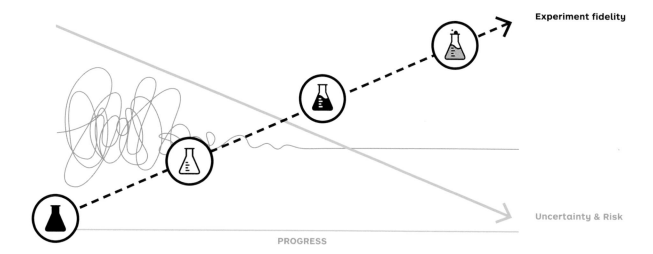

Experiment fidelity

Uncertainty & Risk

PROGRESS

Experiments Reduce the Risk of Uncertainty

As you read through *Testing Business Ideas*, you'll begin to understand how experiments can help you rapidly reduce the risk of uncertainty. Instead of building internally for long periods in a customer-free zone, you'll learn how to incrementally reduce your risk over time. This allows you to build at the right time and at the right fidelity.

"Anyone who isn't embarrassed
by who they were last year
probably isn't learning enough."

———————

Alain de Botton
Philosopher

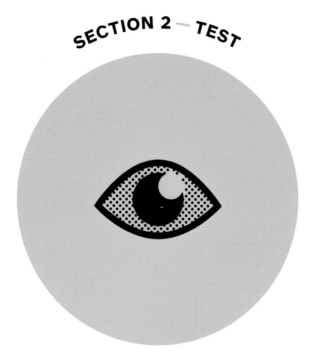

SECTION 2 — TEST

2.3 — LEARN

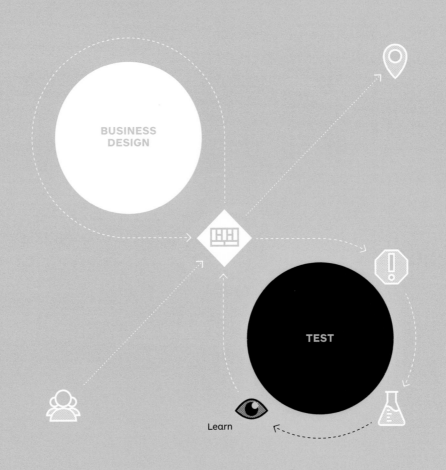

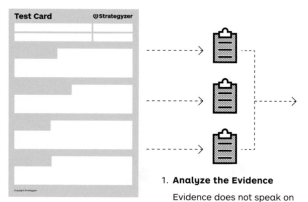

Test Card   ⓊStrategyzer

Learning Card   ⓊStrategyzer

1. **Analyze the Evidence**

   Evidence does not speak on
   its own. Gather the evidence
   you have from different
   experiments for a specific
   hypothesis and analyze it.
   Make sure you distinguish
   between strong and weak
   evidence.

2. **Gain Insights**

   Insights are key learnings
   you get from analyzing
   the data. They allow you
   to support or refute the
   hypotheses you've been
   testing. Your insights help
   you understand how likely
   your idea is to work.

Strength of Evidence

The strength of a piece of evidence determines how reliably the evidence helps support or refute a hypothesis. You can evaluate the strength of evidence by checking four areas. Is the evidence based on...

Evidence

What is Evidence?

Evidence is what you use to support or refute the hypotheses underlying your business idea. It is data that you get from research or generate from business experiments. Evidence can come in many different forms, ranging from weak to strong evidence.

For the purposes of Testing Business Ideas, we focus on your business experiment evidence which we define as:

- data generated from an experiment or collected in the field.
- facts that support or refute a hypothesis.
- possibly of different nature (e.g., quotes, behaviors, conversion rates, orders, purchases...); can be weak/strong.

Weak Evidence		Strong(er) Evidence
1. **Opinions (beliefs)** When people say things like "I would...," "I think _____ is important," "I believe...," or "I like..."		**Facts (events)** When people say things like "Last week I _____," "In that situation I usually _____," or "I spent _____ on."
2. **What people say** What people say in an interview or survey is not necessarily what they do in real life or will do in the future.		**What people do** Observable behavior is generally a good predictor of how people act and what people might do in the future.
3. **Lab settings** When people are aware that you are testing something, they may behave differently than in a real world setting.		**Real world settings** The most reliable predictor of future behavior is what you observe people doing when they are not aware they are being tested.
4. **Small investments** Signing up by email to be informed about an upcoming product release is a small investment and relatively weak evidence of interest.		**Large investments** Pre-purchasing a product or putting one's professional reputation on the line is an important investment and strong evidence of real interest.

Different experiments create different evidence

Customer Interviews

Test Card ⓦStrategyzer

Customer Interviews	*Deadline*
Assigned to Grace Grant	*Duration*

STEP 1: HYPOTHESIS
We believe that | millennial parents prefer curated science projects that fit their kids' education level.
Critical: ▲ ▲ ⚠

STEP 2: TEST
To verify that, we will | interview 20 millennial parents about their kids' science project needs.
Test Cost: | *Data Reliability:*

STEP 3: METRIC
And measure | the top customer jobs, pains, and gains that are not being met with existing solutions.
Time Required:

STEP 4: CRITERIA
We are right if | we are 80% accurate in our top jobs, pains, and gains ranking.

Copyright Strategyzer AG | *The makers of Business Model Generation and Strategyzer*

Transcripts & Quotes

⚖ ● ○ ○ ○ ○
EVIDENCE STRENGTH

"We want our child to have a unique science fair project that stands out, not the same one as every other kid."

"It has to be appropriate for her grade level. The one we tried stated 2nd grade but was way too difficult."

"Many of the kits we find for free online have missing or confusing instructions."

"I'd pay to have a science project kit with everything we need all in a box."

Search Trend Analysis

Test Card ⓦStrategyzer

Search Trend Analysis	*Deadline*
Assigned to Bob Gail	*Duration*

STEP 1: HYPOTHESIS
We believe that | millennial parents prefer curated science projects that fit their kids' education level.
Critical: ▲ ▲ ⚠

STEP 2: TEST
To verify that, we will | perform trend analyses on millennial parents searching online for kids' science project solutions.
Test Cost: | *Data Reliability:*

STEP 3: METRIC
And measure | domestic search volume.
Time Required:

STEP 4: CRITERIA
We are right if | search volume exceeds 10,000 searches a month domestically.

Copyright Strategyzer AG | *The makers of Business Model Generation and Strategyzer*

Search Volume Data

⚖ ● ● ● ○ ○
EVIDENCE STRENGTH

Month of February:

"science fair ideas" had 5k–10k searches.

"kindergarten science fair ideas" had 10k–15k searches.

"first grade science fair ideas" had 1k–5k searches.

"second grade science fair ideas" had less than 1k searches.

"third grade science fair ideas" had less than 1k searches.

Concierge

Test Card ⓦStrategyzer

Concierge	*Deadline*
Assigned to Claire McCain	*Duration*

STEP 1: HYPOTHESIS
We believe that | millennial parents prefer curated science projects that fit their kids' education level.
Critical: ▲ ▲ ⚠

STEP 2: TEST
To verify that, we will | manually curate science project kits for 20 children of millennial parents.
Test Cost: | *Data Reliability:*

STEP 3: METRIC
And measure | time to create, cost to create, cost to ship, and customer satisfaction.
Time Required:

STEP 4: CRITERIA
We are right if | the customer satisfaction score is "partially satisfied" to "very satisfied" for 16 of the 20 parents.

Copyright Strategyzer AG | *The makers of Business Model Generation and Strategyzer*

Concierge Data

⚖ ● ● ● ● ●
EVIDENCE STRENGTH

Time to Create = 2 hours for each kit

Cost to Create = $10–$15

Cost to Ship = $5–$8

Parent Customer Satisfaction Score = Partially Satisfied

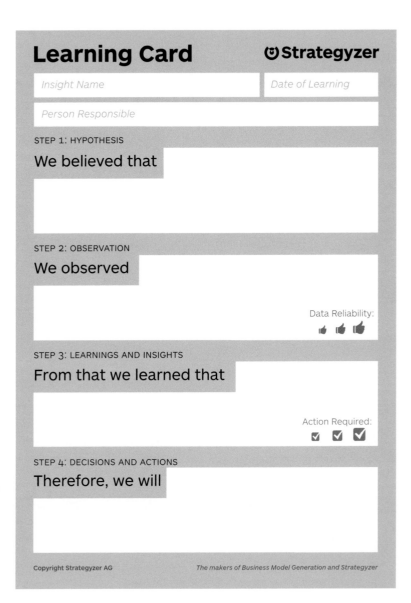

DEFINITION

Insights

What are insights?

There is a difference between looking at something and looking for something. Evidence on its own will not help you reduce risk in your business idea; therefore, we recommend gleaning insights from the evidence your experiments generate.

For the purposes of Testing Business Ideas, business insights are defined as:

- what you learn from studying the evidence.
- learning related to the validity of a hypothesis and potential discovery of new directions.
- the foundation to make informed business decisions and take action.

Customer Interviews

Transcripts & Quotes

Search Trend Analysis

Search Volume Data

Concierge

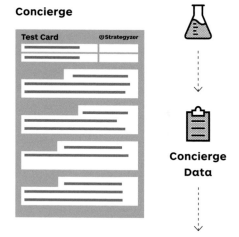

Concierge Data

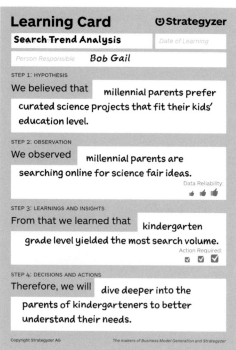

Learning Card   ⊎Strategyzer

Customer Interviews   *Date of Learning*

Person Responsible   **Grace Grant**

STEP 1: HYPOTHESIS

We believed that   millennial parents prefer curated science projects that fit their kids' education level.

STEP 2: OBSERVATION

We observed   millennial parents want their kids to have a unique project with clear instructions that matches their ability.   Data Reliability: 👍 👍 👍

STEP 3: LEARNINGS AND INSIGHTS

From that we learned that   uniqueness was a top job that we had previously not emphasized.   Action Required: ☑ ☑ ☑

STEP 4: DECISIONS AND ACTIONS

Therefore, we will   use the unique customer language in our upcoming landing page's value proposition.

Copyright Strategyzer AG   The makers of Business Model Generation and Strategyzer

Learning Card   ⊎Strategyzer

Search Trend Analysis   *Date of Learning*

Person Responsible   **Bob Gail**

STEP 1: HYPOTHESIS

We believed that   millennial parents prefer curated science projects that fit their kids' education level.

STEP 2: OBSERVATION

We observed   millennial parents are searching online for science fair ideas.   Data Reliability: 👍 👍 👍

STEP 3: LEARNINGS AND INSIGHTS

From that we learned that   kindergarten grade level yielded the most search volume.   Action Required: ☑ ☑ ☑

STEP 4: DECISIONS AND ACTIONS

Therefore, we will   dive deeper into the parents of kindergarteners to better understand their needs.

Copyright Strategyzer AG   The makers of Business Model Generation and Strategyzer

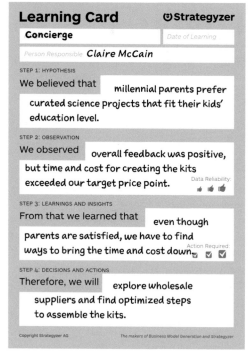

Learning Card   ⊎Strategyzer

Concierge   *Date of Learning*

Person Responsible   **Claire McCain**

STEP 1: HYPOTHESIS

We believed that   millennial parents prefer curated science projects that fit their kids' education level.

STEP 2: OBSERVATION

We observed   overall feedback was positive, but time and cost for creating the kits exceeded our target price point.   Data Reliability: 👍 👍 👍

STEP 3: LEARNINGS AND INSIGHTS

From that we learned that   even though parents are satisfied, we have to find ways to bring the time and cost down.   Action Required: ☑ ☑ ☑

STEP 4: DECISIONS AND ACTIONS

Therefore, we will   explore wholesale suppliers and find optimized steps to assemble the kits.

Copyright Strategyzer AG   The makers of Business Model Generation and Strategyzer

Confidence Level

Your confidence level indicates how much you believe that your evidence is strong enough to support or refute a specific hypothesis.

Not all evidence and insights are equal. You should be more confident about your insights when you've run several experiments with increasingly strong evidence for a specific hypothesis. For example, you might start with interviews to gain some first insights into your customers' jobs, pains, and gains. Then you might run a survey to test your insights on a larger scale with more customers. Finally, you might continue with a simulated sale to generate the strongest type of evidence for customer interest.

There are three dimensions to help you determine your confidence level:

1. **Type and strength of evidence**
   Different types of evidence have different strengths. A quote from an interview is a relatively weak indicator of future behavior. A purchase in a simulated sale is a very strong indicator of future behavior. The type of evidence you've collected for a specific hypothesis will influence how confident you can be about the reliability of your insights.

2. **Number of data points per experiment**
   The more data points you have, the better. Five quotes from personal customer interviews is obviously weaker than 100 quotes. However, those same quotes are likely to be more accurate than 100 data points in an anonymous customer survey.

Type of Test	Strength of Evidence	Number of Data Points	Resulting Evidence Quality
CUSTOMER INTERVIEWS	●○○○○	10 PEOPLE	WEAK
DISCOVERY SURVEY	●●○○○	500 PEOPLE	WEAK
MOCK SALES	●●●●○	250 PEOPLE	VERY STRONG

Hypothesis Confidence Level

How confident are you that you can support or refute a specific hypothesis based on experiments, evidence, and insights?

Very Confident
You can be very confident if you've run several experiments of which at least one is a call-to-action test that produced very strong evidence.

Somewhat Confident
You can be somewhat confident if you've run several experiments that produce strong evidence or a particularly strong call-to-action experiment.

Not Really Confident
You need to run more and stronger experiments if you've only done interviews or surveys in which people say what they will do. They might behave differently in reality.

Not Confident at All
You need to experiment more if you've only run one experiment that produces weak evidence, such as an interview or survey.

3. **Number and type of experiments conducted for the same hypothesis**
Your confidence level should rise with the number of experiments you conduct to test the same hypothesis. Three interview series are better than one. Conducting interviews, surveys, and simulated sales to test the same hypothesis is even better. You achieve the best results when you conduct experiments with increasing strength of evidence, and the more you learn.

"Have a bias toward action—
let's see something happen now.
You can break that big plan into
small steps and take the first step
right away."

—————

Indira Gandhi
Former Prime Minister of India

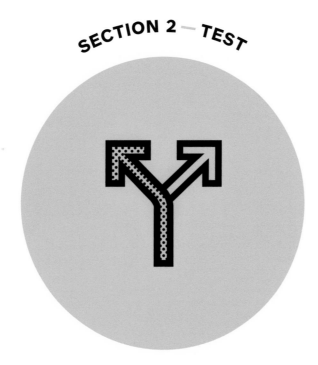

2.4 — DECIDE

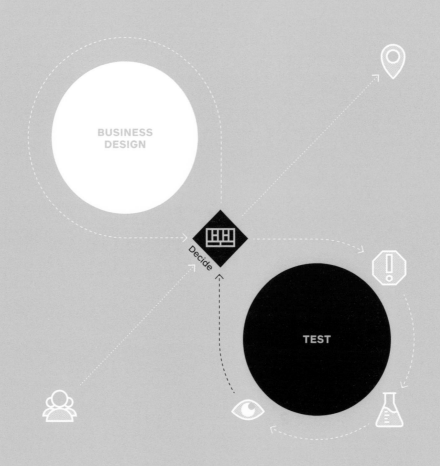

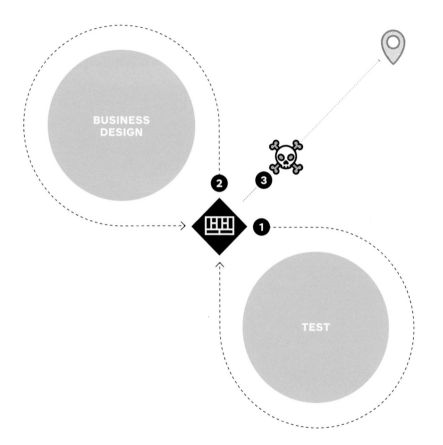

1. **Perservere**

   The decision to continue testing an idea based on evidence and insights. You persevere by further testing the same hypothesis with a stronger experiment, or by moving on to your next important hypothesis.

2. **Pivot**

   The decision to make a significant change to one or more elements of your ideas, value proposition, or business model. A pivot often means that some of your earlier evidence may be irrelevant to your new trajectory. It usually requires retesting elements of your business model that you've already tested.

3. **Kill**

   The decision to kill an idea based on evidence and insights. The evidence might show that an idea won't work in reality or that the profit potential is insufficient.

DEFINITION

Decide

Turning insights into action

Learning faster than everyone else is no longer enough. You need to put that learning into action, because what you've learned has an expiration date. If you feel like this is happening faster than any time in recorded history, you may be correct. People today are exposed to more information in a year than those in the early 1900s experienced in a lifetime. Both markets and technology move so quickly that the insights you've gained can expire within months, weeks, or even days.

  For the purposes of Testing Business Ideas, we define action as:

- next steps to make progress with testing and de-risking a business idea.
- informed decisions based on collected insights.
- decisions to abandon, change, and/or continue testing a business idea.

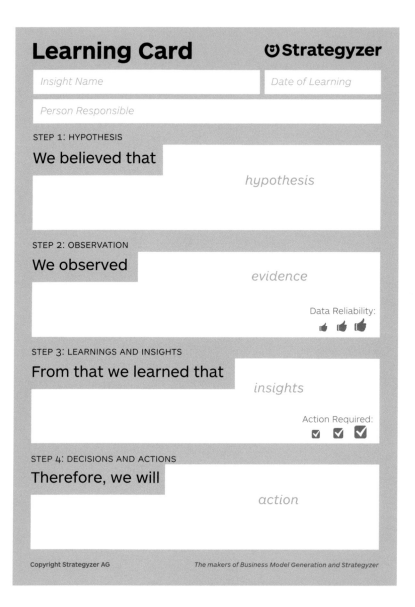

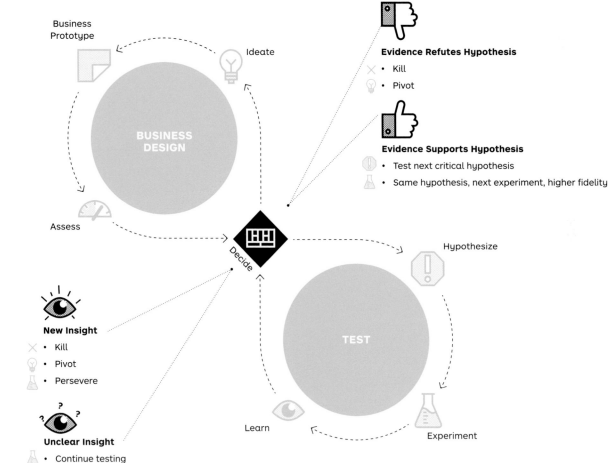

Business
Prototype

Ideate

**BUSINESS
DESIGN**

Assess

Decide

Evidence Refutes Hypothesis
- Kill
- Pivot

Evidence Supports Hypothesis
- Test next critical hypothesis
- Same hypothesis, next experiment, higher fidelity

Hypothesize

TEST

New Insight
- Kill
- Pivot
- Persevere

Unclear Insight
- Continue testing

Learn

Experiment

"The single biggest problem
in communication is the illusion
that it has taken place."

———

George Bernard Shaw
Irish playwright and political activist

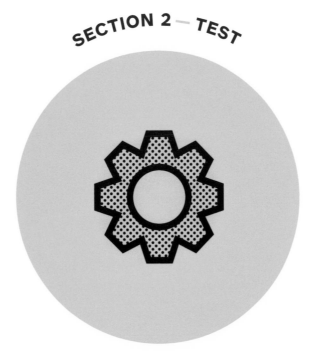

SECTION 2 — TEST

2.5 — MANAGE

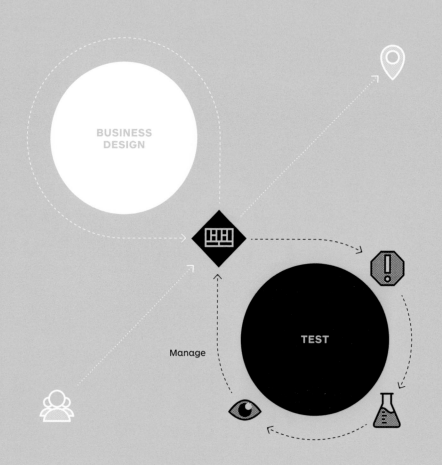

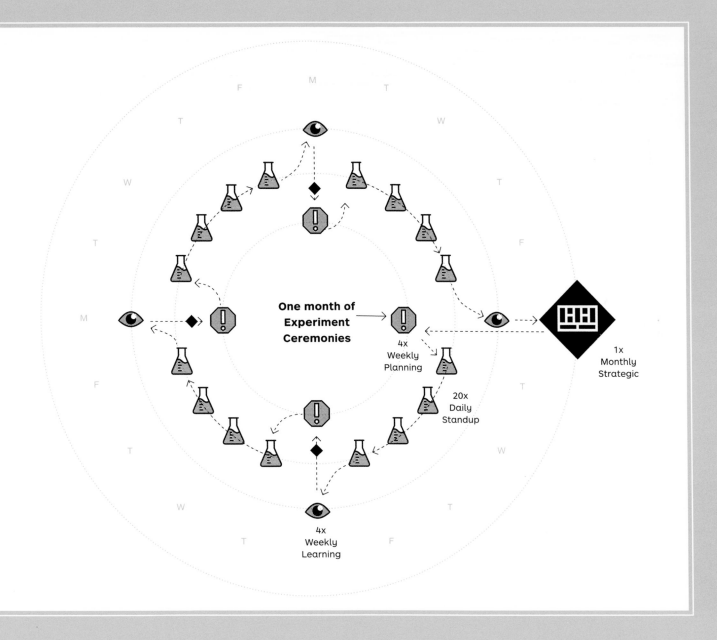

Experiment Ceremonies

Ceremonies help us collaborate and it is no different for experimentation. If your goal is to create a successful new business, you'll need more than one experiment to find your way. This is why we recommend a series of ceremonies to create a repeatable process. Each ceremony informs its connecting ceremony, creating a system.

This series of experiment ceremonies is a result of years of experience working with teams who've made business experimentation a repeatable process. We draw inspiration from agile design thinking and lean methodologies.

Meeting Type	Time		Attendees	Agenda
Planning	60 minutes Weekly	⬡!	● Core Team	• Learning goal • Prioritization • Tasking
Standup	15 minutes Daily	🧪	● Core Team	• Learning goal • Blockers • Help
Learning	60 minutes Weekly	👁	○ Extended Team ● Core Team	• Synthesize evidence • Insights • Actions
Retros	30 minutes Biweekly	↻	● Core Team	• Went well • To fix • To try
Deciding	60 minutes Monthly	◆	◉ Stakeholders ○ Extended Team ● Core Team	• Learnings • Blockers • Decisions

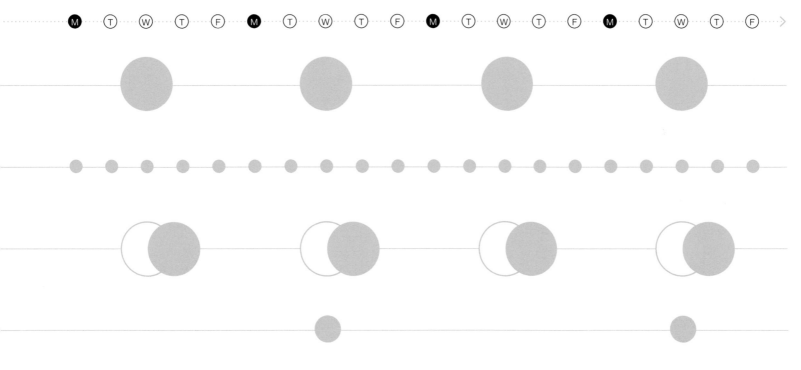

Co-Located or Distributed?

In this rapidly evolving technical world of work, it's no longer a prerequisite that teams need to sit in the same room to be highly effective. Whether you are co-located or distributed, we've witnessed teams adopt these Experiment Ceremonies to help propel their new business ideas.

Co-Located Teams

For Co-Located Teams, we recommend having a space that is semiprivate. It can be difficult to secure a conference room for all of these ceremonies, and it would mean bringing your artifacts in every time if they are physically printed out.

Many teams we've coached pick a wall or have a pod setup that allows them to quickly collaborate and then get back to work.

Distributed Teams

For Distributed Teams, we strongly recommend video chat whenever possible. It's important to make a connection to your team members and be able to see their body language. Luckily for you there are ample options to choose from in video chat.

When reviewing artifacts or conducting exercises, try to use software that shows people editing and moving things in real time. This will prevent confusion and duplication from attendees.

Time Commitment

Based on a 40-hour week, the volume of cermonies can seem overwhelming for your team. In reality, the commitment outside of actually running the experiments is quite modest, and appropriately shouldered by the core team.

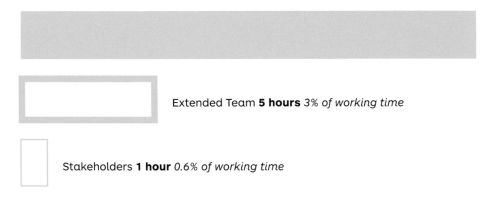

Core Team **15.25 hours** *9% of working time*

Extended Team **5 hours** *3% of working time*

Stakeholders **1 hour** *0.6% of working time*

Time
30–60 minutes
Once a week
After Weekly Learning

Attendees
Core Team

Weekly Planning

Plan and task out the experiments for the upcoming week. While the plan may change, the planning that goes into it is still a valuable exercise.

Agenda

1. Hypotheses to Test
Identify and revisit the hypotheses you are testing. Choose at least one of your important hypotheses to test for the upcoming week.

2. Experiment Prioritization
Once you've defined your hypotheses, prioritize the experiments you'll need to run in order to learn about the hypotheses. Use our experiment library to identify which experiment is best suited for testing desirability, viability, and feasibility.

3. Experiment Tasking
After the experiments have been prioritized, task out the top experiments you've selected to run for the upcoming week. Remember that complex experiments take longer and often require sequential tasks.

TEST

Corporate Team

Core members of the Corporate Team.

Extended Team members are optional, unless you anticipate that their expertise will be needed for the upcoming week. Then they are recommended.

Startup Team

Core members of the Startup Team.

Even if it's only two of you, get into a habit of explaining what's bouncing around your head, so that you can prioritize the most important work.

External contractors are optional, unless you anticipate that their expertise will be needed for the upcoming week. Then they are recommended.

Solopreneur

Solopreneurs benefit from Weekly Planning, even if you are not coordinating with external contractors.

The ritual of planning your work every week will help you keep a cadence and establish a sense of accomplishment.

If you are using external contractors then their attendance is optional, unless you anticipate that their expertise will be needed for the upcoming week's experiments. Then it is recommended.

Time
15 minutes
Every weekday
Morning, same time

Attendees
Core Team

Daily Standups

Stay aligned and focus on your daily work. Many experiments require a series of tasks to complete, and Daily Standups help coordinate your day-to-day work.

Agenda

1. What's the Daily Goal?

Create a daily goal. If your goal is to get an experiment out the door, then it's important to align your tasks to achieve that goal. Remember that daily goals feed into your larger, more ambitious goals for the overall business.

2. How to Achieve That Goal?

Identify the tasks needed to achieve the daily goal and plan your day.

3. What's in the Way?

Identify any blockers that would prevent you from completing experiment tasks for the day or achieving the goal. Some of these can be addressed within the standup if it is quick, otherwise meet after the standup to work through it.

Corporate Team

Core members of the Corporate Team.

Have the Daily Standup in a location where others can see you planning your day. It's a great way to socialize your process to the rest of the organization.

Startup Team

Core members of the Startup Team.

You'll still benefit from Daily Standups. Startups move fast and you can get out of sync rather quickly. This will help you stay aligned and focused on your goals over time.

Solopreneur

Yes, even Solopreneurs need to plan out your day. Daily Standups help you stay organized and aligned with your bigger goals, even if you are not coordinating with external contractors.

Time
30–60 minutes
Once a week
Before Weekly planning

Attendees
Extended Team
Core Team

Weekly Learning

Have a conversation to interpret the evidence and turn it into action. Remember that what you've learned from experiments should inform your overall strategy.

Agenda

1. Gather Evidence

Gather up the evidence your experiments have generated. This includes both qualitative and quantitative types of evidence.

2. Generate Insights

Look for patterns and insights from your evidence. Even qualitative evidence can be quickly themed using techniques such as affinity sorting. Try to keep an open mind. You may find unexpected insights that lead you to new paths to revenue.

3. Revisit Your Strategy

Take the new insights you have and revisit your Business Model Canvas, Value Proposition Canvas, and Assumptions Map. Make any updates needed so that they reflect your current state of learning. This is a crucial step in using what you've learned to inform your strategy. If it feels awkward, don't worry, it's a normal part of being an entrepreneur.

TEST

Corporate Team

Core members of the Corporate Team.

Extended Team members are optional, unless you anticipate that their expertise will be needed for synthesizing the learning. Then they are recommended.

Startup Team

Core members of the Startup Team.

External contractors are optional, unless you anticipate that their expertise will be needed for synthesizing the learning. Then they are recommended.

Solopreneur

If you are using external contractors, they are optional to attend, unless you anticipate that their expertise will be needed for synthesizing the learning. Then they are recommended.

Time
30–60 minutes
Biweekly
After Weekly
Learning/Before
Weekly Planning

Attendees
Core Team

Biweekly Retrospective

Take a step back, breathe, and talk about how you can improve the way you work. In our opinion, this is the most important ceremony. When you stop reflecting, you stop learning and improving.

Agenda

1. What's Going Well

Take five minutes to silently write down what's going well. This gets the retrospective off to a good start as people have space to speak positively about team members and how they are working together.

2. What Needs Improvement

Take five minutes to silently write down what needs improvement. These are things that aren't going well or could be doing better. It's important to frame these items as an opportunity to improve, rather than as a personal attack against a team member.

3. What to Try Next

Come up with three things you'd like to try. It can be one of the items you've previously discussed, or something completely new. This gives you a chance to try out a new way of working that isn't simply rooted in what needs improvement.

Tip
There are plenty of additional retrospective options, such as Speed Boat, Start — Stop — Keep, and Keep — Drop — Add.
*   We recommend trying out a few different formats to see what works best for you.*

Corporate Team

Core members of the Corporate Team.

For Corporate Teams, it's important to detail what you can control inside the team and what may be outside your sphere of influence in the organization.

After the retrospective is completed, have a designated team member communicate any external issues upstream to get help.

If you cannot get them resolved, try to find creative ways to mitigate their impact on the team.

Startup Team

Core members of the Startup Team.

For Startup Teams, keep in mind that as you incorporate improvements into the way you work, it can help build the culture you want to create in your startup.

Cofounders who exhibit the willingness to inspect and adapt how they work will eventually attract employees who want to work that way.

Solopreneur

For Solopreneurs, it can sometimes feel like an isolating experience. Take the time to reflect on how you are working, even if it's only you during the ceremony.

If you are unable to achieve the results you are aiming for, then it's a good idea to try new ways of working to break through.

If you are using external contractors then they are optional to attend, unless you want to check in with them and improve how you are collaborating.

Time
60–90 minutes
Once a month

Attendees
Stakeholders
Extended Team
Core Team

Monthly Stakeholder Reviews
Keep stakeholders in the loop on how you are pivoting, persevering, or killing the idea.

Agenda
1. What You've Learned
Provide an executive summary of what you've learned over the past month. This includes each Weekly Learning Goal and any additional insights generated from experiments. It's important not to overwhelm the attendees with detailed breakdowns of every experiment. Have the information in the appendix to dive deeper if needed.

2. What's Blocking Progress
This is the time to review any impediments that Stakeholders can assist in removing. This includes items from previous Retrospectives that fall outside your influence or control. These should be clearly communicated as requests for assistance.

3. Pivot / Persevere / Kill Decision
Make your recommendation to Stakeholders on whether you should pivot, persevere, or kill the new business idea. This should be based not only on what you've learned, but also what you see as a path forward in your strategy.

Tip
The three major types of pivots we witness are based on the customer, problem, and solution. You can stick with the customer, pivot on the problem. You can stick with the problem and pivot on customer. You can stick with customer and problem, and pivot on the solution.

Corporate Team

Core members of the Corporate Team and Stakeholders.

For Corporate Teams, continue to communicate the progress on what you've learned to Stakeholders. Walk a balance between showing how you are working differently and making progress.

If the Stakeholders take the form of a funding committee, then decisions will be made during the session on whether to fund the effort going forward.

Startup Team

Core members of the Startup Team and Stakeholders.

For Startup Teams, you want to keep investors in the loop on how you are making progress, even if that means sharing your struggles. Great investors realize it's not a linear path to a success. Balaji Srinivasan affectionally calls this the "Idea Maze."

You can choose to communicate this via an email or video update, if your Investors are not physically nearby.

Solopreneur

Solopreneur and an Advisor.

Get on a video call or have coffee with your advisor and share what you've learned and what you're recommending. Although your advisor is not likely an investor, it's still helpful to get an outside opinion on your strategy.

To learn more about the "Idea Maze" visit spark-public.s3.amazonaws.com/startup/lecture_slides/ lecture5-market-wireframing-design.pdf.

Principles of Experiment Flow

Running one experiment is great, but the goal is to reduce the uncertainty in your business. This means running several experiments over time. You want your experiment process to flow, generating the evidence needed to make informed investment decisions.

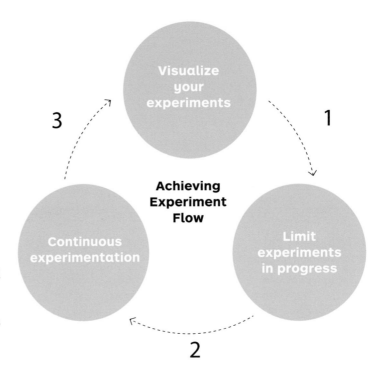

Visualize Your Experiments

*Make your work visible
to yourself and others.*

We've found inspiration from the lean and kanban movements, particularly on this principle. If you keep all this work in your head, you'll never be able to achieve flow. Not only are your teammates unable to read your mind, but much of flow requires you to visualize your work.

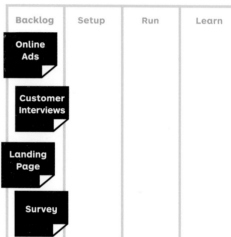

1. Write down your experiments

We recommend only one experiment per sticky, to keep things organized. You don't have to write down hundreds of experiments—only the ones you feel you'll be running over the upcoming weeks.

2. Draw a simple experiment board

This is one of the simplest forms of an experiment board you can create. We've been playing with this format for quite some time and used to like the "Validate" column, which we got originally from Eric Ries. Over time, we've started to back off a bit on that language because teams will set the bar so low on their hypotheses that they'll artificially validate them and move on too quickly. We prefer "Learn" over "Validate."

3. Add your experiments to the Backlog column

Rank your experiments from top to bottom, where the top is the one you are going to do next. Pull them across as you begin to work on each, moving from Setup, to Run, to Learn.

PRINCIPLE #2

Limit Experiments in Progress
Multitasking too many experiments can often lead to trouble.

Teams inherently underestimate how much work it is to run experiments, especially if they've never run them before. So it should come as no surprise that they often pull all the experiments over at once and try to do them all in parallel. This results in slowing the entire process down. It's also difficult to extract insights from a previous experiment to inform your next one.

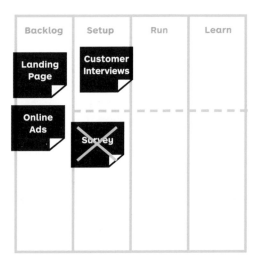

Define work in progress limits for your experiments.

For example, start with a limit of 1 for Setup, Run, and Learn columns. This will prevent the team from pulling a second experiment over until the first is moved to the next column and finally archived.

In this example, the team runs the customer interviews before the survey, instead of trying to do both at once (and slowing everything down). The experiments flow, using what you've learned to inform your next experiment.

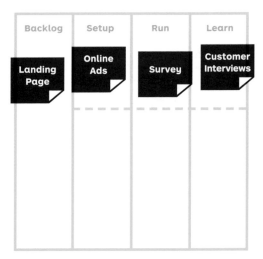

Continuous Experimentation
Continue to experiment over time.

The last principle, which also finds its roots in lean and kanban, is the idea of continuous experimentation. A team that starts with the previous board to achieve flow will eventually outgrow it. You don't want the board to artificially constrain the team from growing and maturing over time. As we recommend in the section on ceremonies (see page 80 and following), have a retrospective every two weeks. This applies to your experiment flow, which can yield interesting artifacts for improvement.

Backlog	Setup		Run	Learn
	In Progress	Waiting		
Survey	Customer Interviews			
Online Ads				
Landing Page				

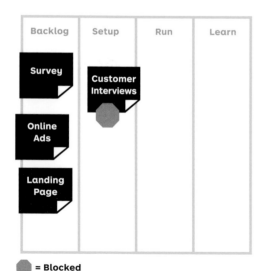

Backlog	Setup	Run	Learn
Survey	Customer Interviews		
Online Ads			
Landing Page			

⬡ = Blocked

Blocker Experiment
As an example, is that the team is trying to line up customer interviews, but the research department won't let them. They state that it's against company policy to talk to customers. That is a "blocker" that's preventing you from making progress on that experiment.

It's a good idea to identify and visualize these, which will help you communicate progress to stakeholders as to why things are slowing down. It's hard to achieve flow when you are blocked.

Splitting Columns Experiment
Another example is that the team has outgrown the initial board and is frustrated that the Setup column doesn't capture the nuances of experimentation.

There is work setting up an experiment, but then you have to run it, and if the team is at capacity the experiment may sit around for a long time waiting to be run. When we talk about the board, it would be great to see which ones are ready to be run and which experiments are still being set up.

Ethics in Experimentation

Are you experimenting with your customers or on them?

This book is about helping you determine if your business idea is desirable, viable, and feasible. What it is *not* is a reason to scam people out of their money. Vaporware was a term that became popular during the late 1980s and much of the 1990s. It described products that never launched, but never really canceled either. Vaporware products managed to get people hyped up, often promising unrealistic expectations. In more severe cases, people even used the lure of vaporware to scam people out of real money. Our goal isn't to recreate the vaporware environment of the 1990s. This is especially important in the era of fake news, when techniques can be weaponized as propaganda to influence entire nations. Context is important when using experiments to de-risk your business. In short, don't be evil.

Experiment Guidelines

Poor communication can destroy any experiment cadence you try to create. You can address this by clearly communicating the details and "the why" behind the experimentation. Teams who've done this repeatedly, over time, find that they are repeating themselves quite a bit. To make things a bit more efficient, they've crafted experiment guidelines to help communicate with those outside of the team. This is particularly effective when working with legal, safety, and compliance departments.

Experiment Guidelines Sample

1. *Our customer segment is _____.*
2. *The total number of customers involved in our experiment is estimated to be _____.*
3. *Our experiment will run from _____ to _____.*
4. *The information currency we are collecting is _____.*
5. *The branding we'll use for the experiment is _____.*
6. *The financial exposure of the experiment is _____.*
7. *We can turn off the experiment by using _____.*

Experi

ments

"The problem happens when you don't put that first note down. Just start!"

———

Herbie Hancock
Jazz musician, composer, and actor

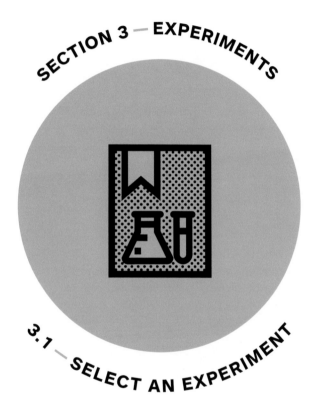

SECTION 3 — EXPERIMENTS

3.1 — SELECT AN EXPERIMENT

Experiment Selection

Pick the right experiment by asking these three questions:

1. **Type of hypothesis: What type of hypothesis are you testing?**
   Pick experiments based on your major learning objective. Some experiments produce better evidence for desirability, some work better for feasibility, and some are more appropriate for viability.

2. **Level of uncertainty: How much evidence do you already have (for a specific hypothesis)?**
   The less you know, the less you should waste time, energy, and money. When you know little, your only goal is to produce evidence that points you in the right direction. Quick and cheap experiments are most appropriate for that goal, despite the generally weak evidence. The more you know, the stronger the evidence should become, which is usually achieved by more costly and lengthier experiments.

3. **Urgency: How much time do you have until the next major decision point or until you run out of money?**
   The selection of the right experiment may depend on the time and money you have available. If you have a major meeting with decision makers or investors coming up, you might need to use quick and cheap experiments to quickly generate evidence on multiple aspects of your idea. When you are running out of money, you need to pick the right experiments to convince decision-makers and investors to extend funding.

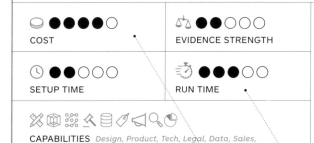

EXPERIMENT NAME / OVERVIEW

Experiment Name

Experiment description

COST ●●●●○

EVIDENCE STRENGTH ●●○○○

SETUP TIME ●●○○○

RUN TIME ●●●○○

DESIRABILITY · FEASIBILITY · VIABILITY

Experiment is ideal for —what it's ideal for

Experiment is not ideal for —what it's not ideal for

CAPABILITIES *Design, Product, Tech, Legal, Data, Sales, Marketing, Research, Finance*

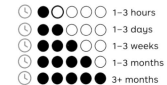

SETUP / RUN TIME

○ ●○○○○ 1–3 hours
○ ●●○○○ 1–3 days
○ ●●●○○ 1–3 weeks
○ ●●●●○ 1–3 months
○ ●●●●● 3+ months

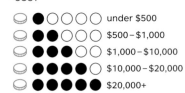

COST

○ ●○○○○ under $500
○ ●●○○○ $500–$1,000
○ ●●●○○ $1,000–$10,000
○ ●●●●○ $10,000–$20,000
○ ●●●●● $20,000+

Rules of thumb

1. **Go cheap and fast at the beginning.**
   Early on, you generally know little. Stick to cheap and quick experiments to pinpoint the right direction. You can afford starting out with weaker evidence, because you will test more later. Ideally, you select an experiment that is cheap, fast, and still produces strong evidence.

2. **Increase the strength of evidence with multiple experiments for the same hypothesis.**
   Run several experiments to support or refute a hypothesis. Try to learn about a hypothesis as fast as possible, then run more experiments to produce stronger evidence for confirmation. Don't make important decisions based on one experiment or weak evidence.

3. **Always pick the experiment that produces the strongest evidence given your constraints.**
   Always select and design the strongest experiment you can, while respecting the context. When uncertainty is high you should go fast and cheap, but that doesn't necessarily mean you can't produce strong evidence.

4. **Reduce uncertainty as much as you can before you build anything.**
   People often think they need to build something to start testing an idea. Quite the contrary. The higher the costs to build something, the more you need to run multiple experiments to show that customers actually have the jobs, pains, and gains you think they have.

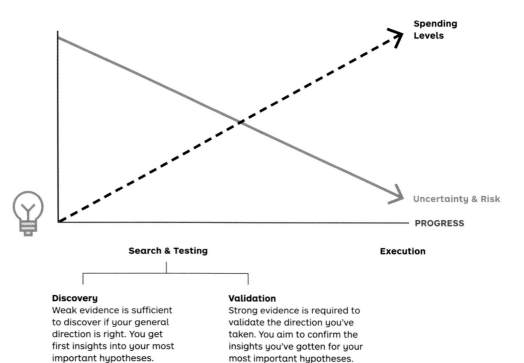

Spending Levels

Uncertainty & Risk

PROGRESS

Search & Testing

Execution

Discovery
Weak evidence is sufficient to discover if your general direction is right. You get first insights into your most important hypotheses.

Validation
Strong evidence is required to validate the direction you've taken. You aim to confirm the insights you've gotten for your most important hypotheses.

Discovery Experiments

Ask these three questions

1. **What type of hypothesis are you testing?**
2. **How much evidence do you already have (for a specific hypothesis)?**
3. **How much time do you have until the next major decision point or until you run out of money?**

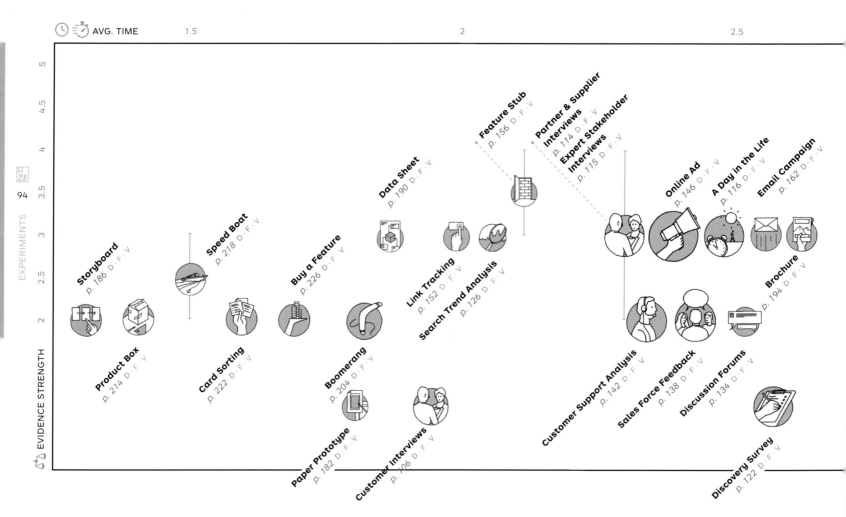

🕐 AVG. TIME   1.5   2   2.5

94

EXPERIMENTS

EVIDENCE STRENGTH

Storyboard *p. 186 D . F . V*

Product Box *p. 214 D . F . V*

Speed Boat *p. 218 D . F . V*

Card Sorting *p. 222 D . F . V*

Buy a Feature *p. 226 D . F . V*

Boomerang *p. 204 D . F . V*

Paper Prototype *p. 182 D . F . V*

Customer Interviews *p. 106 D . F . V*

Data Sheet *p. 190 D . F . V*

Link Tracking *p. 152 D . F . V*

Search Trend Analysis *p. 126 D . F . V*

Feature Stub *p. 156 D . F . V*

Partner & Supplier Interviews *p. 114 D . F . V*

Expert Stakeholder Interviews *p. 115 D . F . V*

Online Ad *p. 146 D . F . V*

A Day in the Life *p. 116 D . F . V*

Email Campaign *p. 162 D . F . V*

Brochure *p. 194 D . F . V*

Customer Support Analysis *p. 142 D . F . V*

Sales Force Feedback *p. 138 D . F . V*

Discussion Forums *p. 134 D . F . V*

Discovery Survey *p. 122 D . F . V*

Rules of thumb

1. **Go cheap and fast early on in your journey.**

2. **Increase the strength of evidence with multiple experiments for the same hypothesis.**

3. **Always pick the experiment that produces the strongest evidence, given your constraints.**

4. **Reduce uncertainty as much as you can before you build anything.**

3   3.5   4

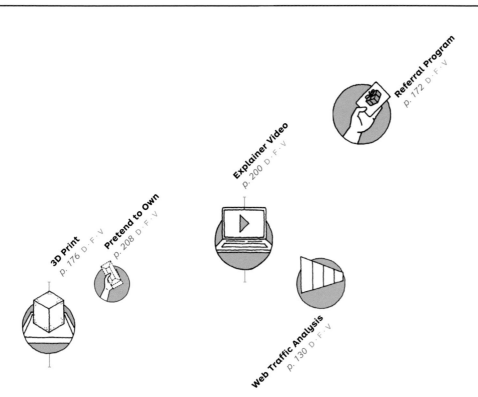

3D Print
P. 176 D · F · V

Pretend to Own
P. 208 D · F · V

Explainer Video
P. 200 D · F · V

Referral Program
P. 172 D · F · V

Web Traffic Analysis
P. 130 D · F · V

Social Media Campaign
P. 168 D · F · V

Validation Experiments

Ask these three questions

1. **What type of hypothesis are you testing?**
2. **How much evidence do you already have (for a specific hypothesis)?**
3. **How much time do you have until the next major decision point or until you run out of money?**

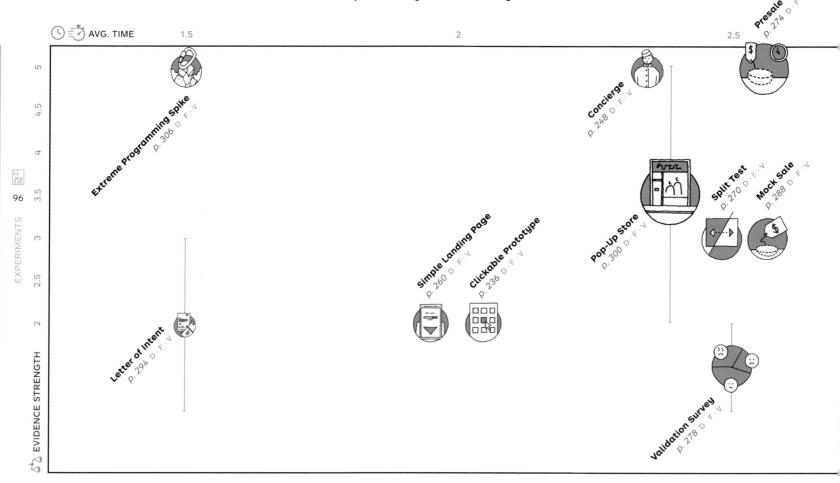

🕐 ⏱️ AVG. TIME   1.5   2   2.5

96

EXPERIMENTS

EVIDENCE STRENGTH

Extreme Programming Spike *p. 306 D · F · V*

Letter of Intent *p. 294 D · F · V*

Simple Landing Page *p. 260 D · F · V*

Clickable Prototype *p. 236 D · F · V*

Concierge *p. 248 D · F · V*

Presale *p. 274 D · F · V*

Pop-Up Store *p. 300 D · F · V*

Split Test *p. 270 D · F · V*

Mock Sale *p. 288 D · F · V*

Validation Survey *p. 278 D · F · V*

Rules of thumb

1. **Go cheap and fast early on in your journey.**

2. **Increase the strength of evidence with multiple experiments for the same hypothesis.**

3. **Always pick the experiment that produces the strongest evidence, given your constraints.**

4. **Reduce uncertainty as much as you can before you build anything.**

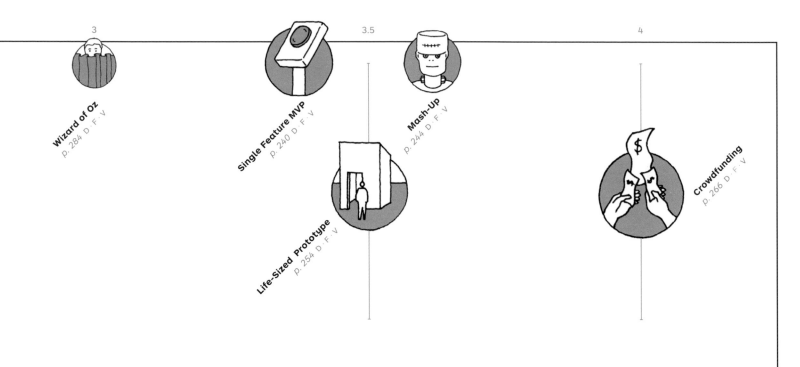

3

Wizard of Oz
p. 284 D · F · V

3.5

Single Feature MVP
p. 240 D · F · V

Mash-Up
p. 244 D · F · V

Life-Sized Prototype
p. 254 D · F · V

4

Crowdfunding
p. 266 D · F · V

DEFINITION

Experiment Sequences

Go beyond pairing with experimentation sequences.

Once you've turned your insights into action, it's time to move on and throw the experiment away, correct? Well, not necessarily. As illustrated in the pairings for each experiment, there are experiments you can run before, during, and after. But what about a sequence of experiments? Great teams are able to gain momentum and build up stronger evidence over time with a series of experiments.

B2B Hardware Sequence

B2B hardware companies search for evidence of customers already hacking together their own solutions to a problem. They use this to inform their design to do the job even better. Then they test it out quickly by integrating standard components with potential customers and crowdfunding it if the signal is strong.

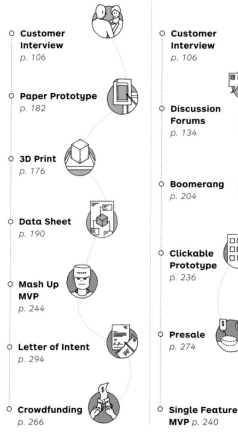

○ **Customer Interview**
p. 106

○ **Paper Prototype**
p. 182

○ **3D Print**
p. 176

○ **Data Sheet**
p. 190

○ **Mash Up MVP**
p. 244

○ **Letter of Intent**
p. 294

○ **Crowdfunding**
p. 266

B2B Software Sequence

B2B software companies look for opportunities where employees are mandated to use subpar software. Many have disrupted incumbents simply by observing where their deficiencies exist and then designing a better experience that solves for a high value customer job, using modern technology.

○ **Customer Interview**
p. 106

○ **Discussion Forums**
p. 134

○ **Boomerang**
p. 204

○ **Clickable Prototype**
p. 236

○ **Presale**
p. 274

○ **Single Feature MVP** p. 240

B2B Services Sequence

B2B services companies often interview stakeholders to research the cost of poorly designed processes and services. They analyze customer support data to see if this is reflected in other areas within the company. Afterward, they create a brochure to communicate the improvement and then deliver the service manually to a handful of customers before scaling.

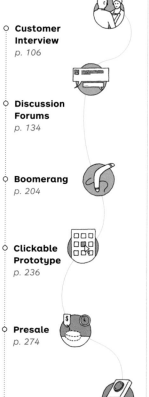
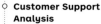

○ **Expert Stakeholder Interviews**
p. 115

○ **Customer Support Analysis**
p. 142

○ **Brochure**
p. 194

○ **Presale**
p. 274

○ **Concierge**
p. 248

B2C Hardware Sequence

Consumer hardware companies have more options now than ever before. They can create Explainer Videos on how their new product will solve an existing problem, then rapidly build using standard hardware components. They will eventually crowdfund the build and distribute to the customer through retail or direct.

 Customer Interview *p. 106*

 Search Trend Analysis *p. 126*

 Paper Prototype *p. 182*

 3D Print *p. 176*

 **Explainer Video** *p. 200*

 **Crowdfunding** *p. 266*

 Pop-Up Store *p. 300*

B2C Software Sequence

The rise of the Internet, open source software, and tools have catapulted new software companies into global markets. Smart B2C companies use the words of their customers in their content to increase conversions. They rapidly prototype experiences and even deliver the value manually before building the product.

 Customer Interview *p. 106*

Online Ad *p. 146*

 Simple Landing Page *p. 260*

 Email Campaign *p. 162*

 Clickable Prototype *p. 236*

 Mock Sale *p. 288*

 **Wizard of Oz** *p. 284*

B2C Services Sequence

B2C services companies start in a specific region by interviewing customers and looking for search volume to determine interest. They can quickly launch ads that drive regional customers to their landing page, then follow it up with an email campaign. Once they've conducted a few presales, B2C services can deliver the value manually to refine it before scaling.

 Customer Interview *p. 106*

 **Search Trend Analysis** *p. 126*

 Online Ad *p. 146*

 Simple Landing Page *p. 260*

Email Campaign *p. 162*

 Presale *p. 274*

 Concierge *p. 248*

B2B2C with B2C Experimentation Sequence

B2B2C companies are in a unique position to use experimentation to inform the supply chain. Many companies we work with go directly to the consumer with their experiments, generate evidence, and then use it in negotiations with their B2B partners. The presence of evidence helps provide leverage, instead of circular conversations based only on opinion.

 Customer Interview *p. 106*

 Online Ad *p. 146*

 Simple Landing Page *p. 260*

 Explainer Video *p. 200*

 Presale *p. 274*

 Concierge *p. 248*

 Buy a Feature *p. 226*

 Data Sheet *p. 190*

 Partner & Supplier Interview *p. 114*

 Letter of Intent *p. 294*

Pop-Up Store *p. 300*

Highly Regulated Sequence

Contrary to popular belief, highly regulated companies can also use experimentation. They need to do so within the constraints of the system and be mindful that not all testing activities involve a catastrophic degree of risk. Companies carve out the extremely high risk areas they are not willing to experiment on and then go after the places in which they can experiment.

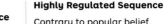 **A Day in the Life** *p. 116*

Validation Survey *p. 278*

Customer Support Analysis *p. 142*

Sales Force Feedback *p. 138*

Storyboard *p. 186*

Explainer Video *p. 200*

Brochure *p. 194*

Partner & Supplier Interview *p. 114*

Data Sheet *p. 190*

Presale *p. 274*

"Knowing your customer
inside and out is mission-critical,
and it takes time."

—————

Sallie Krawcheck
Founder, Ellevest

3.2 — DISCOVERY

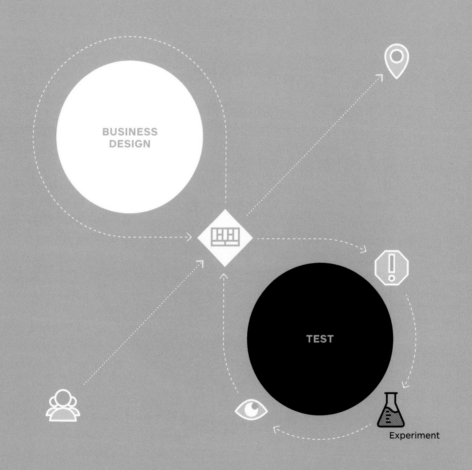

Idea

Business

Search & Testing	Execution

Discovery
Discover if your general direction is right. Test basic hypotheses. Get first insights to course-correct rapidly.

Validation
Validate the direction you've taken. Confirm with strong evidence that your business idea is very likely to work.

Discovery Experiments

◯ COST	◷ SETUP TIME	⏱ RUN TIME	⚖ EVIDENCE STRENGTH	THEME
●●○○○	●●○○○	●●○○○	●○○○○	DESIRABILITY · FEASIBILITY · VIABILITY
●●○○○	●●○○○	●●●○○	●●○○○	DESIRABILITY · FEASIBILITY · VIABILITY
●●○○○	●●○○○	●●●○○	●●●◐○	DESIRABILITY · FEASIBILITY · VIABILITY
●●○○○	●●○○○	●●●○○	●●●○○	DESIRABILITY · FEASIBILITY · VIABILITY
●●○○○	●●○○○	●●●○○	●○○○○	DESIRABILITY · FEASIBILITY · VIABILITY
●○○○○	●●○○○	●●○○○	●●●○○	DESIRABILITY · FEASIBILITY · VIABILITY
●●○○○	●●○○○	●●●○○	●●○○○	DESIRABILITY · FEASIBILITY · VIABILITY
●○○○○	●●○○○	●●●○○	●●○○○	DESIRABILITY · FEASIBILITY · VIABILITY
●●○○○	●●○○○	●●○○○	●●○○○	DESIRABILITY · FEASIBILITY · VIABILITY
●●○○○	●●○○○	●●●○○	●●○○○	DESIRABILITY · FEASIBILITY · VIABILITY
●●●○○	●●○○○	●●●○○	●●●○○	DESIRABILITY · FEASIBILITY · VIABILITY
●○○○○	●○○○○	●●●○○	●●●○○	DESIRABILITY · FEASIBILITY · VIABILITY
●○○○○	●○○○○	●○○○○	●●●○○	DESIRABILITY · FEASIBILITY · VIABILITY
●○○○○	●●○○○	●●○○○	●●●◐○	DESIRABILITY · FEASIBILITY · VIABILITY
●○○○○	●●○○○	●●●○○	●●●○○	DESIRABILITY · FEASIBILITY · VIABILITY
●●○○○	●●●○○	●●●●●	●●●◐○	DESIRABILITY · FEASIBILITY · VIABILITY
●●●○○	●●○○○	●●●●●	●●●●◐	DESIRABILITY · FEASIBILITY · VIABILITY
●●●○○	●●●○○	●●●○○	●●◐○○	DESIRABILITY · FEASIBILITY · VIABILITY
●○○○○	●●○○○	●●○○○	●○○○○	DESIRABILITY · FEASIBILITY · VIABILITY
●●○○○	●●○○○	●○○○○	●●○○○	DESIRABILITY · FEASIBILITY · VIABILITY
●○○○○	●●○○○	●●○○○	●●●○○	DESIRABILITY · FEASIBILITY · VIABILITY
●○○○○	●●●○○	●●○○○	●●●○○	DESIRABILITY · FEASIBILITY · VIABILITY
●●●○○	●●●○○	●●●●○	●●○○○	DESIRABILITY · FEASIBILITY · VIABILITY
●●○○○	●●○○○	●●○○○	●●○○○	DESIRABILITY · FEASIBILITY · VIABILITY
●○○○○	●●○○○	●●●●○	●●○○○	DESIRABILITY · FEASIBILITY · VIABILITY
●●○○○	●●○○○	●○○○○	●●○○○	DESIRABILITY · FEASIBILITY · VIABILITY
●●○○○	●●○○○	●○○○○	●●◐○○	DESIRABILITY · FEASIBILITY · VIABILITY
●●○○○	●●○○○	●○○○○	●●○○○	DESIRABILITY · FEASIBILITY · VIABILITY
●●○○○	●●○○○	●○○○○	●●○○○	DESIRABILITY · FEASIBILITY · VIABILITY

DISCOVERY / EXPLORATION

Customer Interview

An interview that is focused on exploring customer jobs, pains, gains, and willingness to pay.

COST ◯ ● ● ◯ ◯ ◯

EVIDENCE STRENGTH ⚖ ● ◯ ◯ ◯ ◯

SETUP TIME 🕐 ● ● ◯ ◯ ◯

RUN TIME ⏱ ● ● ◯ ◯ ◯

CAPABILITIES *Research*

🔲 ✉ ◐

DESIRABILITY · FEASIBILITY · VIABILITY

Customer Interviews are ideal for gaining qualitative insights into the fit between your value proposition and the customer segment. It's also a good starting point for price testing.

Customer Interviews are not ideal as a substitute for what people will do.

Prepare

☐ Write a script to learn about:

- customers jobs, pains, and gains.

- customers' willingness to buy.

- unmet needs between product and solution.

☐ Find Interviewees.

☐ Select a time frame for your analysis.

Execute

☐ Interviewer asks questions from the script and dives deeper when required.

☐ Scribe takes notes with exact phrasing and notes on body language.

☐ Repeat for 15–20 interviews.

Analyze

☐ Do a 15-minute debrief while impressions are fresh in mind.

☐ Affinity sort the notes.

☐ Perform a ranking analysis.

☐ Update your Value Proposition Canvas.

Cost

Cost is relatively low as customers may not even need to be compensated. In general, remote interviews over video have a lower compensation than scheduled in-person interviews. B2B interviews are typically more expensive than B2C interviews, because the sample size is smaller and may have less free time.

Setup Time

Setup time for customer interviews can be very short or take a few weeks, depending on where your customers are and how accessible. You'll need to create a script, find your customers, and schedule the interviews.

Run Time

Run time for customer interviews is relatively short: they only take 15–30 minutes each. You'll need to have a 15-minute buffer in between each one to recap your findings and make any edits you need to the script.

Evidence Strength

Customer jobs
Customer pains
Customer gains

80% average accuracy ranking on top-3 customer jobs, pains, and gains. You want to be really dialed into your customer segment, so set the bar high.

Customer feedback

Customer jobs, pains, and gains that were not originally in your Customer Profile, but were offered up by your interviewee.

Interview referrals

Referrals are an added bonus. It's a good sign if they occur and it'll save you on acquisition costs for more interviews.

Customer Interviews are relatively weak evidence: it's only what people say and not necessarily what they'll do. However, they are great for qualitative insights to inform your value proposition and customer jobs, pains, and gains for future testing.

Capabilities

Research

While customer interviews can be deceptively difficult to do well, the good news it that almost anyone can do them with practice. It helps if you have a research background, but it isn't required. You'll need to write the script, source candidates, conduct the interview, and synthesize results. A partner makes this all so much easier—otherwise you'll have to record all of the interviews and watch them again.

Requirements

Target Customer

Customer Interviews work best when you are focused on a narrow target audience. Without a customer in mind, you'll end up getting very mixed results and conflicting feedback. It takes much longer to interview everyone, then back your way into a niche customer segment. Instead, we recommend you focus on a niche customer segment before running any customer interviews.

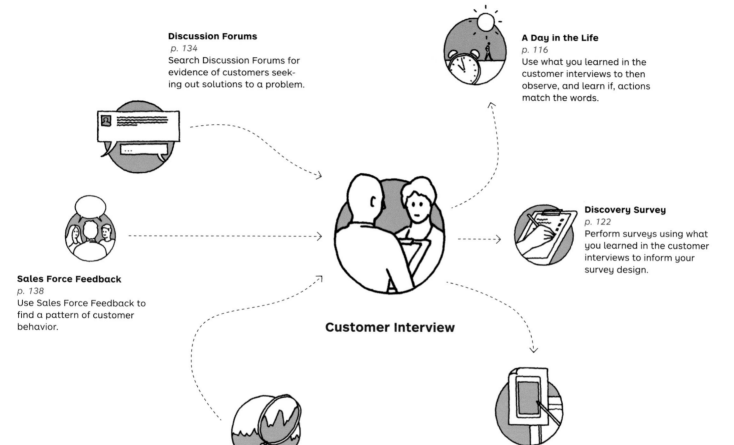

Discussion Forums
p. 134
Search Discussion Forums for evidence of customers seeking out solutions to a problem.

Sales Force Feedback
p. 138
Use Sales Force Feedback to find a pattern of customer behavior.

A Day in the Life
p. 116
Use what you learned in the customer interviews to then observe, and learn if, actions match the words.

Discovery Survey
p. 122
Perform surveys using what you learned in the customer interviews to inform your survey design.

Customer Interview

Search Trend Analysis
p. 126
Search online for volume around a specific job, pain, or gain.

Paper Prototype
p. 182
Sketch out what the solution to the customer jobs, pains, and gains could look like on paper.

CUSTOMER INTERVIEW

109

EXPLORATION

Writing a Script

Scripts are a key part of conducting effective customer interviews, otherwise they often turn into conversations that wander and rarely extract the learning. You need to de-risk your idea. We recommend building your script after you've created your Value Proposition Canvas and ranked the top three customer jobs, pains, and gains.

Sample Script

1. **Introduction & Context**

   "Hello, I am [name] doing research on [idea]"

   "No pressure to make a purchase."

   "Not going to sell you anything."

2. **Have Them Tell a Story**

   "When was the last time you experienced [pain or job]?"

   "What motivated you to do [action]?"

   "How did you solve it?"

   "If not, why?"

3. **Ranking Customer Jobs, Pains, and Gains**

   List the top three customer jobs, pains, and gains.

   Interviewee ranks them based on personal experiences.

   "Are there any others you expected to be on the list?"

4. **Thanks & Wrap Up**

   "What question should I have asked you?"

   "Can you refer me to someone else?"

   "May we contact you in the future?"

   "Thanks!"

Finding Interviewees

B2C Segment

We recommend creating a Value Proposition Canvas for your B2C segment and then brainstorming where you can find them online and offline. Vote as a team where you want to focus your search.

B2B Segment

Same exercise applies to B2B interviewee candidates, although it may be harder to brainstorm where to find them. Luckily there are online and offline locations that, in general, work well for finding B2B interviewees.

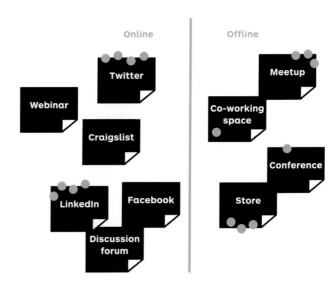

Vetting Interviewees

Vetting interview candidates isn't fail-safe, but overall it'll save you time by screening out those who do not qualify for the interview process. One or two less-than-ideal candidates will always slip through, but it's still better than not qualifying people at all. One way to do so is a simple screener survey to qualify people before scheduling anything.

Screening on Craigslist

Craigslist is a popular website for posting things to buy and sell, but it's also a gold mine for finding customers to interview. Simply go to the Community → Volunteers section of Craigslist and post your research request. In the description, include a survey link for those who are interested in participating. The survey should include qualifying and disqualifying questions.

For example, if you are looking for people who own a bicycle, ask: *"How many bicycles do you own—0, 1, 2, or 3+?"*

If people answer 0, then it saves you from interviewing those who do not own a bicycle. If people answer 3+, they also might not be ideal candidates because they own so many bicycles. Simple screener questions like this will save you and your interviewees hours.

Screening in-person

The offline version of this is very similar, although you'd simply ask these questions in person before diving into the entire interview. If they don't qualify, thank them for their time and move on.

Roles & Responsibilities

We recommend not doing these on your own if at all possible, whether your customer interview is online or in person. It's very difficult and time-consuming to ask the question, actively listen, note body language and response, and then ask the next question. If you get permission to record the interview, it'll take twice as long because you'll need to watch and listen to it all again. Instead, we recommend conducting interviews in pairs.

Scribe

- Takes notes.
- Writes exact quotes when possible without paraphrasing.
- Describes body language.

Interviewer

- Asks questions from script.
- Delves deeper when needed by asking why.
- Thanks and wrap up.

Interviewee

- Answers questions.

15-Minute Debrief

Immediately after each interview is concluded, take 15 minutes to debrief with your partner to quickly recap what you learned and if anything needs to be revised.

Debrief Topics

- What went well with that interview?
- What did we learn from body language?
- Did we bias the candidate in any way?
- Is there anything we want to quickly revise in the script?

Synthesizing Feedback

In addition to the 15-minute debrief, the team should synthesize their notes and update the Value Proposition Canvas to help inform your strategy. One quick way to sort through a lot of qualitative feedback is a technique called Affinity Sorting.

Affinity Sorting

As a team, set aside 30–60 minutes and bring your notes.

- Make sure there is plenty of wall space if meeting in person.
- Write one quote per sticky note.
- Write one insight per sticky note.
- Place the interviewee name or initials on the bottom of the sticky note.
- Place all stickies on the wall.
- Sort them into similar themes.

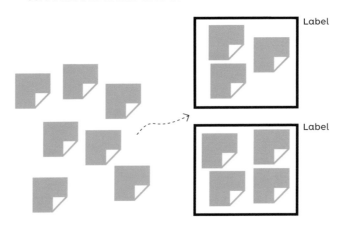

Label

Label

Ranking Analysis

Ranking isn't a perfect science, but it'll give you a sense of how close you are to the ranking in your Customer Profile. The drawback of having interviewees rank is that on its own, you don't know how much they feel the job, pain, or gain, relatively, compared to others. This is why it's important to ask follow-up questions and pick up on body language.

If you've interviewed 10 customers that match your Customer Profile, then ideally you want the customer jobs, pains, and gains ranking from your Customer Profile to be at the 80%+ accuracy rate. Which means 8 out of 10 ranked job 1 as #1, job 2 as #2, job 3 as #3, and so on.

Updating Your Canvas

After you've synthesized the qualitative feedback and analyzed rankings from your first batch of customer interviews, go back to your Value Proposition Canvas and make any edits needed. It's important that your testing inform your strategy.

✔

- ☐ *Ask for permission before recording.*
- ☐ *Qualify the candidate so that you don't waste each other's time.*
- ☐ *Adopt a beginner's mind.*
- ☐ *Listen more than you talk.*
- ☐ *Get facts, not opinions.*
- ☐ *Ask "why" to get real motivations.*
- ☐ *Ask for permission to follow up.*
- ☐ *Ask for referrals to interview.*
- ☐ *Ask if there is anything you should have asked, but didn't.*

✘

- – *Talk more than you listen.*
- – *Pitch the solution.*
- – *Be thinking of the next question to ask, instead of actively listening to the response.*
- – *Nod your head yes or no while the interviewee is speaking.*
- – *Ask only closed ended questions.*
- – *Schedule the interviews back to back, without any time in between to debrief.*
- – *Forget to update your Value Proposition Canvas with your findings.*

CUSTOMER INTERVIEW

113

EXPLORATION

DISCOVERY / EXPLORATION

Partner & Supplier Interviews

Partner & Supplier Interviews are similar to Customer Interviews, but you are focused on whether you can feasibly run the business. You'll be sourcing and interviewing Key Partners to supplement the Key Activities and Key Resources that you cannot do, or do not want to do, in-house.

DESIRABILITY · FEASIBILITY · VIABILITY

 ●●○○○
COST

 ●●○○○
SETUP TIME

 ●●●○○
RUN TIME

 ●●○○ ○

Evidence Strength

●●●●○
# of key partner bids

Response rate = number of partner interviews divided by the number of partner bids provided to you.

Key Partner bids are strong evidence that Key Partners are interested, although many details need to be agreed upon before it is a binding contract.

●●○○○
Key partner feedback

Key Partner quotes and feedback from the interviews.

When Key Partners state what they can deliver, it's relatively strong evidence as long as they check out.

Expert Stakeholder Interviews

Stakeholder Interviews are similar to Customer Interviews, but are focused on getting "buy-in" from key players inside your organization.

DESIRABILITY · FEASIBILITY · VIABILITY

● ● ○ ○ ○
COST

● ● ○ ○ ○
SETUP TIME

● ● ● ○ ○
RUN TIME

⚖ ● ● ○ ○ ○

Evidence Strength

Expert stakeholder feedback

Expert Stakeholder quotes and feedback from the interviews.

When stakeholders state what they wish to see strategically out of the initiative, it's moderately strong evidence. They need to back up their words with actions for it to be stronger.

DISCOVERY / EXPLORATION

A Day in the Life

A method of qualitative research that uses customer ethnography to better understand customer jobs, pains, and gains.

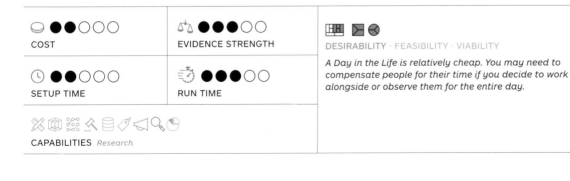

COST
●●○○○

EVIDENCE STRENGTH
●●●○○

SETUP TIME
●●○○○

RUN TIME
●●●○○

CAPABILITIES *Research*

DESIRABILITY · FEASIBILITY · VIABILITY

A Day in the Life is relatively cheap. You may need to compensate people for their time if you decide to work alongside or observe them for the entire day.

1. Prepare

☐ In teams of 2–3, define where and how you plan to observe. Clear your calendar so that you can commit several hours. Identify how to take notes and set the ground rules for not biasing the participants.

2. Permission

☐ Get consent from those who you'd like to observe. Explain the "why" behind the request.

3. Observe

☐ Using the Day in the Life worksheet, capture the customer time, activity, jobs, pains, gains, and notes on what you think. Do not interview or interact with the participants while observing.

4. Analyze

☐ Once the session is over, meet with your team to sort through the notes. Update your Value Proposition Canvas to reflect the latest findings to help inform future experiments.

Cost

A Day in the Life is relatively cheap. You may need to compensate people for their time if you decide to work alongside or observe them for the entire day.

Setup Time

Setup time for A Day in the Life is relatively short. You'll need to define and obtain consent from the participants you observe for the day.

Run Time

Run time for A Day in the Life is a bit longer than other methods, in that you need to spend several hours each day observing customer behavior. This can extend over several days or weeks at a time, depending on the number of participants.

Evidence Strength

●●●○○

Customer jobs
Customer pains
Customer gains

Notes and activities on observed customer jobs, pains, and gains throughout the day.

The grouping and ranking output of A Day in the Life is weak evidence, although it's stronger than inviting people into a lab setting because it's observed behavior in the real world.

●●●○○

Customer quotes

Take note of additional quotes from the customers that are not limited to jobs, pains, and gains.

Customer quotes are relatively weak, but helpful for context and qualitative insights for upcoming experiments.

Capabilities

Research

Almost anyone can use A Day in the Life. It will help if you have research abilities so that you can collect and document the data properly. It's recommended that you have a partner when doing so to compare notes.

Requirements

Consent

A Day in the Life ideally requires consent from those you are observing. It also requires you to coordinate with management and security at the locations in which you observe. For example, if you are going to hang out at a retail store and observe patterns, then speak to the manager first to get permission. If you wish to observe someone who made a purchase, ask them for permission before doing so. Otherwise this can become creepy and you may be escorted out by security.

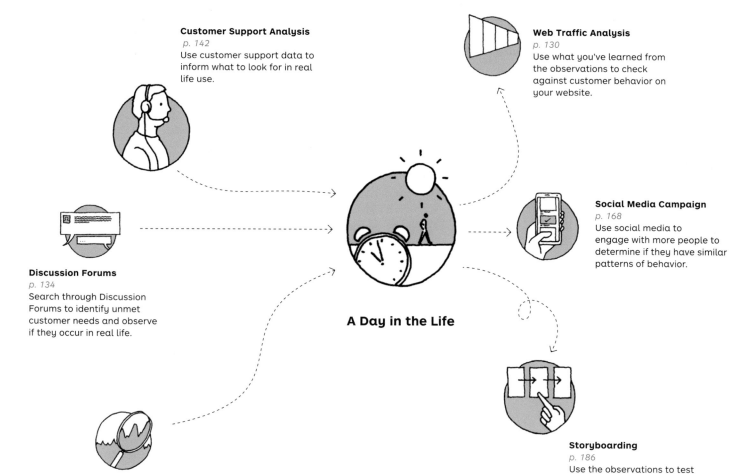

Customer Support Analysis
p. 142
Use customer support data to inform what to look for in real life use.

Web Traffic Analysis
p. 130
Use what you've learned from the observations to check against customer behavior on your website.

Discussion Forums
p. 134
Search through Discussion Forums to identify unmet customer needs and observe if they occur in real life.

A Day in the Life

Social Media Campaign
p. 168
Use social media to engage with more people to determine if they have similar patterns of behavior.

Storyboarding
p. 186
Use the observations to test sequences of solutions using illustrations.

Search Trend Analysis
p. 126
Use what you've found people searching for online and observe if this is happening in day-to-day usage.

A DAY IN THE LIFE

EXPLORATION

119

A DAY IN THE LIFE
Closing the Say/Do Gap
Intuit's Follow-Me-Home Program

Intuit creates financial, accounting, and tax preparation solutions for small businesses, accountants, and individuals, such as TurboTax, Quick-Books, and Mint.com. Intuit is located in the heart of Silicon Valley (Mountain View, California) and is well known for pushing the boundaries of customer-centric problem solving.

Can you give us a brief explanation of the Follow-Me-Home Program at Intuit?
The Follow-Me-Home is one technique from Intuit's "Design for Delight" program, that teaches our employees the skills required to create awesome products for our customers. Design for Delight includes three core principles: Deep Customer Empathy, Go Broad to Go Narrow, and Rapid Experimentation with Customers. The Follow-Me-Home is the most powerful technique from the Design for Delight principle, Deep Customer Empathy. There is nothing more effective than observing a customer when and where they are actually experiencing the pain and problems we are trying to solve.

We teach the Follow-Me-Home technique to each and every employee in the company, and each new person who joins Intuit learns the technique as part of their onboarding process. In fact, each new hire conducts at least two Follow-Me-Homes within the first few weeks of starting their career at Intuit, regardless of their function or level of seniority. From new engineers, to seasoned HR personnel, to product managers, to our most senior leaders, everyone is expected to learn how do to a Follow-Me-Home.

How did it get started?
Intuit's founder, Scott Cook, was inspired by a similar technique used by Toyota. In the early days of Intuit, Scott suspected he could use this technique to improve Intuit's products, and so he began testing the Follow-Me-Home approach while building our early products such as Quicken and QuickBooks. In those days software was installed on a physical computer via floppy discs (sounds crazy), so Scott and our product teams asked real customers if they could watch them install the software after it was purchased.

Through observation, product teams uncovered new insights, and complete surprises about how customers actually used our software in the real world. These insights often led to product improvements, so the Follow-Me-Home principles were codified, then shared with our employees. The Follow-Me-Home technique continues to evolve with the times, but the spirit remains the same—go observe customers where they are experiencing the pain or problems about which you need to learn.

What's your role in the program?
My team reports to Diego Rodriguez, Intuit's Chief Product and Design Officer. Our mission is to nurture Intuit's culture of innovation, through programs such as Design for Delight, our network of expert Innovation Catalyst Coaches, and high-impact training. Our job is to ensure each and every employee has the opportunity to learn and apply the most effective innovations skills to their daily work, such as Follow-Me-Homes, and we continuously improve these skills as the world changes.

We partner with other organizations such as HR, Learning and Development, and functional communities to achieve this goal, but our team's specialty is ensuring Intuit's innovation flame always burns bright. I work with an amazing team who are all dedicated to this goal, so my job is to simply continue learning and improving as a team. There are always ways we can get better.

What do you find most challenging about training employees in this technique?
Techniques like Follow-Me-Home can be learned by anyone, but just like any new skill, it takes consistent practice to master. In the early stages of learning people often misunderstand the details of how to execute a Follow-Me-Home, and it takes time for best practice to become second nature.

For example, one VERY important aspect of a great Follow-Me-Home is the focus on observation, versus traditional interviewing — i.e., talking. We teach people to focus first on what they observe a customer actually doing in a real situation, using their real tools, rather than overly scripting a simulation, or asking questions. Once observation is complete, only then should you ask interview-like questions, and when you ask questions focus on the "why" behind the observed behaviors, not speculation or opinions. When people first learn how to conduct a Follow-Me-Home, they typically ask way too many questions, and do not focus on simply observing the behaviors in question. That's just one example.

We also know that not everyone is comfortable "getting outside the building" to speak with people who are complete strangers. It does take a bit of courage to go try a Follow-Me-Home the first few times, so getting people over their initial reluctance is something we focus on, as well as encouraging them to practice often. The good news is that the vast majority of people tell us Follow-Me-Homes are transformative, and they often begin doing Follow-Me-Homes on their own. They end up loving the technique.

How do you see programs like this evolving in the future?
We've already improved our approach to Follow-Me-Homes over the years, and we'll continue to do so as the world around us evolves. For example, Intuit has an increasing number of customers all over the world. We've adapted the Follow-Me-Home so we can conduct them remotely, using video camera and screen share technology. We've also tweaked the approach to ensure we respect the cultures and traditions of the locations we visit. As the world continues to get flatter, and technology changes, we'll continue to adapt our approach. However, the spirit remains the same. Go observe for yourself.

What advice would you give readers who'd like to try this at their organization?
The simple answer is to just try it. Start small, trying it yourself on a few projects so you can learn what works and what does not work in the context of your organization. Then you build on what you learned to scale a formal program, or just continue using the technique yourself. You just might become the most effective person in your organization.

People who read this book are familiar with innovation best practices, so I simply suggest you apply these best practices to your future Follow-Me-Home program as if it is a "new product." Remember that Follow-Me-Homes are just one of the many skills required to be an effective innovator, so Follow-Me-Homes won't make you successful in a vacuum. You will likely need to develop supporting programs, and a culture which embraces these types of techniques. The good news is Follow-Me-Homes and the related skills are extremely fast to execute, flexible, and much cheaper than a failed product launch. Get out there and try it.

— *Bennett Blank*
Innovation Leader, Intuit Inc.

DISCOVERY / EXPLORATION

Discovery Survey

An open-ended questionnaire used in the collection of information
from a sample of customers.

COST

EVIDENCE STRENGTH

SETUP TIME

 RUN TIME

CAPABILITIES *Product / Marketing / Research*

DESIRABILITY · FEASIBILITY · VIABILITY

*Discovery Survey is ideal for uncovering your value proposition
and customer jobs, pains, and gains.*

*Discovery Survey is not ideal for determining what people will
do, only what they say they'll do.*

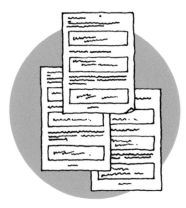

Sample Survey Questions

- *When was the last time you have [insert scenario here]?*
- *Can you explain what happened and how it impacted you?*
- *What other options did you explore? Why?*
- *If you could wave a magic wand, what would you have liked to have happened?*
- *What question do you wish we would have asked you?*

Prepare

☐ Define your goal for the survey and what you are trying to learn.

☐ Identify your target audience for the survey.

☐ Assuming a 10–20% response rate and calculate how many people should receive the survey.

☐ Set a start and stop date for the survey.

☐ Create your survey.

Execute

☐ Send your survey to customers.

Analyze

☐ Use Affinity Sorting to cluster responses into themes. Don't label before you sort; allow the labels to emerge from the sorting.

☐ Use word clouds or a text analyzer to quickly visualize which words and phrases customers use most frequently.

☐ Review the themes and quotes with your team and dot vote on the 1–3 themes you want to explore in more detail in upcoming experiments.

☐ Update your Value Proposition Canvas based on your findings.

Cost

Discovery surveys are not very expensive and there are several free and low-cost services that you can use to send them to your customers. Much of the cost comes from reaching the target audience. It gets more expensive if you are targeting professionals or are in the B2B space. Your sample size gets smaller; therefore you may end up spending time and money to reach your audience.

Setup Time

Discovery surveys do not take very long to set up and configure. Many of the questions are open-ended. It should only take a few hours to a day at most.

Run Time

Much of the run time on a discovery survey depends on the size of your customer pool and how easy it is to reach them. It shouldn't take more than a few days, but could take longer if you aren't able to get enough results.

Evidence Strength

●○○○○

# of free text answer responses
Insights

Look for repeating patterns in the responses to the survey. By the fifth survey response with a similar target customer, you should start seeing the same thing written in different ways.

●○○○○

 # people willing to be contacted after the survey
Valid Emails

Ideally you have a small percentage, around 10%, who want to be contacted in the future.

Capabilities

Product / Marketing / Research

Discovery surveys require the ability to write open-ended survey questions without a negative tone. You'll also need to be able to identify the audience and interpret the results by Affinity Sorting or using word clouds to find patterns in the feedback.

Requirements

Qualitative Source Material

Surveys are generally more impactful when you already have qualitative insights from other methods that don't scale. Use that material to inform your survey design.

Access to an Audience

Getting in front of the right audience is just as important as your survey design. If you have an existing site with lots of traffic, then you can leverage that to get to your audience. If you do not have this luxury or are going after a new market, then brainstorm channels to use before designing your survey.

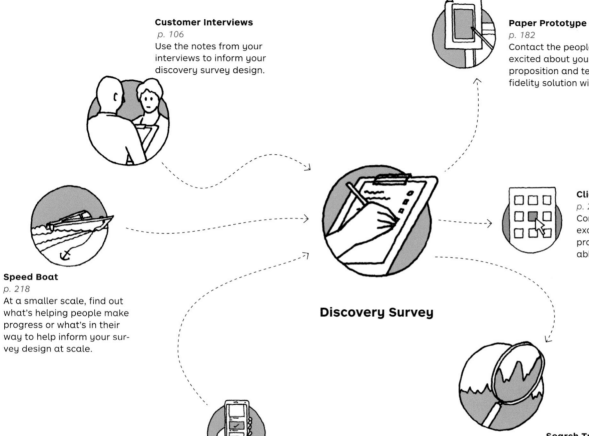

Customer Interviews
p. 106
Use the notes from your interviews to inform your discovery survey design.

Paper Prototype
p. 182
Contact the people who are excited about your value proposition and test your low fidelity solution with them.

Speed Boat
p. 218
At a smaller scale, find out what's helping people make progress or what's in their way to help inform your survey design at scale.

Discovery Survey

Clickable Prototype
p. 236
Contact the people who are excited about your value proposition and test a clickable prototype with them.

Social Media Campaign
p. 168
Use social media to acquire an audience for your discovery survey.

Search Trend Analysis
p. 126
Use the jobs, pains, and gains people listed to find out if these are popular search trends online.

DISCOVERY SURVEY

EXPLORATION

125

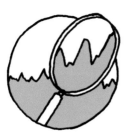

DISCOVERY / DATA ANALYSIS

Search Trend Analysis

The use of search data to investigate particular interactions among online searchers, the search engine, or the content during searching episodes.

COST	EVIDENCE STRENGTH
⊖ ●○○○○	⚖ ●●●○○

 DESIRABILITY · FEASIBILITY · VIABILITY

SETUP TIME	RUN TIME
🕐 ●●○○○	⏱ ●●○○○

Search Trend Analysis is ideal for performing your own market research, especially on newer trends, instead of relying on third party market research data.

CAPABILITIES *Marketing / Research / Data*

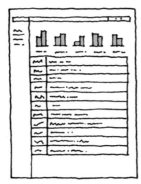 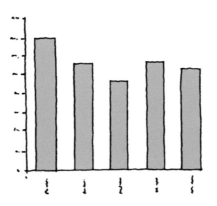 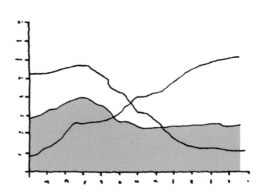

Prepare

☐ Identify what tools to use (Google Trends, Google Keyword Planner, etc.)

☐ Define a geographical area for your search.

☐ List the topics you want to explore such as:

- people trying to solve for customer jobs.

- individuals needing to address a customer pain.

- people wanting to create a customer gain.

- customers who are unhappy with an existing solution.

Execute

☐ Search for phrases related to your topics.

☐ Take screenshots and export your results.

☐ Write down notes alongside your research on what surprised you.

Analyze

☐ Gather your findings.

☐ Consider focusing on problem size over market size. What has the highest search volume on a typical problem? Would that be a meaningful business opportunity for you?

☐ Select the top 1–3 volume searches you want to explore in more detail in upcoming experiments.

Cost

The cost of performing your own Search Trend Analysis is relatively cheap, since there are existing free and low-cost tools. Both Google Trends and Google Keyword Planner are currently free to use.

Setup Time

Setup Time to perform Search Trend Analysis is relatively short, from a few minutes to a few hours. You'll need to define the criteria for your search and choose a tool.

Run Time

Run Time to perform Search Trend Analysis is also relatively short, from a few hours to a few days. It largely depends on the number of topics and geographic locations you are exploring. The more you have, the longer it'll take to do well.

Evidence Strength

●●●○○

Search Volume

# of searches for keyword within a certain period of time

Search Volume varies across geographic location, time, and industry. You'll want to compare your results against the others to get an overall feel for the level of interest.

●●●○○

Related Queries

Queries that users also searched for, in addition to the one you entered

If conducted properly, strength of evidence on search volume and related queries can be stronger than other smaller qualitative research methods.

Capabilities

Marketing / Research / Data

Search Trend Analysis can be performed by almost anyone who is willing to learn online trend analysis tools. Most of them, such as Google Trends and Google Keyword Planner, will have contextual help to walk you through the process. You'll still need to be able to interpret the results, so having a marketing, research, and data background will be beneficial.

Requirements

Online Customers

Search Trend Analysis can be a powerful way to uncover customer jobs, pains, gains, and even their willingness to pay for a solution. However, they must have performed searches online to generate this evidence. If you are targeting a niche, B2B, or mainly offline customer, your searches are not going to return any significant volume.

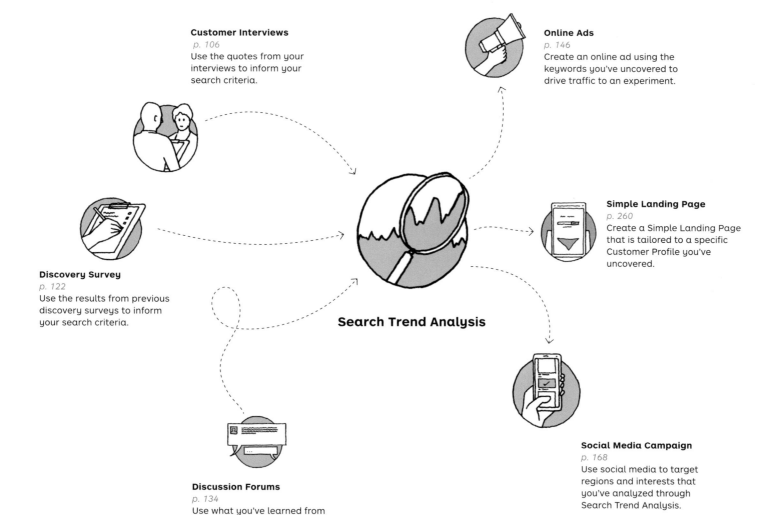

Customer Interviews
p. 106
Use the quotes from your interviews to inform your search criteria.

Online Ads
p. 146
Create an online ad using the keywords you've uncovered to drive traffic to an experiment.

Discovery Survey
p. 122
Use the results from previous discovery surveys to inform your search criteria.

Simple Landing Page
p. 260
Create a Simple Landing Page that is tailored to a specific Customer Profile you've uncovered.

Search Trend Analysis

Discussion Forums
p. 134
Use what you've learned from browsing discussion forums to better inform your search criteria to determine problem size.

Social Media Campaign
p. 168
Use social media to target regions and interests that you've analyzed through Search Trend Analysis.

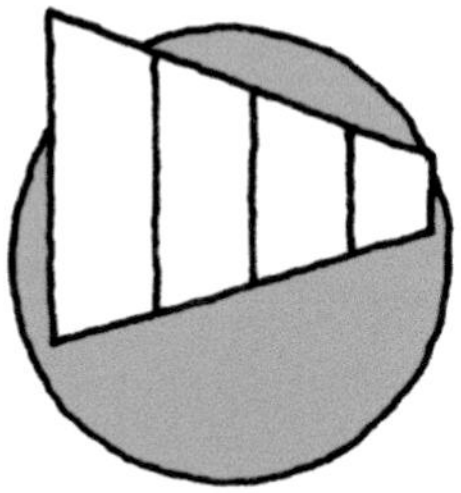

DISCOVERY / DATA ANALYSIS

Web Traffic Analysis

The use of website data collection, reporting, and analysis to look for customer behavior patterns.

COST ●●○○○	EVIDENCE STRENGTH ●●●●○
SETUP TIME ●●○○○	RUN TIME ●●●○○
CAPABILITIES *Technology / Data*	

DESIRABILITY · FEASIBILITY · VIABILITY

The use of website data collection, reporting, and analysis to look for customer behavior patterns.

Prepare

☐ Create your focus area and what customer event it applies to:

- Increasing signups.
- Increasing downloads.
- Increasing # of purchases.

☐ Identify the steps leading up to that event.

☐ Select a time frame for your analysis.

Execute

☐ Using your web analytics software, run your analysis on the defined path.

☐ Note the drop-off points and percentages of each.

Analyze

☐ What are the biggest drop-offs in your flow?

☐ What experiments can you run to improve that number?

Cost

The cost of performing web traffic analysis is relatively cheap, especially if you use a free tool like Google Analytics. If you require more in-depth, event-level tracking and want to pay for a tool, they can vary widely in cost. Some start out very cheap, but as your customer traffic scales the cost can increase with it. If you are looking for heat map analysis of how people use the pages, there are low-cost options for that as well.

Setup Time

Setup time to perform web traffic analysis is relatively short, from a few hours to a few days. You'll need to integrate the tool into your website and log into the dashboard to view the data. Depending on the tool, it may take a day or more for the data to appear.

Run Time

Run time to perform web traffic analysis is unfortunately rather long, typically from weeks to months. It largely depends on the amount of traffic you have, but essentially you don't want to make large risky decisions based on a few days' worth of data.

Evidence Strength

●○○○○
# of sessions

Number of interactions with your website within a given time frame, for a specific user. Usually within a 30-minute period.

●●○○○
# of drop-offs

Drop-offs occur when a user drops out of the flow you've defined. You'll want to analyze the percent of drop-offs at which step and whether they left the site entirely.

How many customers you have on the site and where they are dropping off is relatively strong evidence, as it is measuring what they do. You don't know why they are doing it until you ask them.

●●●●○
Amount of attention

Attention can be a number of different user actions, usually including time spent on page and where they clicked. Users don't always click on buttons and links, so having heat map data can give you amazing insights into how you are gaining or losing attention in your site.

Attention is also relatively strong evidence, and yet, like session and drop-offs, it only tells you the "what" and not the "why."

Capabilities
Technology / Data

The learning curve on web traffic analysis can get steep rather quickly, especially once you go beyond the basics of user behavior. We suggest having the technical capability to integrate the analytics software and the data awareness of being able to analyze the results. For example, the heat map data will show you where people clicked, but you'll want to slice that data by source to see if people coming from online ads click differently than those who come from an email campaign.

Requirements
Traffic

Web traffic analysis requires an existing website with active users, otherwise you won't be able to collect any evidence. Similar to the simple landing page, we recommend driving traffic to your site using:

- Online ads
- Social media campaigns
- Email campaigns
- Word of mouth
- Discussion forums

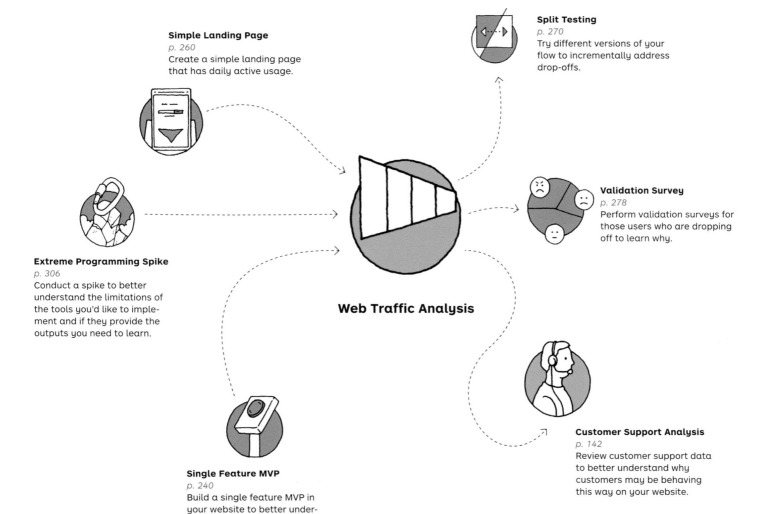

Simple Landing Page
p. 260
Create a simple landing page
that has daily active usage.

Split Testing
p. 270
Try different versions of your
flow to incrementally address
drop-offs.

Extreme Programming Spike
p. 306
Conduct a spike to better
understand the limitations of
the tools you'd like to implement and if they provide the
outputs you need to learn.

Web Traffic Analysis

Validation Survey
p. 278
Perform validation surveys for
those users who are dropping
off to learn why.

Single Feature MVP
p. 240
Build a single feature MVP in
your website to better understand onboarding flow and
getting customers to use it.

Customer Support Analysis
p. 142
Review customer support data
to better understand why
customers may be behaving
this way on your website.

DISCOVERY / DATA ANALYSIS

Discussion Forums

The use of discussion forums to uncover unmet jobs, pains, and gains
in a product or service.

○●○○○○
COST

⚖ ●●●○○○
EVIDENCE STRENGTH

🕐 ●●○○○
SETUP TIME

⏱ ●●●○○
RUN TIME

▦ ▨ ◕
DESIRABILITY · FEASIBILITY · VIABILITY

*Discussion Forums are ideal for finding unmet needs in your
existing product or a competitor's product.*

✂ ⬡ ⠿ ⚒ 🗄 🏷 📢 🔍 📊
CAPABILITIES *Research / Data*

Prepare

☐ Identify what discussion forums you want to use for your analysis (internal vs. external).

☐ Define the questions you want to answer such as, is there evidence that:

- you are not solving for top customer jobs?

- you are not addressing major customer pains?

- you are not creating customer gains?

- customers are creating their own work-around solutions to address your product deficiencies?

Execute

☐ Search for phrases related to your questions on discussion forums.

☐ Take screenshots and export your results.

☐ Write down notes about sense of urgency and tone in the forum threads.

Analyze

☐ Update your Value Proposition Canvas based on your findings.

☐ Contact the forum posters in direct messages to learn if they'll speak to you in more detail.

☐ If yes, then run experiments with them to help close the gap.

Cost

Cost is relatively cheap, since you are basically analyzing online discussion forums to find unmet needs. If it's your own discussion forum, this should be relatively cost effective and analytics may even be already built into your software. If you are analyzing a competitor's or other community discussion boards, you'll likely be web scraping them with low-cost tools or just doing it manually yourself. You'll save on the cost by manually doing so but it might take much longer.

Setup Time

Setup time to analyze discussion forums is relatively short. It'll require you to define the questions you want to answer and identify which discussion forums to analyze.

Run Time

Run time for analyzing discussion forums is also relatively short. It takes a bit longer if you decide not to use a web scraping tool, so we'd recommend automating it if possible to shorten run time. You'll want to look for patterns of unmet customer jobs, pains, and gains.

Evidence Strength

●●●○○

Types of work-arounds

Look for a pattern of work-arounds or ways to hack the product to get it to do what people need. This can provide insights into improvements.

Similar to Steve Blank's "built a solution to solve the problem," it's strong evidence if people are hacking together their own methods to solve problems the product doesn't fully address.

●●○○○

Types of feature requests

Look for a pattern in the top three features requested on the discussion forums and what pains and underlying jobs they could solve.

Feature requests are relatively weak evidence, in that you'll need to perform more experiments around the underlying job or pain the proposed feature is intended to solve.

Capabilities

Research / Data

You'll need to be able to identify discussion forums, gather data, and analyze it. In doing so, it'll help to be able to understand how to scrape online websites and what questions you'll want to answer from looking through the data. It'll help if you have data and research capabilities when doing so.

Requirements

Discussion Forum Data

The most important requirement for analyzing discussion forum data is having existing discussion forums to analyze the questions you need to answer. If you feel there are unmet needs in a competitor's product, go to community and support forums where their customers post topics. If you have your own discussion forums, they should also be a great source of data.

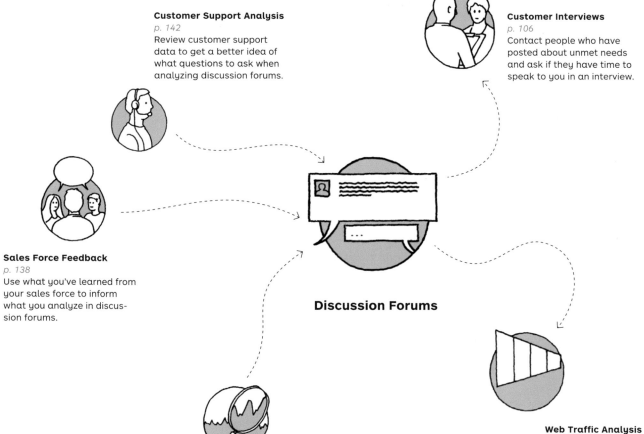

Customer Support Analysis
p. 142
Review customer support
data to get a better idea of
what questions to ask when
analyzing discussion forums.

Customer Interviews
p. 106
Contact people who have
posted about unmet needs
and ask if they have time to
speak to you in an interview.

Sales Force Feedback
p. 138
Use what you've learned from
your sales force to inform
what you analyze in discussion forums.

Discussion Forums

Search Trend Analysis
p. 126
Search the web to see how
people are responding to your
product or a competitor's
product.

Web Traffic Analysis
p. 130
Use what you've learned
from the discussion forums
to check against customer
behavior on your website.

DISCOVERY / DATA ANALYSIS

Sales Force Feedback

The use of sales force feedback to uncover unmet jobs, pains, and gains in your product or service.

COST ◔●●○○○

EVIDENCE STRENGTH ⚖ ●●◉○○

SETUP TIME 🕐 ●●○○○

RUN TIME ⏱ ●●●○○

CAPABILITIES *Sales / Research / Data*

DESIRABILITY · FEASIBILITY · VIABILITY

Sales force feedback is ideal for businesses that use a group of people to conduct sales.

Prepare

☐ Identify the questions you'd like answered from your sales force:

- Are you are solving for top customer jobs?

- Are you addressing major customer pains?

- Are you creating customer gains?

☐ If you have a complex B2B business, then segment your questions into the additional roles of:

- decision makers.

- economic buyers.

- recommenders.

- influencers.

☐ Schedule sessions with your sales force to answer the questions.

Execute

☐ Discuss with your sales force their thoughts on these questions.

☐ Have them bring up any evidence to support their answers from sales calls, dashboards, emails, and so on.

☐ Thank them for their time to help improve the experience.

Analyze

☐ Update your Value Proposition Canvas based on your findings.

☐ Use what you've learned to identify experiments to improve fit.

Cost

Cost is relatively cheap, with much of it focused around collecting the data in a usable way from your existing sales force. The analysis of the sale force feedback data can be done without expensive software or consultants.

Setup Time

Setup time to sort through sales force feedback is relatively short. You'll need to define the time period you'll analyze and what you are specifically looking for in the feedback.

Run Time

Run time for analyzing sales force feedback is also relatively short once you set it up. You'll want to look for patterns of unmet jobs, pains, and gains.

Evidence Strength

# of near misses
Near miss feedback

When your sales group has successfully closed, what almost prevented the sale from occurring? You'll want to log how many sales were almost lost and what customers had to say about what "almost prevented them from purchasing" to better understand fit.

Customer feedback on why they almost didn't purchase, but ultimately did, is a gold mine of relatively strong evidence. It's stronger than most feedback because they've just converted.

Types of feature requests

Look for a pattern in the top three features requested in the sales process and what pains and underlying jobs they could solve.

Feature requests are relatively weak evidence, in that you'll need to perform more experiments around the underlying job or pain the proposed feature is intended to solve.

Capabilities

Research / Data

You'll need to be able to gather, sort, and analyze sales force feedback. In doing so, it'll help to be able to understand how sales operate and what questions you'll want to answer.

Requirements

Sales Force Data

The most important requirement for analyzing sales force feedback is having an engaged sales force that can either provide feedback to you in verbal form or through the customer relationship management (CRM) software.

Customer Interviews
p. 106
Use the notes from your interviews to inform the search for unmet jobs, pains, and gains in the sales force feedback.

Buy a Feature
p. 226
Invite those people who did not convert to participate in an exercise to better understand the features they need.

Split Test
p. 270
Run a Split Test in your sales process to test out different versions of your value proposition to customers.

Validation Survey
p. 278
Use survey findings to inform the search for unmet jobs, pains, and gains in the sales force feedback.

Sales Force Feedback

Expert Stakeholder Interviews
p. 115
Use the notes from stakeholders to better understand if their needs translate into sales.

SALES FORCE FEEDBACK

141

DATA ANALYSIS

DISCOVERY / DATA ANALYSIS

Customer Support Analysis

The use of customer support data to uncover unmet jobs, pains, and gains in your product or service.

◯ ●●◯◯◯
COST

⚖ ●●◯◯◯
EVIDENCE STRENGTH

🕐 ●●◯◯◯
SETUP TIME

⏱ ●●●◯◯
RUN TIME

CAPABILITIES Sales / Marketing / Research / Data

⊞ ✉ ◉

DESIRABILITY · FEASIBILITY · VIABILITY

Customer support analysis is ideal for businesses that already have a substantial amount of existing customers.

Prepare

☐ Identify the questions you'd like answered from your customer support data:

- Are you are solving for top customer jobs?
- Are you addressing major customer pains?
- Are you creating customer gains?

☐ Schedule sessions with your customer support team to answer these questions.

Execute

☐ Discuss with your customer support team —their thoughts on these questions.

☐ Have them bring up any evidence to support their answers from customer support calls, dashboards, emails, and so on.

☐ Thank them for their time to help improve the experience.

Analyze

☐ Update your Value Proposition Canvas based on your findings.

☐ Use what you've learned to identify experiments to improve fit.

Cost

Cost is relatively cheap, in that most of the cost is incurred by simply gathering the customer data over time. The analysis of that data can be done without expensive software or consultants.

Setup Time

Setup time for customer support analysis is relatively short once you have the data. You'll need to define the time period you'll analyze and what you are specifically looking for in the data.

Run Time

Run time for customer support analysis is also relatively short once you have the data and have defined what you are looking for in the data. You'll want to look for patterns of unmet jobs, pains, and gains.

Evidence Strength

Customer feedback

Customer quotes during customer support calls that refer to jobs they are trying to accomplish, pains they feel aren't addressed, and unmet gains.

Customer feedback in customer support data is relatively weak evidence on its own, but can be used to inform future experiments.

●●○○○

Types of feature requests

Look for a pattern in the top three features requested and what pains and underlying jobs they could solve.

Feature requests are relatively weak evidence, in that you'll need to perform more experiments around the underlying job or pain the proposed feature is intended to solve.

Capabilities

Research / Marketing / Sales / Data

You'll need to be able to gather, sort, and analyze customer support data. In doing so, it'll help to be able to understand how sales operates, how your product is marketed, and what questions you'll want to answer from looking at the data.

Requirements

Customer Support Data

The most important requirement for customer support analysis is already having customer support data to analyze. This can be in many forms, whether it is recorded calls from your support team to emails or bug/feature requests submitted. The data you analyze should consist of more than one-off, anecdotal conversations with a handful of customers.

Customer Interviews
p. 106
Use the notes from your interviews to inform the search for unmet jobs, pains, and gains in the support data.

Web Traffic Analysis
p. 130
Use what you've learned from the support data to check against customer behavior on your website.

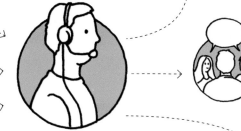

Sales Force Feedback
p. 138
Cross reference what you've found in customer support data against feedback from your sales force.

Validation Survey
p. 278
Use survey findings to inform the search for unmet jobs, pains, and gains in the support data.

Customer Support Analysis

Expert Stakeholder Interviews
p. 115
Use the notes from stakeholders to better understand if their needs translate to what you are hearing from customers.

Speed Boat
p. 218
Rather than have customers simply point out what they feel the product lacks, invite them in for a speed boat exercise to better understand what helps them go faster and what slows them down in regard to the product.

CUSTOMER SUPPORT ANALYSIS

DATA ANALYSIS

DISCOVERY / INTEREST DISCOVERY

Online Ad

An online advertisement that clearly articulates a value proposition
for a targeted customer segment with a simple call to action.

COST ●●●○○

EVIDENCE STRENGTH ●●●○○

SETUP TIME ●●○○○

RUN TIME ●●●○○

CAPABILITIES *Design / Product / Marketing*

DESIRABILITY · FEASIBILITY · VIABILITY

*Online ads are ideal for quickly testing your value proposition
at scale with customers online.*

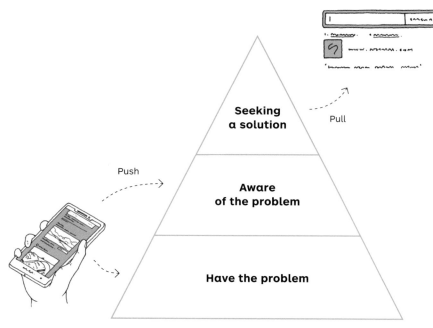

Seeking
a solution

Pull

Push

Aware
of the problem

Have the problem

Adapted from Steve Blank, Earlyvangelists

Finding Target Customers

Finding target customers online can be challenging, but it is possible with creativity and resilience. You can start thinking about this early, even before your experiment design.

For example, when creating your Value Proposition Canvas, take time to brainstorm different places to find your target customers online. Then as a team, vote on the ones you'd like to test first.

What Stage Are Your Customers?

After prioritizing places to find your target customers, you'll want to customize your approach based on the state of the customer. You can use Steve Blank's model to help inform your strategy for engaging with customers.

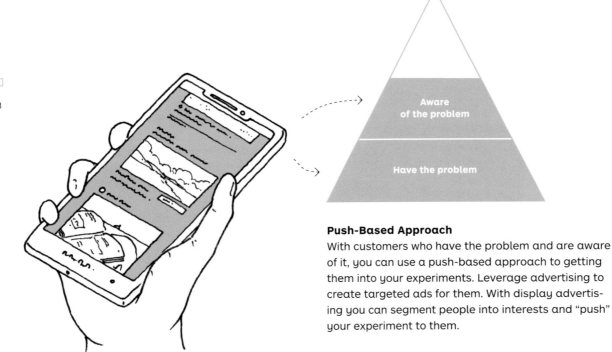

Push-Based Approach

With customers who have the problem and are aware of it, you can use a push-based approach to getting them into your experiments. Leverage advertising to create targeted ads for them. With display advertising you can segment people into interests and "push" your experiment to them.

SOCIAL MEDIA AD

Prepare

☐ Define on which social media platforms you'll run the ad.

☐ Create your target audience, ad campaign length, and budget.

☐ Choose CPC (cost per click) option.

☐ Include your business name and logo.

☐ Craft a value statement from your Value Proposition Canvas to properly communicate your offering.

☐ Create a compelling image that reinforces your value statement.

☐ Include the destination URL that directs to a landing.

Execute

☐ Once approved, run your social media ad.

☐ Monitor how it performs daily with:

• ad spend.

• impressions.

• click through rate.

• comments and shares.

Analyze

☐ Analyze your ad performance daily.

☐ If you are spending a large amount of money for a very low click through rate, pause the campaign, iterate on your text and images, then run the campaign again.

SEARCH ONLY AD

Prepare

- ☐ Define on which search platforms you'll run the ad.
- ☐ Create your target audience, ad campaign length, and budget.
- ☐ Choose CPC (cost per click) option.
- ☐ Craft a value statement from your Value Proposition Canvas to properly communicate your offering.
- ☐ Include the destination URL that directs to a landing page.
- ☐ Craft a shorter version of your value statement as a value headline.
- ☐ Submit your ad for approval.

Execute

- ☐ Once approved, run your search only ad.
- ☐ Monitor how it performs daily with:
  - • ad spend.
  - • impressions.
  - • click through rate.

Analyze

- ☐ Analyze your ad performance daily.
- ☐ If you are spending a large amount of money for a very low click through rate, pause the campaign, iterate on your text and images, then run the campaign again.

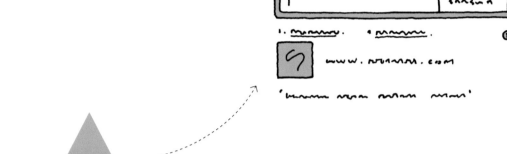

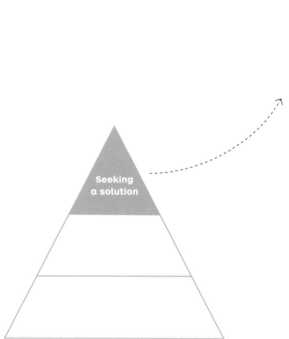

Pull-Based Approach

In contrast to push-based acquisition, you can take a slightly different approach for those already seeking a solution to the problem. You will need to get in front of them when they are seeking it.

Pull-based acquisition means ensuring your experiment is displayed when people go online to search for a solution to their problems. Using online search advertising you can narrow in on the key search terms and "pull" them to your value proposition as they actively seek a solution.

Cost

Online ads can vary in cost, depending on whether you are doing display versus search, the keywords, and the average cost per click for your industry. Overall you should stay away from very expensive online ads early on in your journey. You don't want to get addicted to paid acquisition and have trouble scaling your business later on.

Setup Time

If your ad is text only, you can create it in a few minutes. If your ad contains imagery, it might take longer to find and create the right image for the ad.

Run Time

Depending on the platform, it may take 1–3 days for your ad to be approved. Once it's approved, you'll usually run your ad for at least a week to see how it performs day-to-day.

Evidence Strength

# of unique views
# of clicks

Click through rate = clicks that your ad receives divided by the number of times your ad is shown. CTR varies per industry, so research online to see what a comparable CTR is for your product.

Users clicking ads is a relatively weak strength of evidence, but it it necessary to test acquisition channels. It can also be combined with conversions on a simple landing page to make the evidence stronger overall.

Capabilities

Design / Product / Marketing

Running online ads is much easier than it used to be, mostly because online ad platforms give you a step-by-step experience for managing them. You'll still need to be able to design an ad that conveys your value proposition well, with the right call to action and target audience. This means you'll need product, marketing, and design skills — otherwise your ads will not convert.

Requirements

Destination

You are going to need a destination for the target audience to visit once they click the ad. Most of the time this is some type of landing page. Platforms have become more restrictive over the years, so the page will need to match the overall value proposition of the ad and meet the site's ad destination requirements. Be sure to review these before running your ads, otherwise they'll get rejected in the approval process.

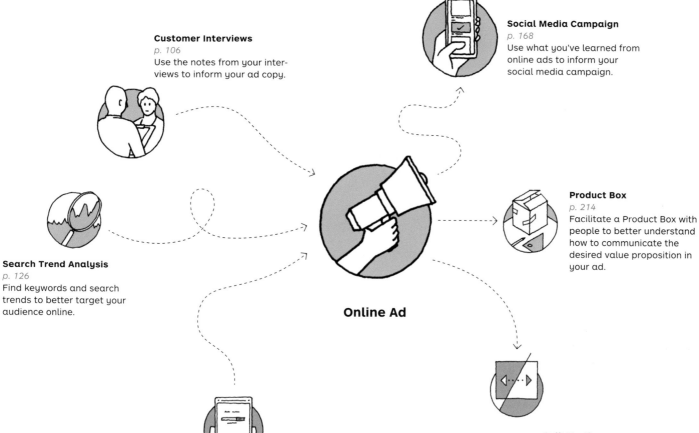

Customer Interviews
p. 106
Use the notes from your interviews to inform your ad copy.

Social Media Campaign
p. 168
Use what you've learned from online ads to inform your social media campaign.

Search Trend Analysis
p. 126
Find keywords and search trends to better target your audience online.

Product Box
p. 214
Facilitate a Product Box with people to better understand how to communicate the desired value proposition in your ad.

Online Ad

Simple Landing Page
p. 260
Create a simple landing page to act as your destination for your ads.

Split Testing
p. 270
Try different versions of your ads to see what resonates best with customers.

DISCOVERY / INTEREST DISCOVERY

Link Tracking

A unique, trackable hyperlink to gain more detailed information about your value proposition.

⬤●○○○○
COST

⚖ ●●●○○
EVIDENCE STRENGTH

🕐 ●○○○○
SETUP TIME

⏱ ●●●○○
RUN TIME

▦ ✉ ◈
DESIRABILITY · FEASIBILITY · VIABILITY

Link tracking is ideal for testing customer actions to gather quantitative data.

✂◻⚹⚒🗄✎📢🔍◔
CAPABILITIES *Technology / Data*

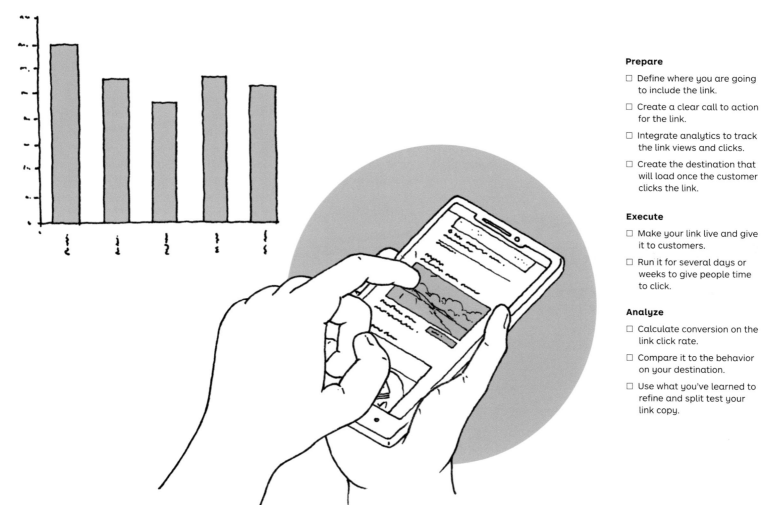

Prepare

☐ Define where you are going to include the link.

☐ Create a clear call to action for the link.

☐ Integrate analytics to track the link views and clicks.

☐ Create the destination that will load once the customer clicks the link.

Execute

☐ Make your link live and give it to customers.

☐ Run it for several days or weeks to give people time to click.

Analyze

☐ Calculate conversion on the link click rate.

☐ Compare it to the behavior on your destination.

☐ Use what you've learned to refine and split test your link copy.

LINK TRACKING

153

INTEREST DISCOVERY

Cost

Link tracking is relatively cheap. Most online web analytics, online ad, and email software provide the ability to track unique URL links.

Setup Time

The setup time for link tracking is relatively short if you use existing software. You'll need to create the links for your different digital media formats.

Run Time

The run time for link tracking is usually over a few weeks. It'll take time for people to view it and decide to click, or not.

Evidence Strength

# of unique views

Click rate = percentage of people who viewed your link divided by the number of people who clicked on your link.

Click rates vary by industry. Use industry guidelines to determine what the average is for your experiment.

Link clicks are an average strength of evidence. You'll learn what they do, but you won't know why unless you talk to them.

Capabilities

Technology / Data

Link tracking doesn't require deep expertise, as most software already has it included. You'll need to be able to create links with tracking and interpret the results.

Requirements

Call to Action

Link tracking isn't going to be very successful without a clear call to action and value proposition. You'll want to clearly communicate this in your content and imagery, while providing a link that brings the customer to a web page.

Customer Interviews
p. 106
Gather email addresses from
your customer interviews to
send a follow-up email with
link tracking.

Split Test
p. 270
Use link tracking analysis
to create different version
to Split Test.

Link Tracking

Online Ad
p. 146
Create an online ad with
clickable links to track click
through rate (CTR).

Simple Landing Page
p. 260
Include link tracking in your
landing page to understand
how customers who clicked
online ads converted on your
page.

Email Campaign
p. 162
Include link tracking to
understand how many people
clicked the links in your email
campaign.

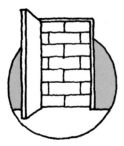

DISCOVERY / INTEREST DISCOVERY

Feature Stub

A small test of an upcoming feature that includes the very beginning of the experience, usually in the form of a button.

⊖ ● ○ ○ ○ ○
COST

⚖ ● ● ● ○ ○
EVIDENCE STRENGTH

🕐 ● ● ○ ○ ○
SETUP TIME

 ● ● ○ ○ ○
RUN TIME

▦ ✉ ◔
DESIRABILITY · FEASIBILITY · VIABILITY

Feature Stub is ideal for rapidly testing the desirability of a new feature of an already existing offering.

Feature Stub is not ideal for testing mission critical functionality for your product.

CAPABILITIES *Design / Product / Technology*

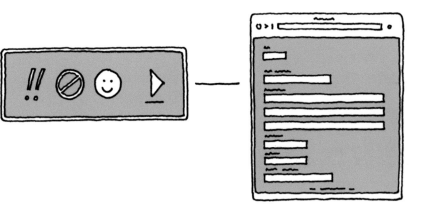

Prepare

☐ Decide where you are going to include the Feature Stub: preferably in the part of your product where your customers would need it most in the workflow.

☐ Define the length and schedule for the Feature Stub.

☐ Create the Feature Stub, using the same visual styling as the rest of the product.

☐ When clicked, launch a popup that states the feature isn't completed yet.

☐ Include a "learn more" link to determine if people are interested enough to click again. Optionally, it can display a survey that asks how interested and has an email signup.

☐ Integrate analytics to track views and clicks.

☐ Implement a feature toggle that allows you to quickly turn it on and off. This is a very important step!

Execute

☐ Toggle your Feature Stub on.

☐ Monitor the activity usage of the link very closely, by the hour.

☐ Toggle the Feature Stub off once you've reached the end of the schedule.

Analyze

☐ Calculate conversion rates on your button, learn more, and surveys. Did these reach your success criteria?

☐ Review the findings with your team to determine whether the feature is still worth pursuing.

Cost

Feature Stubs are usually very cheap, since you are not building out an entire feature but merely the entry point for it.

Setup Time

It should only take few hours to set up a Feature Stub in your existing product or service. If it takes longer than that, you may need to rethink your architecture when it comes to implementing experiments.

Run Time

Feature Stubs should never be run for more than 1–3 days. They are designed as a short experiment to quickly gather evidence.

Anything longer will frustrate your customers, since they'll continue to expect it to work.

Evidence Strength

# of unique views
# of button clicks
Button % Conversion Rates

You can calculate the conversion rate by taking the number of unique views divided by button clicks = conversion rate. Aim for a 15% conversion on button click.

Button views and clicks are relatively weak evidence, although they do signal interest in the feature.

of "learn more" clicks
Learn More % Conversion Rates

You can calculate the conversion rate by taking the number of unique "learn more" views divided by link clicks = conversion rate. Aim for a 5% conversion on learn more click.

Clicking to learn more is a bit stronger than simply closing the popup.

# of surveys completed
Survey Feedback

You can calculate the conversion rate by taking the number of unique learn more clicks divided by completions = conversion rate. Aim for a 3% conversion on survey completion.

Filling out the survey from the learn more link is a bit stronger than closing the popup. You can learn valuable insights from people voluntarily clicking on and filling out a survey on a feature they'd love to see in the product.

Capabilities

Design / Product / Technology

You'll need to be able design a button that fits into the existing product. You'll also need the button to launch a window stating that the feature isn't ready yet and optionally asks the customer to fill out a survey. Analytics will be important—you'll need to measure its performance.

Requirements

Existing Product

Feature Stubs require a product that already has daily active users. If you don't already have one with a steady stream of users, it will be difficult to gauge customer interest. They have to see it in the context of the product for the evidence to be believable.

Integration and Analytics

Feature Stubs need to be toggled off and on at a moment's notice. Make sure you have this capability and that it works before launching one. In addition, you'll need analytics to measure feature interest.

Buy a Feature
p. 226
Facilitate an exercise with customers to decide if the feature would even be a priority for them.

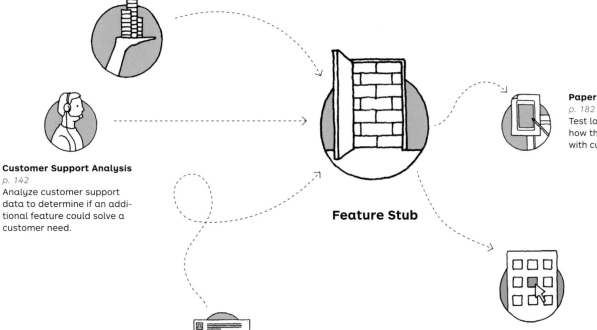

Customer Support Analysis
p. 142
Analyze customer support data to determine if an additional feature could solve a customer need.

Feature Stub

Paper Prototype
p. 182
Test low fidelity versions of how the feature could function with customers.

Clickable Prototype
p. 236
Test clickable prototypes of how the feature could work with customers.

Discussion Forums
p. 134
Search through discussion forums to see if customers are using creative work-arounds to address your product deficiencies.

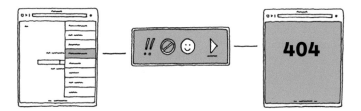

DISCOVERY / INTEREST DISCOVERY

404 Test

Another faster, and somewhat riskier, variation of a Feature Stub is the 404 test. It is very similar, except you do not put anything behind the button or link whatsoever. Hence, the 404 test name, as it generates 404 errors each time it is clicked. To learn if a feature is desirable, you simply count the number of 404 errors generated.

This variant has trade-offs since, on one hand, you can test something as quickly as possible at scale with customers. On the other hand, it gives the impression that your product is broken.

When running a 404 test, do not run it for more than a few hours.

COST

SETUP TIME

RUN TIME

EVIDENCE STRENGTH

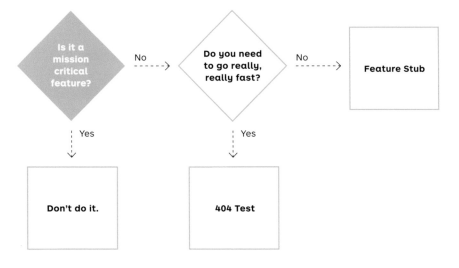

The notion of doing a quick test, solves umpteen meetings' worth of powerful debate and logical argument.
— Stephen Kaufer, CEO of TripAdvisor

Endless Meetings

Have you ever been in a meeting where team members debated over whether a feature would be a good idea to build for your customers?

Without evidence, the conversation goes in circles, using only opinions for decision-making.

A Feature Stub will generate data to help you gauge demand.

What if the test is a wild success and customers reach out to you asking when they can use the feature? It then helps break the circular meetings of opinion on the feature.

What if the test is a dud and no one even clicks on it? Then it also helps move the conversation forward.

It's not so much about being right and able to gloat in the meeting to your peers that your prediction was correct, but instead to use data to help move the conversation forward. Making progress is far more important than being correct in these scenarios, and a Feature Stub is a great way to make progress.

DISCOVERY / INTEREST DISCOVERY

Email Campaign

Email messages that are deployed across a specific period of time
to customers.

COST

○ ● ○ ○ ○ ○

EVIDENCE STRENGTH

● ● ● ○ ○

SETUP TIME

● ● ○ ○ ○

RUN TIME

● ● ● ○ ○

CAPABILITIES *Design / Product / Marketing*

DESIRABILITY · FEASIBILITY · VIABILITY

*Email campaigns are ideal for quickly testing your
value proposition with a customer segment.*

*Email campaigns are not ideal as a replacement
for face-to-face customer interaction.*

Prepare

☐ Define your email campaign goal.

☐ Create your series of "drip emails" to incrementally deliver value to the customer over a period of days or weeks.

☐ Send test emails internally to review content and images.

Execute

☐ Run your email campaign with customers.

☐ Be responsive to customers who reply.

Analyze

☐ Analyze which emails are performing best.

☐ What type of content is driving the most opens?

☐ What type of content is driving the most clicks?

☐ What type of content is driving the most reply emails?

☐ Recap with your team and decide what revisions you'd like to make for your next campaign.

Cost

Email campaigns are relatively cheap: there are several services that make it cost effective to manage the creation, distribution, and analysis of emails across large numbers of subscribers.

Setup Time

Using today's email tools, it only takes minutes to a few hours to craft an email campaign. You can create auto-drip emails to send on a schedule over time without manually having to intervene.

Run Time

Depending on the nature of the email campaign, it can take 1–2 days or 3–4 weeks.

Evidence Strength

Opens

Clicks

Bounces

Unsubscribes

Open rate = unique clicks divided by the number of unique opens.

Click rate = percentage of people who clicked on at least one link in your email message.

Open and click rates vary by industry. Use industry guidelines to determine what the average is for your experiment. They can be found in most email service tools as part of the reports package.

Email opens and clicks are an average strength of evidence.

Capabilities

Design / Product / Marketing

Email campaigns are relatively easy to create and manage now that many dedicated tools and services exist. You'll still need to be able to write clear, coherent copy with compelling images and a strong call to action. Much of the formatting can be taken care of by online templates.

Requirements

Subscriber List

Email campaigns require subscribers before you can effectively use them. You can acquire subscribers from a number of different sources including:

- Social media campaigns
- Website signup
- Blog posts with email signup
- Word of mouth
- Discussion forums

Campaign Goal

Email campaigns need a goal, otherwise you can't be confident that it's helping you make progress. Goals can vary from driving traffic to a page for conversions, onboarding new customers, building trust, and learning customers needs to re-engaging existing or lost customers. Create a goal before putting in the effort to create the email campaign.

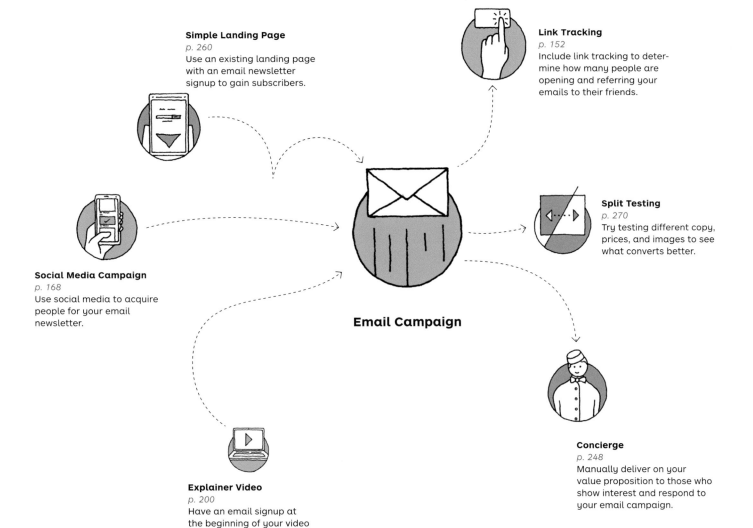

Simple Landing Page
p. 260
Use an existing landing page with an email newsletter signup to gain subscribers.

Link Tracking
p. 152
Include link tracking to determine how many people are opening and referring your emails to their friends.

Social Media Campaign
p. 168
Use social media to acquire people for your email newsletter.

Email Campaign

Split Testing
p. 270
Try testing different copy, prices, and images to see what converts better.

Explainer Video
p. 200
Have an email signup at the beginning of your video as currency to watch it.

Concierge
p. 248
Manually deliver on your value proposition to those who show interest and respond to your email campaign.

DISCOVERY

166

EXPERIMENTS

EMAIL CAMPAIGN

Share, Discover, Discuss New Products
Product Hunt

Product Hunt is a website that lets users share and discover new products. The website has grown tremendously over the years since it's inception in 2013. Product Hunt has become the place to launch your new product, but curiously enough it all started off in a Philz Coffee as a 20-minute experiment by Ryan Hoover, mainly using email.

Hypothesis

Ryan believed that product people would join an online community to share, discover, and discuss new and interesting products.

Experiment

Creating the first version of Product Hunt as an email campaign.

In only 20 minutes, Ryan created a group on Linkydink, a link-sharing tool built by the folks over at Makeshift. At the time, it allowed people to share links with a group and send them out as a daily email. He then invited a few of his startup friends to contribute to the group. To promote it, Ryan announced the experiment on Quibb (a technology focused, online community) and Twitter.

Evidence

Opens, clicks and shares.

Within two weeks, over 200 people had subscribed to product discoveries from 30 hand-picked contributors, consisting of startup founders, venture capitalists, and prominent bloggers.

Ryan also received several unsolicited emails and in-person conversations expressing their love and support of the project.

Insights

There is a there, there.

The response was overwhelmingly positive and unlike most email that is opened and clicked (or not), Ryan had an audience openly contributing and sharing links over email. He had built up a network over the years of hungry entrepreneurs and product people. Clearly there was an unmet need of a community for product enthusiasts, based on the sheer volume of activity from his email list.

Actions

Turning user behavior from email into a platform.

Ryan used what he learned from the experiment to inform the design and technology of Product Hunt as a community platform.

Since then, Product Hunt graduated from Y Combinator (YC S14) and was acquired by AngelList for a reported $20 million in 2016. It's become the place where makers and startups launch their new product to a global community of founders, journalists, investors, and enthusiastic people in technology.

DISCOVERY / INTEREST DISCOVERY

Social Media Campaign

Social media messages that are deployed across a specific period of time to customers.

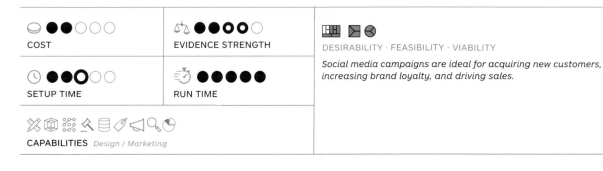

◯●●◯◯◯
COST

⚖ ●●●◯◯◯
EVIDENCE STRENGTH

🕐 ●●◯◯◯
SETUP TIME

⏱ ●●●●●
RUN TIME

⊞ ⊠ ◉
DESIRABILITY · FEASIBILITY · VIABILITY

Social media campaigns are ideal for acquiring new customers, increasing brand loyalty, and driving sales.

CAPABILITIES *Design / Marketing*

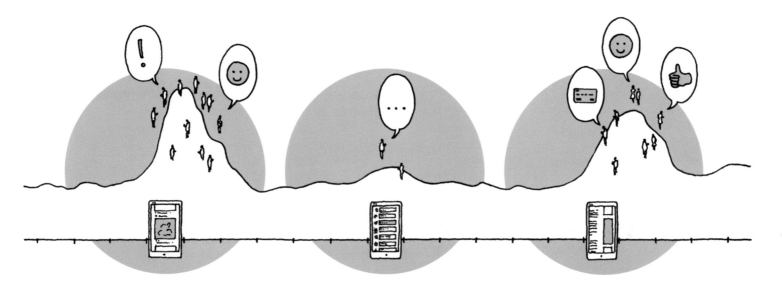

Prepare

☐ Define your social media campaign goal.

☐ Identify the platforms to use for your campaign.

☐ Create your content calendar and schedule.

☐ Create your social media content.

Execute

☐ Post your content across platforms per your schedule.

☐ Monitor, respond, and engage with those who comment.

Analyze

☐ Analyze which posts and platforms are performing best.

☐ What type of content is driving the most shares?

☐ What type of content is driving the most clicks?

☐ What type of content is driving the most comments?

☐ What type of content is driving the most conversions?

☐ Recap with your team and decide what revisions you'd like to make for your next campaign.

 ●●○○○

Cost

Social media campaigns are moderately cheap to produce if you are doing the work yourself and not paying for social media ads. However, costs can go up rather quickly ($5k to $20k a month), if you are paying people to manage and create content.

 ●●●○○

Setup Time

Setup time for a social media campaign can take days or weeks, depending on how much content you need to create. Setup time increases as well if you are running it across multiple platforms.

 ●●●○○

Run Time

Run Time for a social media campaign is long, usually several weeks or months. You'll need time to post, read, and respond over social media. You'll also need to measure the effectiveness it has toward your business goals.

 ●●●○○

Evidence Strength

●●○○○

# of views
# of shares
# of comments

Engagement is how customers are viewing, sharing, and commenting on your social media posts.

   Social media engagement is rather weak evidence. You can learn qualitative insights from the comments to inform your value proposition.

 ●●●○○

# of clicks

Click through rate is the number of views your social media post receives divided by the number who clicked.

 ●●●●○

# of conversions

Conversion rate is the number who clicked on the social media link divided by the number who used it to sign up or make a purchase.

   Conversions are strong evidence and can help you determine what social media platform works best for driving business.

Capabilities

Design / Marketing

Social media campaigns require a great deal of marketing and design: marketing to create, respond, and manage social media across multiple platforms; design to help shape and visualize the content before it is posted.

Requirements

Content

Social media campaigns are not simply posting here and there, they are about scheduling content over weeks and months. Without content, your campaign will not be successful. Make sure you have a plan and the resources to create the content before jumping into your campaign.

Explainer Video
p. 200
Use the social media
campaign to drive traffic
to your video.

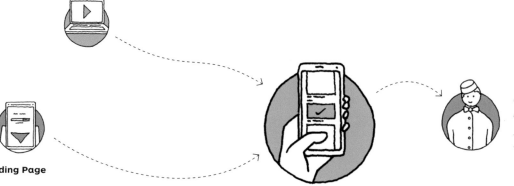

Simple Landing Page
p. 260
Use a landing page for as
the destination for your social
media links.

Concierge
p. 248
Deliver value manually to
those who converted from
the social media campaign.

Social Media Campaign

DISCOVERY / INTEREST DISCOVERY

Referral Program

A method of promoting products or services to new customers through referrals, by word of mouth, or through digital codes.

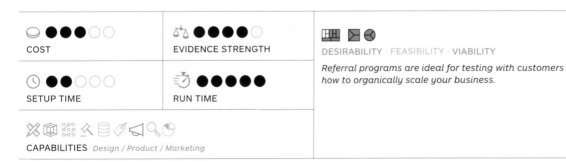

COST
●●●○○

EVIDENCE STRENGTH
●●●●○

SETUP TIME
●●○○○

RUN TIME
●●●●●

DESIRABILITY · FEASIBILITY · VIABILITY

Referral programs are ideal for testing with customers how to organically scale your business.

CAPABILITIES *Design / Product / Marketing*

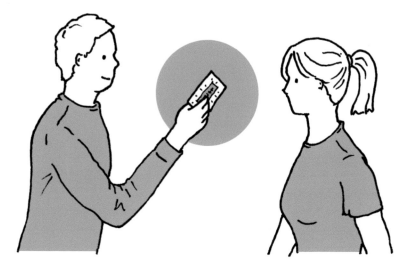

Prepare

☐ Define your referral program conversion goal.

☐ Identify the advocates you'll send the referral codes to.

☐ Create the unique codes and integrate analytics.

Execute

☐ Provide your advocates with the referral codes.

☐ Run it for several weeks to give friends time to consider and click.

Analyze

☐ Calculate advocate share rate.

☐ Calculate friend click through rate.

☐ Calculate friend conversion rate.

☐ Compare the conversion rate to your previously defined goal.

☐ Use what you've learned to refine and Split Test the referral program.

Cost

Referral programs are moderately cheap. You'll need to incentivize customers (advocates) for making referrals, which will incur cost in the way of discounts for both the advocate and the customer (friend) being referred. Low cost software can help you manage referrals, so that you have analytics on how the program is performing.

Setup Time

Setup time for a referral program is short. You'll need to configure your referral codes and choose which advocates to send them to.

Run Time

Run time for a referral program is long, usually several weeks or months. You'll need time for advocates to refer and for their friends to decide whether or not to act on the referral.

Evidence Strength

●●●●○

# of advocates
# of advocate shares

Advocates are the customers you provide referral codes to for sharing. The number of shares is how many customers actively shared the code with friends.

Advocate share rate is the number of advocates who received a code divided by the number who shared it with a friend. Target 15%–20%.

Advocates agreeing to accept and share a code is relatively strong evidence. They are acting to refer friends to your product.

●●●●○

# of friends
# of friend clicks
# of friend conversions

Friends are the people who received the code from the advocate.

Friend click through rate is the number of friends who received the code divided by the number who clicked on it. Percent varies by channel. Target 50%–80%.

Friend conversion rate is the number who clicked on the code divided by the number who used it to sign up or make a purchase. Target 5%–15%.

Friends accepting the referral code and converting is strong evidence. They are acting on a referral for an incentive, so it remains to be seen if they will stay over time.

Capabilities

Design / Product / Marketing

Referral programs mostly require product and marketing capabilities. You'll need to clearly communicate why you are offering the discount and how your friends would benefit from it. You'll need design skills if you have custom emails, social media posts, or landing pages dedicated to the program.

Requirements

Passionate Customers

Customers usually do not start out passionate about your product. It takes time for them to be satisfied and grow into passionate customers. Therefore, we recommend that you gauge this before randomly sending out referral codes. You'll want to give codes to those who you think will actually refer their friends to your product and speak to it in a positive light.

Link Tracking
p. 152
Have link tracking already in place to determine which customers are the most active.

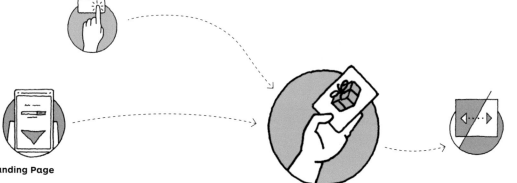

Simple Landing Page
p. 260
Use a landing page for testing the demand of your referral program.

Split Test
p. 270
Use analytics to Split Test different discount codes and determine which media converts better with friends.

Referral Program

Email Campaign
p. 162
Use email to distribute your referral program to advocates.

Social Media Campaign
p. 168
Use social media to distribute your referral program.

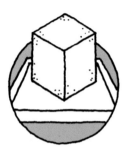

DISCOVERY / DISCUSSION PROTOTYPES

3D Print

Rapidly prototyping a physical object from a three-dimensional digital model by using a 3D printer.

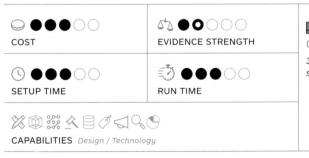

COST ●●●○○

EVIDENCE STRENGTH ●●◐○○○

SETUP TIME ●●●○○

RUN TIME ●●●○○

CAPABILITIES *Design / Technology*

DESIRABILITY · FEASIBILITY · VIABILITY

3D print is ideal for rapidly testing iterations of your physical solution with customers.

Prepare

☐ Gather your previous low fidelity evidence to support the 3D print.

☐ Model the print in 3D modeling software.

☐ Create a 3D print using a printer.

☐ Source customers and schedule the interactive session.

Execute

☐ Show the 3D print to customers.

☐ One person on the team conducts the interview.

☐ Another person on the team takes notes on customer quotes, jobs, pains, gains, and body language.

☐ Wrap up the interview by asking if it is ok to contact them in the future with higher fidelity solutions.

Analyze

☐ Review your notes with the team.

☐ Update your Value Proposition Canvas based on what you've learned.

☐ Use what you've learned to refine and iterate on your 3D print for the next round of testing.

3D PRINT

177

DISCUSSION PROTOTYPES

● ● ● ○ ○
Cost

3D prints are moderately cheap. If you are printing small basic prototypes to test with customers, it can be less expensive. The more complex and larger the 3D print, the more costly it will be.

 ● ● ● ○ ○
Setup Time

The setup time for a 3D print can take days or weeks, depending on your ability to model it out and your access to a printer.

 ● ● ● ○ ○
Run Time

Run time for a 3D print is relatively short. You'll want customers interacting with the prototype to better understand the fit between your value proposition and customer jobs, pains, and gains.

 ● ● ○ ○ ○ ○
Evidence Strength

● ● ○ ○ ○

Customer jobs
Customer pains
Customer gains

Customer jobs, pains, and gains and how the prototype could solve for them.

The evidence is relatively weak evidence—they need to suspend belief and imagine using it in real world scenarios.

● ○ ○ ○ ○

Customer feedback
Customer Quotes

Take note of additional quotes from the customers that are not limited to customer jobs, pains, and gains.

Customer quotes are relatively weak, but helpful for context and qualitative insights for upcoming experiments.

Capabilities

Design / Technology

You'll need to be able to model the 3D print in software, then create it using a 3D printer. Some software is easier to learn that others, but the learning curve can be quite steep if you don't have a design background. We suggest getting help from a 3D modeling expert. With regards to 3D printers, don't rush out and purchase one. Maker spaces and workshops usually allow members to rent time for creating 3D prints.

Requirements

Sketches to Model

Before planning to create a 3D print, make sure you've spent time testing faster, lower fidelity experiments. For example, you should have at least placed paper prototypes in front of customers to receive feedback. That feedback should help inform your design and solution. It doesn't necessarily mean you make all of the changes customers requested.

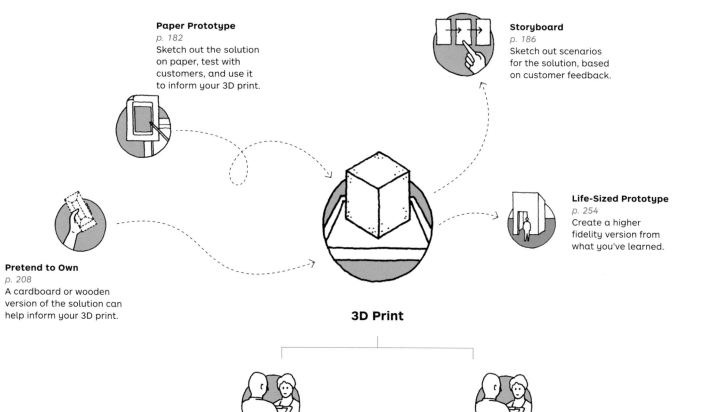

Paper Prototype
p. 182
Sketch out the solution on paper, test with customers, and use it to inform your 3D print.

Storyboard
p. 186
Sketch out scenarios for the solution, based on customer feedback.

Life-Sized Prototype
p. 254
Create a higher fidelity version from what you've learned.

Pretend to Own
p. 208
A cardboard or wooden version of the solution can help inform your 3D print.

3D Print

Customer Interviews
p. 106
Interview your customers while they interact with the 3D print to learn about customer jobs, pains, and gains.

Partner & Supplier Interviews
p. 114
Interview your partners and suppliers to get feedback on the feasibility of your solution.

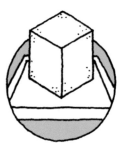

3D PRINT
3D Printing with CubeSats
The National Security Agency

The National Security Agency (NSA) is a world leader in cryptology (the art and science of making and breaking codes) that helps protect sensitive national security information, even in space! If you're like most people, the word "satellite" conjures up images of a bus-sized object weighing several tons and costing hundreds of millions of dollars orbiting the Earth for several years.

CubeSats, on the other hand, are a newer type of satellite that measure only 10 cm × 10 cm × 11.35 cm, weigh less than 2 kg, and utilize commercial off-the-shelf components. An Innovation Corps (I-Corps) team from NSA's Cybersecurity Solutions Group had an idea for creating a new type of cryptographic device to secure uplink and downlink communications from CubeSats. Their solution had dramatically smaller size, weight, power, and price characteristics as compared to existing products designed and certified for use with those expensive bus-sized satellites.

Hypothesis

The NSA team believed that...

Resisting the urge to start building an early version of their encryption device, these intrapreneurs "got out of the building" to validate the desirability of their product. Finding broad demand for CubeSat encryption by external customers, they sought to determine if they could get the "buy-in" of some key internal stakeholders who unfortunately didn't see the need for a new solution. If we can help them see the need, thought the entrepreneurs, then they will authorize and fund our project.

Experiment

The team set out to devise a way to help these stakeholders quickly and unequivocally see the need for a new solution. After a few failed attempts, the team and their coach wondered if using a 3D-printer to create a life-sized mockup of the CubeSat might help them see it. They were ready the next day!

Evidence

The stakeholders immediately saw the need for a new solution after seeing how the currently certified encryption product simply wouldn't fit in the 3D printed mock-up!

Actions

The team was resourced, and they confidently began building their solution that will be tested in orbit in 2019.

DISCOVERY / DISCUSSION PROTOTYPES

Paper Prototype

Sketched interface on paper, manipulated by another person
to represent the software's reactions to the customer interaction.

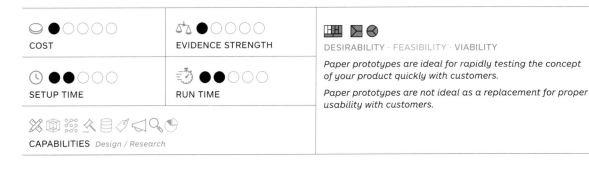

○ ● ○ ○ ○ ○
COST

⚖ ● ○ ○ ○ ○
EVIDENCE STRENGTH

🕐 ● ● ○ ○ ○
SETUP TIME

⏱ ● ● ○ ○ ○
RUN TIME

CAPABILITIES *Design / Research*

DESIRABILITY · FEASIBILITY · VIABILITY

*Paper prototypes are ideal for rapidly testing the concept
of your product quickly with customers.*

*Paper prototypes are not ideal as a replacement for proper
usability with customers.*

Prepare

- ☐ Define the goals of your paper prototype experiment
- ☐ Determine the target audience to test with, preferably a group that isn't cold and has context for your offering.
- ☐ Write your script.
- ☐ Create your paper prototype sketches.
- ☐ Test it internally to make sure the flow works.
- ☐ Schedule your Paper Prototype experiments with target customers.

Execute

- ☐ Explain to the customers that this is an exercise to get their feedback on what you are planning to deliver. Make sure they understand that you value their input.
- ☐ Have one person conduct the interviews and interact with the customer.
- ☐ Have another person write notes and act as a scribe.
- ☐ Wrap up and thank the participants.

Analyze

- ☐ Place the paper prototypes on the wall and place your notes, observations, and quotes around them.
- ☐ Where did they get stuck or confused?
- ☐ What did they get excited about?
- ☐ Use this feedback to inform your next higher fidelity experiment of the experience.

Cost

Paper prototypes are very cheap. You are sketching out what the solution could be and simulating the experience with paper. Your paper prototype should not be an expensive endeavor. If you purchase stencils or apps to assist in the process it can add a small amount of cost.

Setup Time

Setup time for a paper prototype is relatively short. It should only take a few hours to a few days to create your paper prototype. It'll most likely take you longer to find customers to test with than to create the paper prototype itself.

Run Time

Run time for a paper prototype is also a few days to a week. You'll want to rapidly test the paper prototype with target customers, to get feedback on the value proposition and flow of the solution.

Evidence Strength

●○○○○

Task completion
Task completion percentage
Time to complete tasks

   Manual task completion is not necessarily strong evidence, but it will provide glimpses into where customers could get confused.

●○○○○

Customer feedback

Customer quotes on the value proposition and usefulness of the imagined solution.

   Customer quotes on paper prototypes are relatively weak, but can be helpful to inform your higher fidelity experiments.

Capabilities

Design / Research

In addition to an imagination, you'll need some design skills to sketch out the product. You'll also want to write a coherent script and record the sessions.

Requirements

An Imagined Product

Paper prototyping requires a great deal of imagination and creativity. You'll need to be able to sketch out the flow of the product and manually replicate customer interactions. This will require you to think through the experience first, before putting it in front of potential customers.

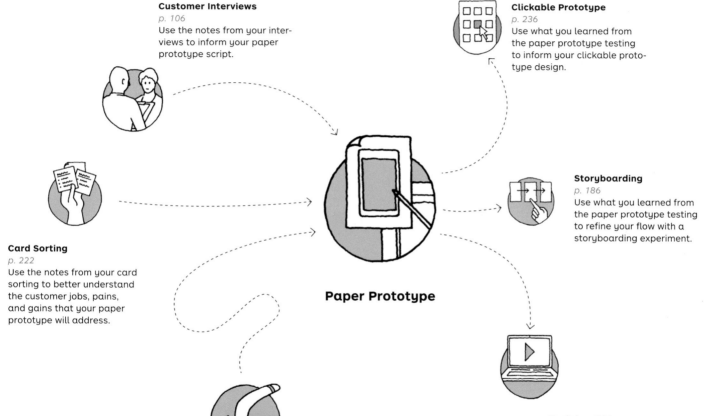

Customer Interviews
p. 106
Use the notes from your interviews to inform your paper prototype script.

Card Sorting
p. 222
Use the notes from your card sorting to better understand the customer jobs, pains, and gains that your paper prototype will address.

Boomerang
p. 204
Use the notes from your Boomerang testing to shape how the paper prototype can address unmet needs.

Paper Prototype

Clickable Prototype
p. 236
Use what you learned from the paper prototype testing to inform your clickable prototype design.

Storyboarding
p. 186
Use what you learned from the paper prototype testing to refine your flow with a storyboarding experiment.

Explainer Video
p. 200
Use the notes from your paper prototype testing to inform your higher fidelity Explainer Video.

DISCOVERY / DISCUSSION PROTOTYPES

Storyboard

Illustrations displayed in sequence for the purpose of visualizing
an interactive experience.

⊖ ●●○○○
COST

⚖ ●●○○○
EVIDENCE STRENGTH

🕐 ●●○○○
SETUP TIME

⏱ ●○○○○
RUN TIME

CAPABILITIES *Design / Research*

DESIRABILITY · FEASIBILITY · VIABILITY

*Storyboards are ideal for brainstorming scenarios of different
value propositions and solutions with customers.*

Prepare

☐ Gather your supplies: paper, poster paper, sharpie, and sticky notes.

☐ Book a room with lots of wall and table space.

☐ Define the customer segment and overall value proposition.

☐ Invite your team members and schedule the interactive session.

Execute

☐ Have the team members brainstorm 8–12 alternative value propositions.

☐ Sketch out storyboards on poster paper that describe how the customer will experience the value proposition.

☐ Take notes on customer quotes, the jobs, pains, and gains mentioned for each scenario.

☐ Have an illustrator help visualize the customer experiences as a single illustration for each scenario.

Analyze

☐ Review your notes with the team.

☐ Update your Value Proposition Canvas or create new ones based based on what you've learned.

☐ Use your sketches in customer interviews.

Cost

Storyboarding is relatively cheap. If you are facilitating it in person, you'll need a lot of wall space, markers, and poster paper. If you are facilitating it remotely over video, you'll need low cost or free, virtual white-boarding software.

Setup Time

Setup time for storyboarding is relatively short. You'll need to gather the supplies and recruit customers.

Run Time

Run time for storyboarding is a few hours. You'll be facilitating it with customers to illustrate value propositions and scenarios.

Evidence Strength

●●○○○

Customer jobs
Customer pains
Customer gains

Illustrations of customer scenarios as to how they'd experience different value propositions.
Top three ranked jobs, pains, and gains.
Themes of jobs, pains, and gains.

   The illustrations are relatively weak evidence, in that it's a lab environment. However, these can help inform higher fidelity feature experiments that focus on action.

●●○○○

Customer feedback
Customer Quotes

Take note of additional quotes from the customers that are not limited to jobs, pains, and gains.

   Customer quotes are relatively weak, but helpful for context and qualitative insights for upcoming experiments.

Capabilities

Design / Research

Almost anyone can facilitate storyboarding with some practice. It will help if you have design and research abilities on your team.

Requirements

Customer Segment

Storyboarding works best if you already have a specific customer segment in mind. It's meant to help you visualize various interactive experiences, but they can be too wide if you don't narrow in on a customer segment first.

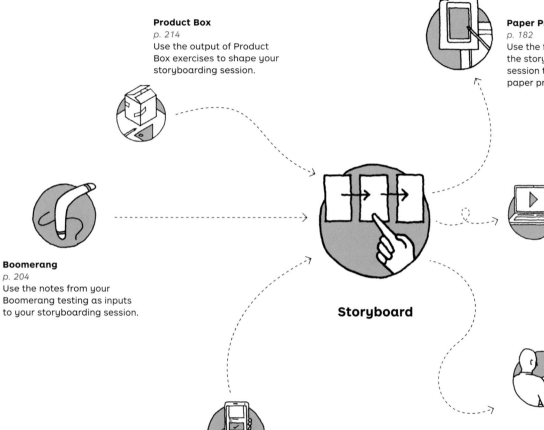

Product Box
p. 214
Use the output of Product
Box exercises to shape your
storyboarding session.

Paper Prototype
p. 182
Use the feedback from
the storyboarding
session to inform your
paper prototype design.

Boomerang
p. 204
Use the notes from your
Boomerang testing as inputs
to your storyboarding session.

Explainer Video
p. 200
Animate the illustrations as a
higher fidelity Explainer Video
to test with customers.

Storyboard

Social Media Campaign
p. 168
Use social media to recruit
people for your storyboarding
session.

Customer Interviews
p. 106
Use the sketches from
your storyboarding in
customer interviews.

STORYBOARD

DISCUSSION PROTOTYPES

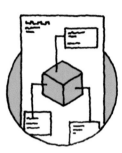

DISCOVERY / DISCUSSION PROTOTYPES

Data Sheet

One page physical or digital sheet with specifications
of your value proposition.

◷ ●○○○○○
COST

⚖ ●●●○○
EVIDENCE STRENGTH

◔ ●●○○○
SETUP TIME

⏱ ●●○○○
RUN TIME

✂ ▦ ⚒ 🗄 🏷 📢 🔍 📊
CAPABILITIES *Design / Technology / Marketing*

▦ ✉

DESIRABILITY · FEASIBILITY · VIABILITY

*Data sheets are ideal for distilling down your specifications
into a single page for testing with customers and key partners.*

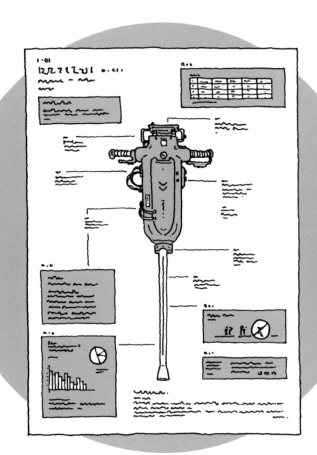

Prepare

- ☐ Define your value proposition and solution specifications.
- ☐ Create your data sheet.
- ☐ Source customers and key partners and schedule the interviews.

Execute

- ☐ Show the data sheet to customers.
- ☐ One person on the team conducts the interview.
- ☐ Another person on the team takes notes on customer quotes, jobs, pains, gains, and body language.
- ☐ Wrap up the interview by asking if it is okay to contact them in the future with higher fidelity solutions or the opportunity to buy.

Analyze

- ☐ Review your notes with the team.
- ☐ Update your Value Proposition Canvas based on what you've learned.
- ☐ Use what you've learned to refine and inform your higher fidelity experiments.

Connections

- • Use the value proposition from your Value Map as your title.
- • Include the product/service from your Value Map.
- • Expand on the product/service specifications and illustrate details.
- • Include the top three gain creators from your Value Map.
- • Include the top three pain relievers from your Value Map.

Cost

A data sheet is very cheap. If it's physical, you'll need basic word processor or office software to create the physical one page document and print it. If it's digital, you'll need basic web software to include the specifications in your web page or email.

Setup Time

Setup time for a data sheet is a few hours to a day to set up and create. This includes the time needed to gather your specifications and properly format them. You'll need to recruit customers and key partners if you are planning on showing it in person.

Run Time

Testing your data sheet with customers and key partners is generally quick and only takes about 15 minutes each.

Evidence Strength

Customer feedback
Partner feedback

Customer and partner quotes when reviewing the data sheet.

Feedback is weak but generally good for qualitative insights.

Capabilities

Design / Research

Data sheets require basic design skills to effectively convey the information about the value proposition and technical specifications. You'll need to include your value proposition and the technical specifications of the solution as well as source customers and/or key partners.

Requirements

A data sheet will require you to have specifications and a specific value proposition. You'll want to think through how it performs technically and what the benefits are, before creating a data sheet. You'll also need a target customer or key partner to have in mind for testing purposes.

Product Box
p. 214
Inform your data sheet by facilitating a Product Box exercise with your potential customers.

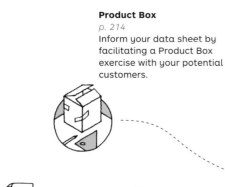

3D Print
p. 176
Create a 3D print of your solution based on what you learned from testing the data sheet.

Paper Prototype
p. 182
Use the feedback from a paper prototype to inform your data sheet.

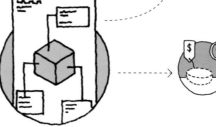

Presale
p. 274
Conduct presales with the people who showed interest in the data sheet.

Data Sheet

Customer Interviews
p. 106
Share your data sheet in customer interviews to get feedback on how it solves for jobs, pains, and gains.

Partner & Supplier Interviews
p. 114
Interview your key partners and suppliers to get feedback on the feasibility of your data sheet.

Simple Landing Page
p. 260
Include the data sheet in your landing page to clearly communicate the detailed specifications of your solution.

DISCOVERY / DISCUSSION PROTOTYPES

Brochure

Mocked up physical brochure of your imagined value proposition.

COST	EVIDENCE STRENGTH
◯ ● ◯ ◯ ◯ ◯	⚖ ● ● ● ◯ ◯

SETUP TIME	RUN TIME
🕐 ● ● ● ◯ ◯	⏱ ● ● ◯ ◯ ◯

CAPABILITIES *Marketing / Research*

DESIRABILITY · FEASIBILITY · VIABILITY

Physical brochures are ideal for testing your value proposition in person with customers who are difficult to find online.

Prepare

☐ Design your brochure, using the connections from your Value Proposition Canvas.

☐ Create your plan on where to find target customers.

Execute

☐ Show the brochure to customers.

☐ One person on the team conducts the interview.

☐ Another person on the team takes notes on customer quotes, jobs, pains, gains, and body language.

☐ Count how many viewed the brochure and how many accepted it.

☐ Wrap up the interview stating that if they want to learn more or purchase to contact you using the information on the brochure.

Analyze

☐ Review your notes with the team.

☐ Update your Value Proposition Canvas based on what you've learned.

☐ Keep track of how many people contact you from the brochure information.

☐ Use what you've learned to refine and inform your higher fidelity experiments.

Connections

• The value proposition comes from your Value Map.

• The solution comes from the Value Map product and service. Position this under the value proposition so that customers understand how you are going to deliver.

• Pains come from your Customer Profile. Take the top three voted pains from the canvas and include them in the inside of the brochure.

BROCHURE

195

DISCUSSION PROTOTYPES

Cost

Physical brochure costs are low if you can use a word processor and have basic design skills. The costs increase if you decide to outsource the creation of the physical brochure to a professional agency or designer.

Setup Time

If you have the skills, a brochure should only take 1–2 days to set up and create. This includes the time needed to define the brochure hypothesis, pull in concepts from your Value Proposition Canvas, write the content, and include the graphics. If you do not have the skills, it can take 1–2 weeks instead.

Run Time

Testing your brochure with customers is generally quick and only takes about 15 minutes. Your brochures can be used with interviews wherever your customers are located physically, whether that be on the street, a cafe, or at a conference.

Evidence Strength

# of brochure views
# of brochures taken
# of interviews
# of people who contact you
Email % Conversion Rates
Phone % Conversion Rates

You can calculate the conversion rate by taking the number people given a brochure divided by number who took action = conversion rate.

Brochure conversion rates vary by industry and segment; however, if you target a very specific segment for your brochure, you should look for a strong signal of 15% or more on the call-to-action conversion.

When customers take action to reach out, it's a good signal that you are on the right path. This is different than a landing page where people are giving up their email. On a brochure with a call to action, it takes more initiative on the customer's side to take the brochure home, read through it, and then call or email you to find out more about the value proposition you are offering.

Capabilities

Marketing / Research

Brochures require design skills to create a compelling visual experience, with high quality images and styling. If you are unable to do so, you may get false negatives in your testing — people won't believe your value proposition is real. The other important aspect of the brochure is the copy and content. You'll need to be able to write clear, concise sentences that resonate with your customers.

Requirements

Acquisition Plan

Brochures are different than online digital experiments — you need to physically interact with people to distribute them. Have a plan about what you are trying to achieve and where to find your customers before finalizing a brochure. Brainstorm locations to visit, such as:

- Conferences.
- Meetups.
- Events.
- Cafes.
- Stores.
- Door-to-door.

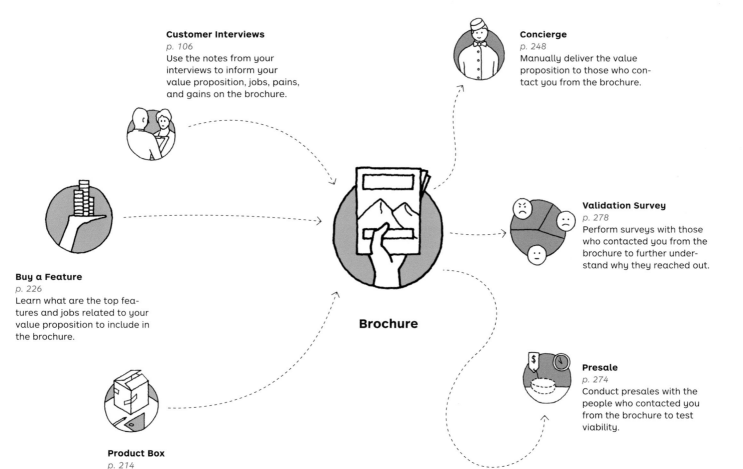

Customer Interviews
p. 106
Use the notes from your interviews to inform your value proposition, jobs, pains, and gains on the brochure.

Concierge
p. 248
Manually deliver the value proposition to those who contact you from the brochure.

Buy a Feature
p. 226
Learn what are the top features and jobs related to your value proposition to include in the brochure.

Validation Survey
p. 278
Perform surveys with those who contacted you from the brochure to further understand why they reached out.

Brochure

Product Box
p. 214
Inform your brochure's value proposition by first facilitating a Product Box exercise with your potential customers.

Presale
p. 274
Conduct presales with the people who contacted you from the brochure to test viability.

BROCHURE
A New Type of Insurance
Farm and Ranch Insurance

American Family Insurance is a private mutual company that focuses on property, casualty, and auto insurance. As an insurance company, they understand risk very well and do not want to build complex insurance offerings that no one will buy. In this example, the Commercial Farm Ranch division was searching for fit for new market risk protection offerings.

In the past, this team had used Facebook/Google Ads to drive traffic to a landing page, which is a great combination but it was difficult to target farmers online, and the team wasn't getting enough qualitative insights. So they decided to go analog and face-to-face at a large farmer convention.

Hypothesis

The Farm and Ranch team believed that...
We believe that farmers desire a new type of financial/insurance risk protection offering.

Experiment

Going analog with physical brochures.
The team went to a farming trade show in Missouri and handed out professional physical marketing brochures with a clearly articulated value proposition and solution. They had a call to action of getting in touch with the team via a phone call or email for more information.

The team screened for small/mid-sized cattle and corn farmers.

Their target metric was that 20% of the target farmers (small/mid sized cattle or corn farmers) would take initiative and call or email.

Evidence

Conversions using a brochure.
15% target farmers who received the brochure called or emailed requesting more info.

Qualitative learnings talking to the farmers and getting reaction to the brochure in face-to-face conversations.

Insights

Segmenting different types of farmers for a stronger value proposition.
Cattle farmers' pain points seemed greater based on metrics and emotion in conversations compared to corn farmers.

The farmers' current way to solve the problem was to go to a bank and get another loan/line of credit but that felt risky to them.

Several farmer focused banks/credit unions were interested in the the concept. The team could explore this as a channel.

Actions

Narrowing in on cattle farmers.
The team refined the value proposition and marketing to be more cattle-farmer specific. Next they reran the experiment to see if focusing on a more niche customer segment would get a more decisive validation signal.

DISCOVERY / DISCUSSION PROTOTYPES

Explainer Video

A short video that focuses on explaining a business idea in a simple, engaging, and compelling way.

●●●○○	⚖ ●●◉○○
COST	EVIDENCE STRENGTH
⏱ ●●●○○	⏱ ●●●●○
SETUP TIME	RUN TIME

CAPABILITIES *Design / Product / Technology*

🖥 ✉ ◉

DESIRABILITY · FEASIBILITY · VIABILITY

An Explainer Video is ideal for quickly explaining your value proposition at scale with customers.

Prepare

☐ Write a script for your Explainer Video.

☐ Use the connections from your Value Proposition Canvas to inform the script and visuals.

☐ Create your Explainer Video.

☐ Upload it on a social media platform, video platform, email, or landing page.

☐ Test that the video analytics and CTA links work.

Execute

☐ Make your video live to the public.

☐ Drive traffic to your video.

☐ If comments are enabled, engage with the public on questions they have about the solution.

Analyze

☐ How many views and shares does the video receive?

☐ What is your click through rate?

☐ Are people that land on your destination from the video converting?

☐ Use what you've learned to tailor the video content. It's quite common to have different versions of the video depending on your target customer and platform.

Connections

• Lead with the top pain from your Customer Profile.

• Introduce your solution to the pain from your Value Map.

• Illustrate the gain from the Customer Profile you receive from solving the pain.

• Close with a call-to-action link to gauge desirability.

● ● ● ○ ○

Cost

The cost of running an Explainer Video is relatively cheap, but can get expensive quickly depending on the production value. There are many products that'll enable you to create an Explainer Video that looks good enough, but if you want to stand out, it'll likely cost you for professional videography. You should also consider how you'll drive traffic to the Explainer Video as part of the cost.

 ● ● ● ○ ○

Setup Time

Good Explainer Videos take a few days or weeks to set up. You'll need to think through how to clearly convey your value proposition, write a script, and do multiple takes and edits.

 ● ● ● ● ○

Run Time

Run time for Explainer Videos is relatively long, from several weeks to months, unless it goes viral. While viral videos get a lot of buzz, they tend to be the outliers. Many Explainer Videos require a great deal of work to drive traffic to them, both with paid advertising and social media.

 ● ● ● ○ ○

Evidence Strength

● ● ○ ○ ○

# of unique views

How many unique views you receive and from what referral source.

# of shares

How many shares of the video there are and via what platform.

Views and shares are relatively weak evidence.

● ● ● ○ ○

# of clicks

Click through rate = clicks that your video receives divided by the number of views.

Clicks are stronger evidence in that people are clicking to learn more.

● ● ○ ○ ○

Comments

Viewer comments on the video with regard to availability, price, and how it works.

Comments are relatively weak evidence but at times good for qualitative insights.

Capabilities

Design / Product / Technology

You'll need to be able to write a script for a compelling Explainer Video, create the video, edit it, and then share and promote it to your target audience. The Explainer Video will need a clear call to action, usually at the end, to encourage your audience to click and learn more.

Requirements

Traffic

Explainer Videos need traffic to generate evidence, regardless whether they exist on a video hosting platform or a landing page. Drive traffic to your Explainer Video using:

- Online ads.
- Social media campaigns.
- Email campaigns.
- Redirecting existing traffic.
- Word of mouth.
- Discussion forums.

Data Sheet
p. 190
Create a data sheet that explains the performance and specifications of your proposed solution.

Email Campaign
p. 162
Contact the people who signed up and interview them to learn why they liked the video.

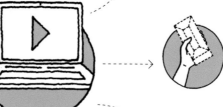

Pretend to Own
p. 208
Create a nonfunctioning prototype of your solution and see if you have the desire to use it in real world situations.

Storyboarding
p. 186
Test out different sequences of events using illustrations to inform your Explainer Video.

Explainer Video

Simple Landing Page
p. 260
Create a simple landing page as a destination for the call-to-action link at the end of your Explainer Video.

Card Sorting
p. 222
Facilitate a card sorting exercise to better understand different sequences to solve for customer needs.

DISCOVERY / DISCUSSION PROTOTYPES

Boomerang

Performing a customer test on an existing competitor's product to gather insights on the value proposition.

 ●●○○○
COST

⚖ ●○○○○
EVIDENCE STRENGTH

🕐 ●●○○○
SETUP TIME

⏱ ●●○○○
RUN TIME

CAPABILITIES *Product / Marketing / Research*

▦ ▷ ◐
DESIRABILITY · FEASIBILITY · VIABILITY

Boomerang is ideal for finding unmet needs with potential customers in an existing market, without building anything.

Boomerang is not ideal for stripping away branding and testing a product as if it's your own.

Prepare

- ☐ Identify a product to test that has unmet needs related to your idea.
- ☐ Create a script for customer testing.
- ☐ Recruit customers who agree to test the product and be recorded.
- ☐ Schedule the Boomerang sessions.
- ☐ Prepare the Boomerang location with a competitor's product.

Execute

- ☐ Share the script and explain the goal.
- ☐ Record the session and take notes on what they say, where they get stuck, and how long it takes them to complete tasks.
- ☐ Wrap up and thank the participants.

Analyze

- ☐ Review your notes with the team.
  - Which tasks were unfinished? Took the longest? Caused the most frustration?
- ☐ Create a Value Proposition Canvas for the competition indicating where they are misaligned.
- ☐ Use this information to inform your upcoming experiments to learn more.

Perils of Rebranding Competitor Products as Yours

Over time we've observed Boomerang tests and variants of it, sometimes called Imposter Judo. While, at times, these techniques vary widely in definition, we have come to a consensus that it is too risky to rebrand a competitor's product entirely for customer testing purposes.

The technique usually involves creating a clone of the competitor's, stripping away the branding and replacing it with your branding, or a fabricated brand.

This has legal and ethical implications which we advise against, especially for established corporations or those operating in heavily regulated environments.

Interestingly enough, we've seen both corporations and startups use Boomerang testing with branding intact to get an idea of unmet needs.

Corporations have pointed their Boomerang testing at a hot up-and-coming startup.

Startups have pointed their Boomerang testing at entrenched established corporations.

●●○○○○
Cost

Boomerang is a low cost experiment involving pointing people to your competitor's product and not building anything. Any incurred costs would be associated with sourcing people to test with and recording the sessions.

 ●●○○○○
Setup Time

Setup time for a Boomerang is short, in that you only need to find and schedule people to participate in the test.

 ●●○○○○
Run Time

Run time for a Boomerang is short, as the sessions should not last more than 30 minutes each. Even if you schedule several of these, it should only take a few days to complete.

 ●●○○○
Evidence Strength

●●●○○

Task completion
Time to complete the task

Task completion rate = tasks completed divided by tasks attempted.

Average time to complete a task.

In the evidence you are looking for unmet gaps and needs when it comes to the espoused value proposition versus what it really takes for an average customer.

Evidence for measuring tasks in existing competitors' products is relatively strong — you are measuring actual behavior in the product.

●○○○○

Customer feedback

Customer quotes with regards to ease of use and unmet needs.
Look for gaps in what the customer wants and expects the product to do versus what it does in reality.

Customer feedback is relatively weak evidence, but it is helpful in determining unmet needs to explore.

Capabilities
Product / Marketing / Research

Boomerang capabilities include the ability to select an applicable product, craft a script, recruit an audience to test with, record the sessions, and synthesize the results. Many of these capabilities reside within product and marketing and research. Like interviews, these are best performed in pairs when possible.

Requirements
Existing Product

Before you schedule a Boomerang experiment, you'll need to identify the existing product to use for the testing. It needs to be a product from which you can extract learning to inform your new idea, otherwise the feedback you'll collect will not be useful.

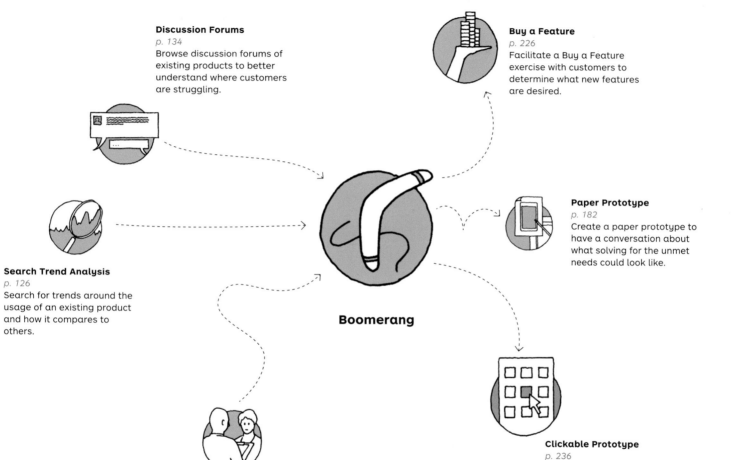

Discussion Forums
p. 134
Browse discussion forums of existing products to better understand where customers are struggling.

Buy a Feature
p. 226
Facilitate a Buy a Feature exercise with customers to determine what new features are desired.

Paper Prototype
p. 182
Create a paper prototype to have a conversation about what solving for the unmet needs could look like.

Search Trend Analysis
p. 126
Search for trends around the usage of an existing product and how it compares to others.

Boomerang

Clickable Prototype
p. 236
Create a clickable prototype that simulates customers' expectations.

Customer Interviews
p. 106
Perform customer interviews on people who are already using the competitor's product.

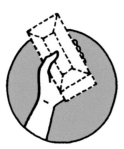

DISCOVERY / INTERACTION PROTOTYPE

Pretend to Own

Creating a nonfunctioning, low fidelity prototype of the solution to determine whether it fits into the day-to-day life of the customer. Sometimes called a Pinocchio experiment.

COST
○ ● ○ ○ ○ ○

EVIDENCE STRENGTH
● ● ○ ○ ○

SETUP TIME
● ● ○ ○ ○

RUN TIME
● ● ● ● ○

CAPABILITIES *Design / Research*

DESIRABILITY · FEASIBILITY · VIABILITY

Pretend to Own is ideal for generating your own evidence on the potential usefulness of an idea.

Prepare

☐ Sketch out the product idea on a piece of paper.

☐ Gather the materials you'd need to make a Pretend to Own experiment of the product.

☐ Time box the amount of time to create it so that you do not over-iterate internally.

☐ Create your Pretend to Own product.

☐ Create an experiment log to track your metrics.

Execute

☐ Run your Pretend to Own experiment, acting as though it was a functioning product.

☐ Track your usage in an experiment log.

Analyze

☐ Review your log for events:

• How many times did you engage with it?

• Were there certain aspects of it that made it difficult or cumbersome?

☐ Use your findings to inform your higher fidelity experiment.

Cost

Cost of Pretend to Own is very cheap, in that you are using readily available material such as wood and paper. Cost can increase with size and complexity.

Setup Time

Setup time for Pretend to Own is a few minutes to a few hours. You don't want to iterate on the design internally very much at all, but instead have the bare bones shape and user interface.

Run Time

Run time for Pretend to Own can be several weeks to several months, depending on the nature of your idea. You'll want to test it over time, in order to forget that it isn't real (almost).

Evidence

When do you use it?
Engagement Logbook

Keep a spreadsheet that tracks the amount of time it was available and the number of occurrences in which you thought it would be of use to you.

Document the types of uses and in what scenarios they occurred. Overall engagement is a relatively weak strength of evidence, but you'll learn firsthand insights that can help shape the idea and value proposition.

Capabilities

Design / Research

Basic design and research skills are helpful when running a Pretend to Own experiment. You'll need to be able to create a rough replica and then log your activities over time.

Requirements

Pretend to Own doesn't require a great deal to get started: simply an idea that you want to validate and some creativity on how to create a nonfunctioning replica of it.

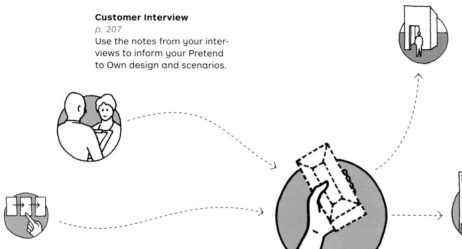

Customer Interview
p. 207
Use the notes from your interviews to inform your Pretend to Own design and scenarios.

Life Sized Prototype
p. 254
Create a higher fidelity, life-sized prototype of the solution.

Storyboarding
p. 186
Test out different sequences of events using illustrations to inform your Pretend to Own.

Pretend to Own

Data Sheet
p. 190
Write up a data sheet on what the specifications should be for the solution.

Brochure
p. 194
Create a brochure that conveys the value proposition of the solution to test with customers.

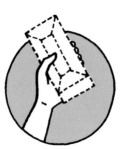

PRETEND TO OWN
Wooden Palm Pilot
Palm

Before the Palm Pilot was created, Jeff Hawkins wanted to gauge the desirability of the product. He had seen personal digital assistants in the past that were feasible, but not desirable. These ultimately led to large expensive failures.

Jeff Hawkins cut a block of wood to fit the overall size of the envisioned product and printed out a simple user interface, like the one he envisioned. He taped the printout over the wooden block and used a wooden chopstick as the stylus. This was rough enough that it only took hours to create. He then carried it around in his pocket at work for months to determine the desirability of the value proposition in the real world.

When someone asked for a meeting or email, he would pull the wood block out of his pocket, tap on it with the chopstick and then put it away.

After several instances when he felt it would've been useful to have the real product, only then did he decide to go forward with the product development of the Palm Pilot.

Evidence
Palm Pilot Engagement Logbook

- Carried the device in my pocket 95% of the time
- Pulled it out to use it an average of 12 times
- For scheduling appointments: 55% of the time
- To look up phone numbers or addresses: 25% of the time
- To add to or check a to-do list: 15% of the time
- To take notes: 5% of the time

Adapted from The Right It *by Alberto Savoia*

✓

☐ *Create your nonfunctioning replica as soon as possible in the design process.*

☐ *Be thrifty and use low cost, commonly available craft materials.*

☐ *Use your creative inspiration to pretend it functions in real life.*

☐ *Keep a logbook of your interactions, whether they be physical or digital.*

✗

– *Spend a lot of money and time creating the replica.*

– *Choose extremely large and expensive products for this technique.*

– *Be embarrassed to carry it around in real world scenarios.*

– *Forget to have fun in the process.*

DISCOVERY / PREFERENCE & PRIORITIZATION

Product Box

A facilitation technique used with customers to visualize value propositions, main features, and key benefits in the physical form of a box.

COST
● ● ● ○ ○ ○

EVIDENCE STRENGTH
● ● ● ○ ○ ○

SETUP TIME
● ● ● ○ ○ ○

RUN TIME
● ● ○ ○ ○ ○

DESIRABILITY · FEASIBILITY · VIABILITY

Product Box is ideal for refining your value proposition and narrowing in on key features to your solution.

CAPABILITIES *Design / Product / Research*

Prepare

☐ Recruit 15–20 target customers.

☐ Set up the room with boxes and supplies for each table.

Execute

☐ Set the stage by defining the area to explore.

☐ Have each table design a box for a product idea they would buy.

☐ Have them include messaging, features, and benefits of the imaginary product.

☐ Each team has to imagine selling the imaginary product at a trade show. Have them take turns pitching the product to you, a skeptical customer.

☐ Take notes during the pitches on key messaging, features, benefits.

Analyze

☐ Debrief with your team. What aspects did the teams emphasize over others?

☐ Use what you've learned to update your Value Proposition Canvas. This can be the basis of future experiments.

To learn more about Product Box we highly recommend reading Innovation Games *by Luke Hohmann.*

Cost

Running a Product Box experiment is relatively cheap. The materials you need are low cost and widely available at craft stores. You'll need cardboard boxes and supplies to decorate the box, colored markers, paper, and stickers.

Setup Time

Setup time for Product Box is relatively short, in that you'll need to recruit customers to participate. You'll need to purchase the supplies and set up the room.

Run Time

Run time for Product Box is very short. You can facilitate it in less than 1 hour.

Evidence Strength

Value propositions
Customer jobs
Customer pains
Customer gains

Collect and organize the key customer jobs, pains, and gains offered up by the participants. Highlight the top three of each.

Take note of the messaging of the value propositions from the participants, as these can inform your own messaging.

Artifacts produced by Product Box are relatively weak evidence, but they can be used to shape and inform your upcoming experiments.

Customer feedback
Customer Quotes

Take note of additional quotes from the customers that are not limited to jobs, pains, and gains.

Customer quotes are relatively weak evidence, but helpful for context and qualitative insights for upcoming experiments.

Capabilities

Design / Product / Research

Almost anyone can facilitate a Product Box with some practice. It will help though if you have design, research, and product abilities— you'll want to assess the outputs and provide inspiration when needed.

Requirements

Idea and Target Customer

Product Box requirements are not expansive, although ideally you'll want to have an idea and target customer in mind. Without this, the session will likely go very wide and the results will be difficult to interpret.

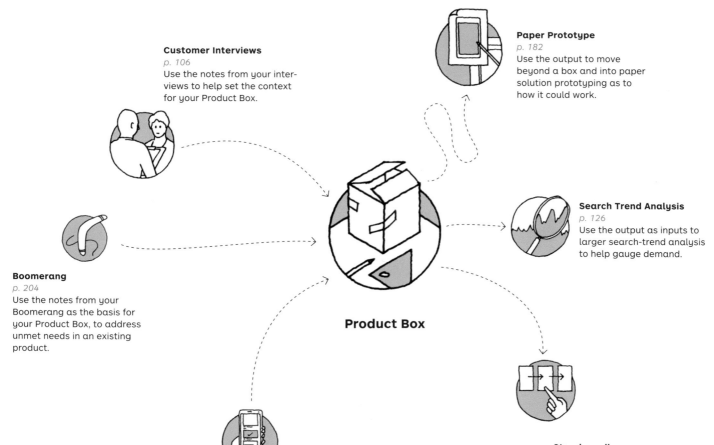

Customer Interviews
p. 106
Use the notes from your interviews to help set the context
for your Product Box.

Paper Prototype
p. 182
Use the output to move
beyond a box and into paper
solution prototyping as to
how it could work.

Boomerang
p. 204
Use the notes from your
Boomerang as the basis for
your Product Box, to address
unmet needs in an existing
product.

Search Trend Analysis
p. 126
Use the output as inputs to
larger search-trend analysis
to help gauge demand.

Product Box

Social Media Campaign
p. 168
Use social media to recruit
people for your Product Box
session.

Storyboarding
p. 186
Use the output to test
sequences of solutions using
illustrations.

DISCOVERY / PREFERENCE & PRIORITIZATION

Speed Boat

A visual game technique used with customers to identify
what's inhibiting progress.

◯ ●●◯◯◯
COST

⚖ ●●◉◯◯
EVIDENCE STRENGTH

🔲 ▶️ ⊘
DESIRABILITY · FEASIBILITY · VIABILITY

*Speed Boat is ideal for going beyond conversations
and having a visual representation of what's slowing your
customers down and learning how it impacts feasibility.*

🕐 ●●◯◯◯
SETUP TIME

 ●◯◯◯◯
RUN TIME

✂️📦 ⚙️ ⟰ 🗄 🔖 📣 🔍 📊
CAPABILITIES *Design / Product / Technology*

1. Recruit

☐ Recruit 15–20 customers who use your existing product for the exercise.

2. Prepare

☐ If it's in person, you'll want a picture of a speed boat and cards. If it's remote, then you'll need to set up a virtual whiteboard that has a speed boat and virtual cards which customers can write on digitally.

3. Facilitate

☐ Give each customer a few minutes to think before writing down anchors. After they've placed them near the speed boat, note their location. Anchors that are in groups, repeating the same thing in different ways, are clustered together. If they are deeper below the speed boat, then it means they are slowing things down more so than others. Be mindful to review each card with the group, but refrain from trying to solve or provide feedback. Doing so will bias the group and the exercise.

4. Analyze

☐ Once Speed Boat has concluded and the customers have left, assign a severity and urgency to each anchor as a team. Some you may want to address right away while others you may ignore entirely. These results, after you've processed the anchors, should be inputs into your upcoming experiments.

To learn more about Speed Boat we highly recommend reading Innovation Games *by Luke Hohmann.*

●●○○○○

Cost

Running a Speed Boat experiment is relatively cheap. The materials you need are a picture of a speed boat, writing utensils, and note cards. If you choose to run this remotely, then you'll need to use a virtual product, which could slightly increase cost.

 ●●○○○○

Setup Time

Setup time for Speed Boat is relatively short, in that you'll need to recruit customers to participate. You'll also want to review any existing support data that could help inform what to look for during the experiment.

 ●○○○○○

Run Time

Run time for Speed Boat is very short. It takes 1–2 hours to facilitate with multiple customers involved.

 ●●●○○○

Evidence

●●●○○

# of anchors
Severity
Urgency
# of severe and urgent anchors
The higher number of severe and urgent anchors, the bigger gap you have between your Value Map and your Customer Profile.

Artifacts produced by Speed Boat are still relatively weak evidence, but it's stronger than simply talking to customers. You are unpacking what specifically is keeping your product from living up to its value proposition.

●●○○○

Customer feedback
Customer Quotes
In addition to the anchors, you'll want to collect customer quotes to better understand their context when struggling with the product.

Customer quotes are relatively weak evidence, but helpful for context and qualitative insights on your product.

Capabilities

Design / Product / Technology

In addition to facilitation capabilities, which are not necessarily role specific, you'll need the right people in the room to assign severity and urgency to the anchors. Not all anchors are created equal, and some you'll want to fix right away while others you may ignore entirely.

Requirements

Facilitation Skills

Speed Boat requires some degree of facilitation skills, especially with a group of customers who are about to complain about your product. You'll need to check your ego at the door and have the skills to extract the specific anchors. If you feel you are unable to do so because you are too close to the product, then we recommend bringing in a neutral third-party facilitator to lead the session.

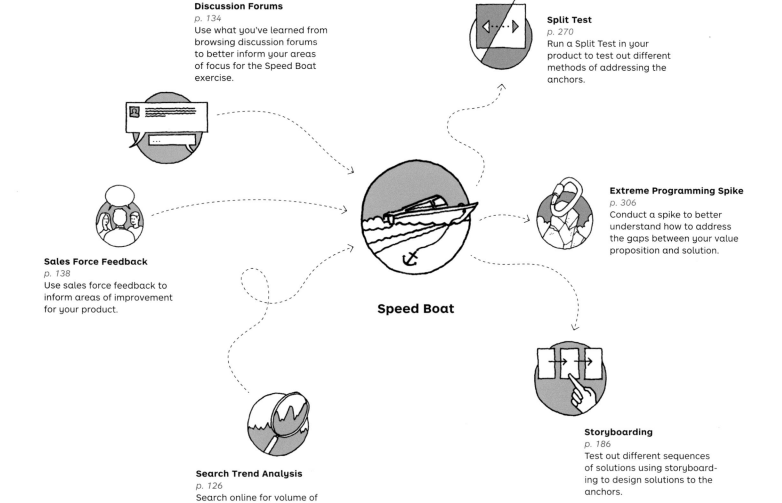

Discussion Forums
p. 134
Use what you've learned from browsing discussion forums to better inform your areas of focus for the Speed Boat exercise.

Split Test
p. 270
Run a Split Test in your product to test out different methods of addressing the anchors.

Sales Force Feedback
p. 138
Use sales force feedback to inform areas of improvement for your product.

Speed Boat

Extreme Programming Spike
p. 306
Conduct a spike to better understand how to address the gaps between your value proposition and solution.

Storyboarding
p. 186
Test out different sequences of solutions using storyboarding to design solutions to the anchors.

Search Trend Analysis
p. 126
Search online for volume of customers who are complaining about your product.

SPEEDB BOAT

221

PREFERENCE & PRIORITIZATION

DISCOVERY / DISCUSSION PROTOTYPES

Card Sorting

A technique in user experience design in which a person uses cards with customers to generate insights.

⬭ ●●○○○	⚖ ●●○○○	▦ ✉ ◔
COST	**EVIDENCE STRENGTH**	DESIRABILITY · FEASIBILITY · VIABILITY
🕐 ●●○○○	⏱ ●○○○○	*Card sorting is ideal for getting insights into customer jobs, pains, gains, and value propositions.*
SETUP TIME	**RUN TIME**	

CAPABILITIES *Marketing / Research*

1. Recruit

☐ Recruit 15–20 existing or target customers for the card sorting session.

2. Prepare

☐ If it's in person, you'll need cards you've created for customer jobs, pains, and gains as well as blank cards for customers to fill out. If it's remote, then you'll need to set up a virtual whiteboard that has cards you've already created as well as blank ones.

3. Facilitate

☐ Explain the categories of customer jobs, pains, and gains that you've witnessed in the market. Have the participants map the existing cards to each category and rank them. Encourage them to talk out loud as they do so. Ask if there are any missing and, if so, have the participants write them down and include them in the ranking. Have an additional person take notes on your side during the session for qualitative insights.

4. Analyze

☐ Once card sorting is concluded, identify any themes you've found and calculate how the participants have ranked the top three jobs, pains, and gains. Update or create your Value Proposition Canvas to reflect the latest findings to help inform future experiments.

Cost

Running a card sorting experiment is relatively cheap. If you are facilitating it in person, then the only materials you need are note cards. If you are facilitating it remotely over video, then you'll need low-cost or free virtual white-boarding software.

Setup Time

Setup time for card sorting is relatively short. You'll need to define the content of the cards and recruit customers.

Run Time

Run time for card sorting is very short. You can facilitate it in less than 1 hour.

Evidence

Customer jobs
Customer pains
Customer gains
Top three ranked jobs, pains, and gains.
Themes of jobs, pains, and gains.

The grouping and ranking output of card sorting is relatively weak evidence, in that it's a lab environment. However it can help inform higher fidelity feature experiments that focus on action.

Customer feedback
Customer Quotes

Take note of additional quotes from the customers that are not limited to jobs, pains, and gains.

Customer quotes are relatively weak evidence, but helpful for context and qualitative insights for upcoming experiments.

Capabilities

Marketing / Research

Almost anyone can facilitate a card sorting session with some practice. It will help if you have marketing and research abilities, in that you'll want to recruit the right customers and analyze the categories and rankings created.

Requirements

Target Customer

Card sorting works best with existing customers, but it can also be used for learning about a potential niche customer as well. Both will require you to put thought into customer jobs, pains, and gains so that the output can be used to inform your Value Proposition Canvas and future experiments.

DISCOVERY

EXPERIMENTS

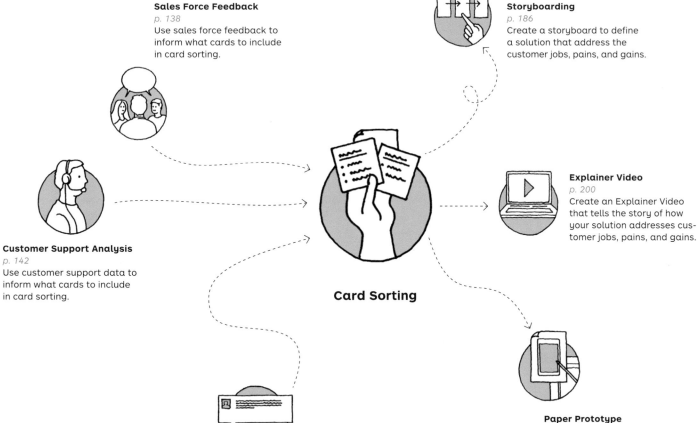

Sales Force Feedback
p. 138
Use sales force feedback to
inform what cards to include
in card sorting.

Storyboarding
p. 186
Create a storyboard to define
a solution that address the
customer jobs, pains, and gains.

Customer Support Analysis
p. 142
Use customer support data to
inform what cards to include
in card sorting.

Explainer Video
p. 200
Create an Explainer Video
that tells the story of how
your solution addresses customer jobs, pains, and gains.

Card Sorting

Discussion Forums
p. 134
Search through discussion
forums to see what unmet
needs customers have to
inform your cards.

Paper Prototype
p. 182
Create a paper prototype
of how the solution could
address the customer jobs,
pains, and gains.

DISCOVERY / DISCUSSION PROTOTYPES

Buy a Feature

A technique where people use pretend currency to buy the features that they would like to be available for a given product.

○ ●●○○○
COST

⚖ ●●○○○
EVIDENCE STRENGTH

🕐 ●●○○○
SETUP TIME

⏱ ●○○○○
RUN TIME

CAPABILITIES *Product / Research / Finance*

DESIRABILITY · FEASIBILITY · VIABILITY

Buy a Feature is ideal for prioritizing features and refining customer jobs, pains, and gains.

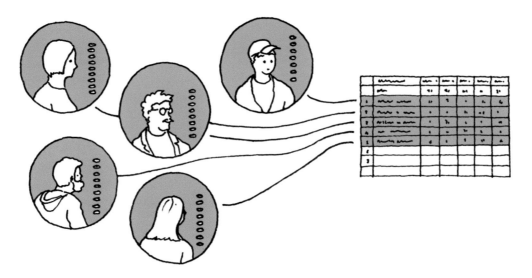

1. Recruit

☐ Recruit 15–20 target customers.

2. Prepare

☐ Set up the room with play money, note cards, and grid paper.

3. Design

☐ Explain that this is a hypothetical setting. Share the list of 15–30 features and available play money budget.

4. Buy

☐ Each customer allocates their budget to the features they want. They can collaborate with others to receive more features. It's important not to bias customers by providing feedback as they choose features.

5. Analyze

☐ Calculate on grid paper which features received the most play money.

To learn more about Buy a Feature we highly recommend reading Innovation Games *by Luke Hohmann.*

Cost

Running a Buy a Feature experiment is relatively cheap. If you are facilitating it in person, then the only materials you need are play money, note cards, and grid paper. If you are facilitating it remotely over video, then you'll need low-cost or free virtual white-boarding software.

Setup Time

Setup time for Buy a Feature can take a few days. You'll need to recruit customers, purchase supplies, and setup the room. Most of your time will be spent defining and pricing the features for the session.

Run Time

Run time for Buy a Feature is very short. You can facilitate it in less than one hour.

Evidence

●●○○○

Feature ranking
Customer jobs
Customer pains
Customer gains

Top three features that were purchased the most by customers.

Take note of any customer jobs, pains, and gains mentioned that are driving the customers' prioritizations.

Buy a Feature is relatively weak evidence—it's a lab environment. However, it can help inform higher fidelity feature experiments that focus on action.

●●○○○

Customer feedback
Customer Quotes

Take note of additional quotes from the customers that are not limited to customer jobs, pains, and gains.

Customer quotes are relatively weak evidence, but helpful for context and qualitative insights for upcoming experiments.

Capabilities

Product / Research / Finance

Almost anyone can facilitate a Buy a Feature with some practice. It will help, however, if you have design, research, and product abilities—you'll want to assess the outputs and provide inspiration when needed.

Requirements

Feature List and Target Customer

Buy a Feature requires you to put significant thought into what features you'd like to include in your product. It also requires customers to have a bit of context about the product, otherwise their rankings will not be very useful to you.

DISCOVERY

228

EXPERIMENTS

Sales Force Feedback
p. 138
Use sales force feedback
to inform what features to
include in Buy a Feature.

Feature Stub
p. 156
Create a Feature Stub for top
ranking features to determine
if people will show interest in
the real world.

Split Test
p. 270
Split Test different top-ranking
features in your product
to measure engagement.

Customer Support Analysis
p. 142
Use customer support data
to inform what features could
address gaps in your product.

Buy a Feature

Clickable Prototype
p. 236
Invite participants back to
test clickable prototypes of
the top ranking features.

Discussion Forums
p. 134
Search through discussion
forums to see what unmet
needs customers have to
inform your feature list.

BUY A FEATURE

229

PREFERENCE & PRIORITIZATION

"Invention is not disruptive.
Only customer adoption
is disruptive."

———

Jeff Bezos
Entrepreneur and philanthropist,
founder of Amazon.com

3.3 — VALIDATION

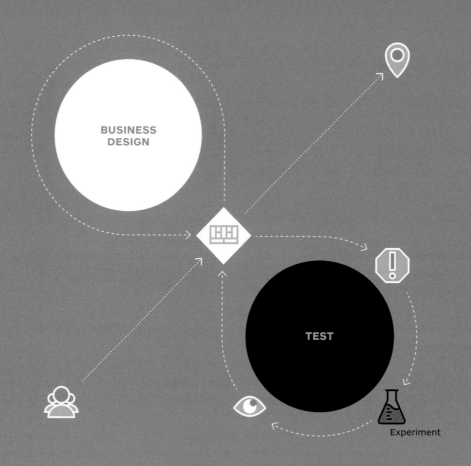

Idea

Search & Testing	Execution

Business

Discovery
Discover if your general direction is right. Test basic hypotheses. Get first insights to course-correct rapidly.

Validation
Validate the direction you've taken. Confirm with strong evidence that your business idea is very likely to work.

Validation Experiments

COST	SETUP TIME	RUN TIME	EVIDENCE STRENGTH	THEME
●●○○○	●●○○○	●●○○○	●●○○○	DESIRABILITY · FEASIBILITY · VIABILITY
●●●●○	●●●○○	●●●●○	●●●●●	DESIRABILITY · FEASIBILITY · VIABILITY
●●●○○	●●●○○	●●●●○	●●●●●	DESIRABILITY · FEASIBILITY · VIABILITY
●○○○○	●●○○○	●●●○○	●●●●●	DESIRABILITY · FEASIBILITY · VIABILITY
●●●●●	●●●●○	●●●○○	●●○○○	DESIRABILITY · FEASIBILITY · VIABILITY
●●○○○	●●○○○	●●●○○	●●○○○	DESIRABILITY · FEASIBILITY · VIABILITY
●●●●●	●●●●○	●●●●○	●●○○○	DESIRABILITY · FEASIBILITY · VIABILITY
●●○○○	●●○○○	●●●○○	●●●○○	DESIRABILITY · FEASIBILITY · VIABILITY
●●●○○	●●○○○	●●●○○	●●●●●	DESIRABILITY · FEASIBILITY · VIABILITY
●●○○○	●●○○○	●●●○○	●○○○○	DESIRABILITY · FEASIBILITY · VIABILITY
●●○○○	●●●○○	●●●○○	●●●●●	DESIRABILITY · FEASIBILITY · VIABILITY
●○○○○	●○○○○	●●●○○	●●●○○	DESIRABILITY · FEASIBILITY · VIABILITY
●○○○○	●○○○○	●●○○○	●●○○○	DESIRABILITY · FEASIBILITY · VIABILITY
●●●●○	●●●○○	●●○○○	●●○○○	DESIRABILITY · FEASIBILITY · VIABILITY
●●○○○	●○○○○	●●○○○	●●●●●	DESIRABILITY · **FEASIBILITY** · VIABILITY

DISCOVERY / INTERACTION PROTOTYPE

Clickable Prototype

Digital interface representation with clickable zones to simulate the software's reactions to customer interaction.

🥠 ●●○○○
COST

⚖ ●●○○○
EVIDENCE STRENGTH

🕐 ●●○○○
SETUP TIME

⏱ ●●○○○
RUN TIME

✂📦⚙⚒🗄✎📢🔍📊
CAPABILITIES *Design / Product / Technology / Research*

DESIRABILITY · FEASIBILITY · VIABILITY

Clickable prototype is ideal for rapidly testing the concept of your product quickly with customers at a higher fidelity than paper.

Clickable prototype is not ideal as a replacement for proper usability with customers.

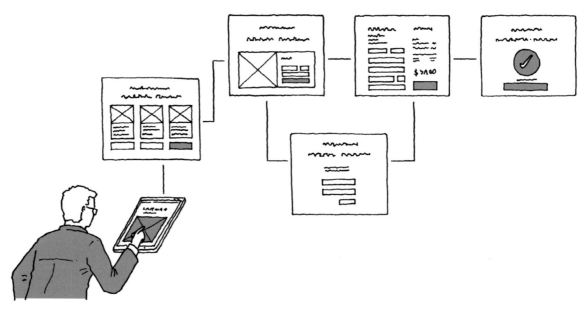

Prepare

☐ Define the goals of your clickable prototype experiment.

☐ Determine the target audience to test with, preferably a group that isn't cold and has no context for your offering.

☐ Write your script.

☐ Create your clickable prototype screens with hot zones.

☐ Test it internally to make sure that the interaction works.

☐ Schedule your clickable prototype experiments with target customers.

Execute

☐ Explain to the customers how this is an exercise to get their feedback on what you are planning to deliver. Make sure they understand that you value their input.

☐ Have one person conduct the interviews and interact with the customer.

☐ Have another person write notes and act as a scribe.

☐ Wrap up and thank the participants.

Analyze

☐ Place the sketches on the wall and place your notes, observations, and quotes around them.

☐ Where did they get stuck or confused?

☐ What did they get excited about?

☐ Use this feedback to inform your next experiment of the experience.

Cost

Clickable prototypes are a little more expensive than paper prototypes, but still relatively cheap. There are many tools and templates that allow you to quickly create a clickable prototype without having to create it from scratch yourself.

Setup Time

Setup time for a clickable prototype is relatively short. It should only take a day or two to create your clickable prototype.

Run Time

Run time for a clickable prototype is also short, as in a few days to a week. You'll want to rapidly test the clickable prototype with target customers, to get feedback on the Value Proposition and flow of the solution.

Evidence

Task completion

Task completion percentage.
Time to complete tasks.

Manual task completion is not necessarily strong evidence, but it is a bit stronger than using paper and will provide glimpses into where customers could get confused.

●●○○○

Customer feedback

Customer quotes on the Value Proposition and usefulness of the imagined solution.

Customer quotes on clickable prototypes are relatively weak evidence, but stronger than feedback on paper prototype experiments.

Capabilities

Design / Product / Technology / Research

In addition to a digital product idea, you'll need design skills to create the appearance of the product in a prototype tool or template. It'll require you to create hot zones that link to other mocked up screens once clicked. You'll also want to write a script and have the sessions recorded.

Requirements

A Digital Product Idea

Clickable prototyping requires that your idea be digital in nature, since your audience will be clicking through a digital experience on a screen. At the point at which you're considering a clickable prototype, you should have a strong opinion on what the flow of the product should look like, but still be open to it being wrong.

Customer Interviews
p. 106
Use the notes from your interviews to inform your clickable prototype script.

Paper Prototype
p. 182
Use the feedback from a paper prototype to inform your clickable prototype.

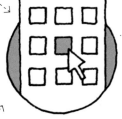

Clickable Prototype

Boomerang
p. 204
Use the notes from your Boomerang testing to shape how the clickable prototype can address unmet needs.

Mash-Up
p. 244
Create a Mash-Up from your clickable prototype experiment with existing technology.

Storyboard
p. 186
Use what you learned from the clickable prototype testing to refine your flow with a storyboarding experiment.

Explainer Video
p. 200
Use the notes from your clickable prototype testing to inform your higher fidelity Explainer Video.

DISCOVERY / INTERACTION PROTOTYPE

Single Feature MVP

A functioning minimum viable product with the single feature needed to test your assumption.

COST	EVIDENCE STRENGTH
⬤⬤⬤⬤◯	⬤⬤⬤⬤⬤

SETUP TIME	RUN TIME
⬤⬤⬤◯◯	⬤⬤⬤⬤◯

CAPABILITIES *Design / Product / Tech / Legal / Marketing / Finance*

DESIRABILITY · FEASIBILITY · VIABILITY

Single Feature MVP is ideal for learning if the core promise of your solution resonates with customers.

Prepare

☐ Design the smallest version of your feature that solves for a high impact customer job.

☐ Test it out internally first to make sure it works.

☐ Acquire customers for your Single Feature MVP.

Execute

☐ Conduct the Single Feature MVP experiment with customers.

☐ Gather satisfaction feedback from the customers.

Analyze

☐ Review your customer satisfaction feedback.

☐ How many customers converted?

☐ What did it cost you to operate this solution?

Cost

Single Feature MVPs are a bit more expensive then low fidelity experiments, because you're creating a higher fidelity version that delivers value to the customer.

Setup Time

Setting up a Single Feature MVP can take 1–3 weeks. You'll need to design, create, and test it out internally before involving customers. You are likely going to charge for this version, so it'll need to do one thing really well.

Run Time

Running a Single Feature MVP experiment can take several weeks or months. You'll want to run it long enough to analyze qualitative and quantitative feedback before prematurely optimizing or trying to scale.

Evidence

●●●●●

Customer satisfaction

Customer quotes and feedback on how satisfied they were after receiving the output from your Single Feature MVP.

Customer satisfaction evidence is strong in this case because you are asking for feedback after the value was delivered to the customer, instead of a hypothetical situation.

●●●●●

# of purchases

Customer purchases from using the Single Feature MVP.

Payments are strong evidence, even if it's only a single feature customers are purchasing.

●●●●●

Cost

How much does it cost to design, create, deliver, and maintain a Single Feature MVP?

The cost it takes you to deliver a Single Feature MVP is strong evidence and a leading indicator of what it'll take to create a viable business in the future.

Capabilities

Design / Product / Technology / Legal / Marketing / Finance

You'll need all of the capabilities to create and deliver the feature to the customer. This is very context specific, depending on whether you are delivering a physical or digital product or service to the end customer.

Requirements

Evidence of Niche Customer Need

This is a longer, more expensive experiment with a higher transaction cost. Before considering a Single Feature MVP, you'll need to have worked through a series of lower fidelity experiments to inform the feature. You should have clear evidence of a specific customer need that the feature will address.

Concierge
p. 248
Use what you've learned from
the Concierge experiment
to inform the design of your
feature.

Wizard of Oz
p. 284
Use what you've learned from
the Wizard of Oz experiment
to inform the design of your
feature.

Simple Landing Page
p. 260
Create a simple landing
page to collect interest in
your Single Feature MVP
experiment.

Customer Interviews
p. 106
Interview the people who
used the feature to better
understand how it satisfied
their needs.

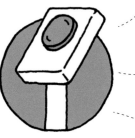

Single Feature MVP

Validation Survey
p. 278
Survey the people who used
the feature to better understand how it satisfied their
needs.

Crowdfunding
p. 266
Create a crowdfunding campaign to fund what it would
take to scale beyond a single
feature.

SINGLE FEATURE MVP

243

INTERACTION PROTOTYPES

DISCOVERY / INTERACTION PROTOTYPE

Mash-Up

A functioning minimum viable product that consists of combining multiple existing services to deliver value.

◯ ●●●◯◯
COST

⚖ ●●●●●
EVIDENCE STRENGTH

🕐 ●●●◯◯
SETUP TIME

⏱ ●●●●◯
RUN TIME

DESIRABILITY · FEASIBILITY · VIABILITY

Mash-Up is ideal for learning if the solution resonates with customers.

CAPABILITIES *Design / Product / Tech / Legal / Marketing / Finance*

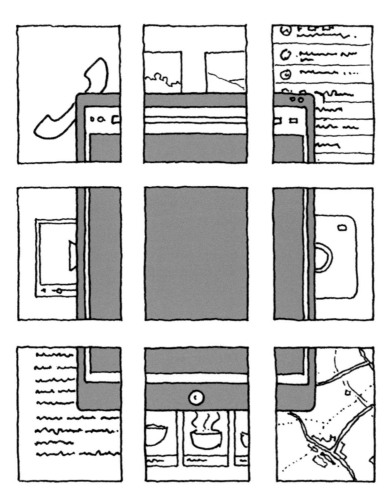

Prepare

☐ Map out the process flow needed to create the customer value.

☐ Assess the market for existing technology products that can be integrated to complete the process.

☐ Integrate the technology pieces and test the output.

☐ Acquire customers for the Mash-Up.

Execute

☐ Conduct the Mash-Up experiment with customers.

☐ Gather satisfaction feedback from customers.

Analyze

☐ Review your customer satisfaction feedback.

☐ How many customers made it through the process and purchased?

☐ Where did they abandon the process?

☐ Are there any gaps where the existing technology fell short of customer expectations?

☐ Only consider building custom solutions as a result, if the experience was unsatisfactory or if the cost of using these solutions doesn't scale.

MASH-UP MVP

245

INTERACTION PROTOTYPES

Cost

Mash-Ups are a bit more expensive then low fidelity experiments, since you need to piece together multiple existing technological components to deliver an overall solution. The costs incurred will be paying for the existing technology and the effort to wire it all together.

Setup Time

Setting up a Mash-Up can take 1–3 weeks. You'll need to evaluate and piece together existing technology.

Run Time

Running a Mash-Up experiment can take several weeks or months. You'll want to run it long enough to analyze qualitative and quantitative feedback before prematurely optimizing or trying to scale.

Evidence

Customer satisfaction

Customer quotes and feedback on how satisfied they were after receiving the output from your Mash-Up.

Customer satisfaction evidence is strong in this case because you are asking for feedback after the value was delivered to the customer, instead of a hypothetical situation.

●●●●●
# of purchases

Customer purchases from using the Mash-Up.

Payments are strong evidence, even if they don't realize it's pieced together behind the scenes with existing technology.

●●●●●
Cost

How much does it cost to design, create, deliver, and maintain a Mash-Up?

The cost it takes you to deliver a Mash-Up is strong evidence and a leading indicator of what it'll take to create a viable business in the future.

Capabilities

Design / Technology / Product / Marketing / Legal / Finance

You'll need to be able assess existing technology, choose the right components, and integrate them together into a solution that can deliver the needed value to customers. It doesn't necessarily mean you need to know how all the technology works, but you'll need to know enough to put it all together behind the scenes. In addition, the Mash-Up will need all of the other characteristics of a legitimate product.

Requirements

A Process to Automate

This is another longer, more expensive experiment with a higher transaction cost. Before considering a Mash-Up, you'll need to have run enough lower fidelity experiments to have an idea of the process you'll need to deliver value to the customer. Use that process knowledge to begin the assessment of what existing technology you could piece together to deliver that value.

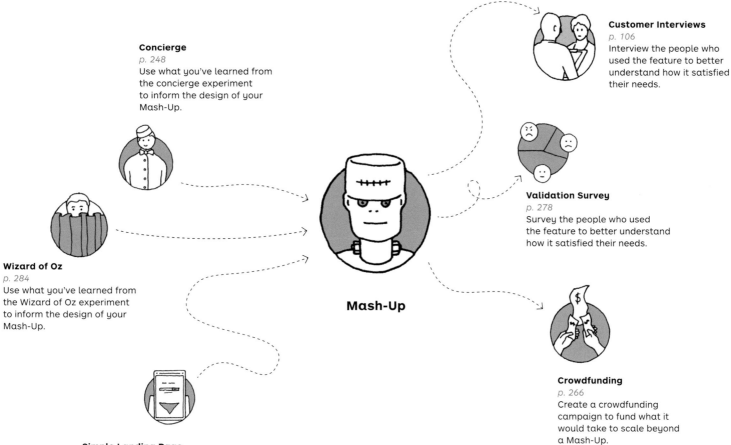

Concierge
p. 248
Use what you've learned from
the concierge experiment
to inform the design of your
Mash-Up.

Customer Interviews
p. 106
Interview the people who
used the feature to better
understand how it satisfied
their needs.

Wizard of Oz
p. 284
Use what you've learned from
the Wizard of Oz experiment
to inform the design of your
Mash-Up.

Mash-Up

Validation Survey
p. 278
Survey the people who used
the feature to better understand
how it satisfied their needs.

Simple Landing Page
p. 260
Create a simple landing page
to collect interest in your
Mash-Up experiment.

Crowdfunding
p. 266
Create a crowdfunding
campaign to fund what it
would take to scale beyond
a Mash-Up.

DISCOVERY / INTERACTION PROTOTYPE

Concierge

Creating a customer experience and delivering value manually, with people instead of using technology. Unlike Wizard of Oz, the people involved are obvious to the customer.

⊖ ●○○○○○ **COST**	⚖ ●●●●● **EVIDENCE STRENGTH**
🕑 ●●○○○ **SETUP TIME**	⏱ ●●●○○ **RUN TIME**

DESIRABILITY · FEASIBILITY · VIABILITY

Concierge is ideal for learning firsthand about steps needed to create, capture, and deliver value to a customer.

Concierge is not ideal for scaling a product or business.

CAPABILITIES *Design / Product / Technology / Legal / Marketing*

Prepare

☐ Plan the steps of creating the product manually.

☐ Create a board to track the orders and steps needed.

☐ Test the steps with someone first to make sure they work.

☐ If taking orders on the web, make sure analytics are integrated. Otherwise, document the numbers on grid paper or excel.

Execute

☐ Receive orders for the concierge experiment.

☐ Conduct the concierge experiment.

☐ Document how long it takes to complete the tasks.

☐ Gather feedback from customers with interviews and surveys.

Analyze

☐ Review your customer feedback.

☐ Review your metrics for:

- Length of time for task completion.
- Where you experienced delays in the process.
- How many purchased.

☐ Use these findings to improve your next concierge experiment and to help inform where to automate the process.

CONCIERGE

249

INTERACTION PROTOTYPES

Cost

As long as you keep the concierge experiments small and simple, they are cheap to run, mostly because you are doing all of the work manually with little to no technology involved. If you try to scale the experiment or make it overly complex, it'll increase the cost.

Setup Time

Setting up a concierge experiment takes a bit longer than other rapid prototyping techniques, because you have to manually plan out all of the steps and acquire customers for it.

Run Time

Running a concierge experiment can take days to weeks, depending on how complex the process is and how many customers you involve in the experiment. It generally takes longer than other rapid prototyping techniques.

Evidence

Customer satisfaction

Customer quotes and feedback on how satisfied they were after receiving the output from your experiment.

Customer satisfaction evidence is strong in this case because you are asking for feedback after the value was delivered to the customer, instead of a hypothetical situation.

# of purchases

Customer purchases from the concierge experiment. What are they willing to pay for a manual experience?

Payments are strong evidence, even if you are manually delivering value.

Time it takes to complete the process

Lead time is the total time measured from customer request to when the order was delivered.

Cycle time is the amount of time spent working on the request. It does not include the time the request sits idle before action was taken on it.

The time it takes for you to complete the concierge experiment is very strong, in that it gives you firsthand knowledge of the steps needed to receive a request and deliver value to a customer.

Capabilities

Design / Technology / Product / Marketing / Legal

You'll need all of the capabilities to manually create and deliver the product to the customer. This is very context specific, depending on whether you are delivering a physical or digital product or service to the end customer.

Requirements

Time

The biggest requirement for a concierge test is time. Your time. The team's time. If you do not make time to run this experiment, it will be frustrating for both you and the customer. Be sure to plan when you will run the Concierge experiment and clear your schedule so that you can give it the attention it will need.

VALIDATION

EXPERIMENTS

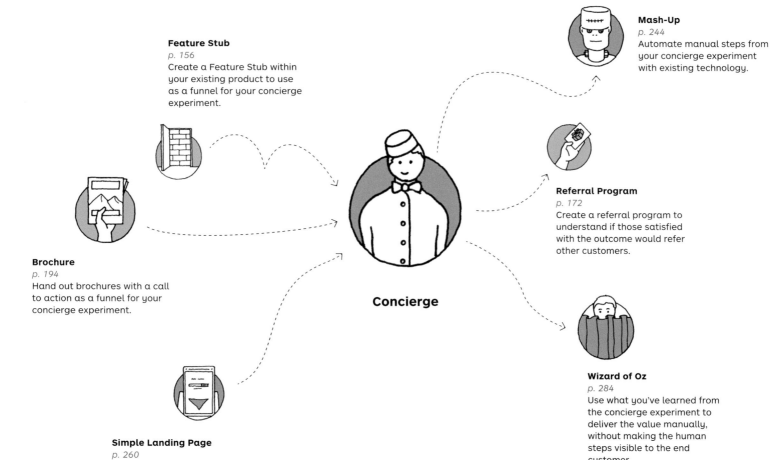

Mash-Up
p. 244
Automate manual steps from your concierge experiment with existing technology.

Feature Stub
p. 156
Create a Feature Stub within your existing product to use as a funnel for your concierge experiment.

Referral Program
p. 172
Create a referral program to understand if those satisfied with the outcome would refer other customers.

Brochure
p. 194
Hand out brochures with a call to action as a funnel for your concierge experiment.

Concierge

Wizard of Oz
p. 284
Use what you've learned from the concierge experiment to deliver the value manually, without making the human steps visible to the end customer.

Simple Landing Page
p. 260
Create a simple landing page to collect interest in your concierge experiment.

CONCIERGE
Buying and Selling a Home
Realtor.com

Realtor.com is a real estate listings web-site operated by Move, Inc. out of Santa Clara, California. It provides buyers and sellers with the information, tools and professional expertise they need throughout the home journey.

As realtor.com teams spoke with people who were looking to sell their home, one of the problems commonly heard was the struggle with timing the process of selling a house with buying a new one. When people move, they end up moving to another zip code or other cities or even other states.

The idea was to aggregate and show the market insights for them with the two markets side by side. Would that be useful for them? Would we extend that into a real feature?

Hypothesis

The realtor.com team believed that sellers on their site who are looking to sell within the next year will also be buying at the same time.

Experiment

Concierge delivery of PDF insights.
The team did a simple concierge experiment that was triggered by a call to action. When clicked, the modal window highlighting a value proposition for insights on timing your ability to buy and sell at the same time appeared. Users would then click through a series of questions. Once complete, Dave Masters (the product manager) manually created the output by piecing together insights from other parts found throughout Realtor.com into a PDF.

Dave would then individually email these PDFs out to the users who signed up. Additionally in his email to them, Dave added a meeting link to further connect to these users in hopes to learn more and see how we could help.

Evidence

80 signups in just a few minutes.
It surpassed expectations quite quickly. Based on site statistical data, the team had estimated that it would generate 30 signups within 3 hours. It generated more than 80 signups in a few minutes, faster than they could even shut it off.

Insights

Hypothesis validated — audience has problem. The team learned that a reasonably large pool of people within their site that had the buying and selling problem.

The team also learned about the challenge with concierge testing. High volume could be a good sign but might require you to do a lot more manual work than you initially set out to do. It's probably worth noting that this type of work requires your ability to execute for these users. When dual-tracking work, you have to anticipate and set aside appropriate time to deliver on this promise and really aim to learn. With the copious amounts of work you might have in your day-to-day, it can be hard to manage it all.

Actions

Persevere by testing in app features.
Knowing the audience mix was roughly the size anticipated, the team felt confident in moving forward with more experiments targeting these users within this app. In fact, the very next experiment was a feature stub that included a link to a nonexistent tab for "Selling-Tools"—a place that the team would begin to put Seller specific features and tests.

DISCOVERY / INTERACTION PROTOTYPE

Life-Sized Prototype

Life-sized prototypes and real-world replicas of service experiences.

COST ●●●●●

EVIDENCE STRENGTH ●●○○○

SETUP TIME ●●●●○

RUN TIME ●●●○○

CAPABILITIES *Design / Product*

DESIRABILITY · FEASIBILITY · VIABILITY

Life-sized prototypes are ideal for testing higher fidelity solutions with customers at a small sample size, before deciding to scale your solution.

Prepare

☐ Gather your previous evidence to support the solution.

☐ Create your life-sized prototype, which is a replica of your proposed solution.

☐ Source customers and schedule the interactive session.

Execute

☐ Show the life-sized prototype to customers.

☐ One person on the team conducts the interview.

☐ Another person on the team takes notes on customer quotes, jobs, pains, gains, and body language.

☐ Wrap up the interview with a call to action or mock sale, to get beyond what the customer says and into what they would do.

Analyze

☐ Review your notes with the team.

☐ Update your Value Proposition Canvas based on what you've learned.

☐ Calculate conversion on mock sales and call to action.

☐ Use what you've learned to refine and iterate on your prototype for the next round of testing.

LIFE-SIZED PROTOTYPE

255

INTERACTION PROTOTYPES

●●●●●

Cost

Life-sized prototypes can be moderately expensive. They need to have a believable level of polish and the bigger the size, the greater the expense.

 ●●●●○

Setup Time

The setup time for a life-sized prototype can be quite long, depending on the size and complexity of your solution. It may take several weeks or months to create a high fidelity replica.

 ●●●○○

Run Time

Run time for a life-sized prototype is relatively short. You'll want customers interacting with the prototype to better understand the fit between your Value Proposition and their customer jobs, pains, and gains.

VALIDATION

256

EXPERIMENTS

 ●●○○○

Evidence

●●●●○

Customer jobs
Customer pains
Customer gains
Customer feedback

Customer jobs, pains, and gains and how the prototype could solve for them.

Take note of additional quotes from the customers that are not limited to customer jobs, pains, and gains.

The evidence is relatively weak evidence—they need to suspend belief and imagine using it in real world scenarios.

●●●●●

# of successful mock sales

You can calculate the mock sale conversion rate by taking the number people who view the price divided by the number of people who filled out payment information.

Payment information submission is very strong evidence.

●●○○○

# of email signups

Conversion rate on people who you interviewed who provided their email address to be contacted when the solution is available.

Customer emails are rather weak evidence, but good for future experiments.

Capabilities

Design / Product

You'll need mostly product and design capabilities to create the life-sized prototype. It doesn't need to be fully operational or have all of the bells and whistles, but it needs to be at a high enough fidelity to interact with customers.

Requirements

Evidence of a Solution

Before considering a life-sized prototype, you'll want to have a significant amount of evidence that a solution is needed.
This means you've gathered and generated evidence of unmet customer jobs, pains, and gains in the market that warrant testing a high fidelity experiment with customers.

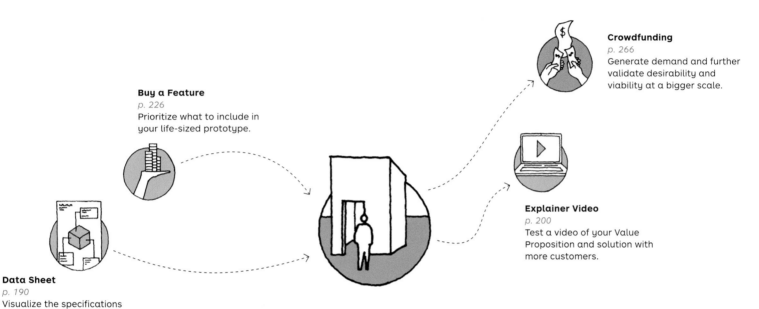

Crowdfunding
p. 266
Generate demand and further validate desirability and viability at a bigger scale.

Buy a Feature
p. 226
Prioritize what to include in your life-sized prototype.

Explainer Video
p. 200
Test a video of your Value Proposition and solution with more customers.

Data Sheet
p. 190
Visualize the specifications to include in your life-sized prototype.

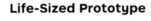

Life-Sized Prototype

Mock Sales
p. 288
Learn if your customers are willing to pay for the solution while they interact with the prototype.

Customer Interviews
p. 106
Interview your customers while they interact with the prototype to learn about customer jobs, pains, and gains.

LIFE-SIZED PROTOTYPE
Validating a Physical Space
Zoku

Zoku is a hive of smart lofts and friendly spaces based in Amsterdam and is viewed by experts as the next evolution of Airbnb. They provide a home base for traveling professionals who are living and working in a city for periods from a few days to a few months. As is the case any time you create a new market, the Zoku team has risky assumptions about their business that need testing.

Hypothesis

The Zoku team believed that traveling professionals would like to stay for weeks and months in a micro-apartment of only 25m² (around 250 square feet).

Experiment

Testing living spaces with customers.

The team built a Life-Sized prototype of the micro-apartment to test with traveling professionals to determine if they'd stay for weeks and months. They sourced 150 traveling professionals, shuttling them over from their workplaces, to interact with the Life-Sized Prototype.

Travelers toured and stayed in the Life-Sized Prototype. The Zoku team interviewed them while they interacted with the physical space, learning about what worked and what didn't in the design.

Evidence

Gathering qualitative feedback on the space.

People were the most enthusiastic about staying when the space used stacking, eliminating internal walls and circulation. If the stairs are in, there is more living space; if the stairs are out it becomes circulation space for the sleeping area. This evidence especially came out when they tested with groups of 4–5 people at once.

Insights

The experience of the space means more than the size of the space.

The experiment helped the Zoku team understand nuances about the prototype. When stacked all the normal home elements (sleeping area, storage area, bathroom and kitchen) on to each other like Tetris/Lego, it resulted in a distinction between secondary space (functional elements) and primary space (living space to move around and put your loose furniture).

During the course of all the validation rounds they learned that "the experience of space" is different from the amount of square feet and can be positively influenced by clear sight lines through the furniture (the shutters in the sleeping area), large windows, and smart lighting.

Actions

Testing space flow with cleaning services.

Using what they had learned from the Life-Sized Prototype testing, the team ran another round of testing with cleaning services for the unit. This helped them learn about the service challenges, specifically with the raised sleeping platform.

VALIDATION / CALL TO ACTION

Simple Landing Page

A simple, digital web page that clearly illustrates your Value Proposition with a call to action.

COST ●●○○○

EVIDENCE STRENGTH ●●○○○

SETUP TIME ●●○○○

RUN TIME ●●●○○

CAPABILITIES *Design / Product / Technology*

DESIRABILITY · FEASIBILITY · VIABILITY

A simple landing page is ideal for determining if your Value Proposition resonates with your customer segment.

Prepare

☐ Choose a template or layout that supports your industry.

☐ Find high quality, royalty-free photos to use for your design.

☐ Purchase a short, memorable domain name that reinforces your brand. If your preferred brand is taken already, which many domains are by now, use a verb in front of the name such as "try" or "get."

☐ Include a Value Proposition statement above the fold in large font, preferably header sized.

☐ Place your call-to-action email signup above the fold, below your Value Proposition statement.

☐ Include customer pains, your solution, and the customer gains below the call-to-action.

☐ Integrate analytics and confirm they are working.

☐ Don't forget website requirements such as logo, brand, contact, terms of service, and cookie and privacy policy information.

Execute

☐ Make your landing page live on the web.

☐ Drive traffic to your page.

Analyze

☐ Review your analytics on how many people:

- viewed your landing page.
- signed up with their email address.
- spent time or engaged with the page by clicking and scrolling.

☐ How did different traffic sources convert? For example, if a specific social media ad or email campaign causes more customers to sign up, you may want to replicate it across other platforms.

☐ Use these findings to refine your Value Proposition and contact those who signed up for interviews.

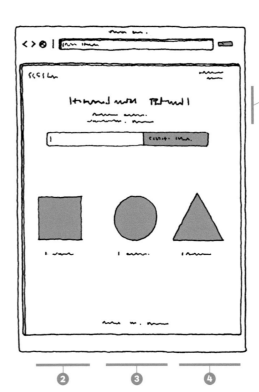

Connections

Value propositions come from your Value Map. Do not create your Value Proposition in a vacuum or neglect the work that you've already done. The Value Map contains hypotheses and your landing page value proposition test is a great way to prove or disprove those hypotheses.

Customer pains come from your Customer Profile. Take the top three voted customer pains from the canvas and include them in the pains description at the bottom left of the landing page.

Solution comes from the Value Map product and service. The visitor needs to know how you are delivering the Value Proposition in a real tangible way. The product and services in the middle column of the page should reflect this.

Gains come from the customer profile. Take the top three voted customer gains from the canvas and include them in the gains description at the bottom right of the landing page.

Cost

Landing pages are relatively cheap to produce, mostly due to the fact that digital tools have evolved and are much easier to use. It's one of the cheapest ways you can test your Value Proposition at scale with potential customers.

Setup Time

Landing pages can be deceptively difficult to do, mostly because you are distilling down all the customer jobs, pains, and gains into short easy-to-understand statements. Still, it shouldn't take more than a few days at most to design a landing page.

Run Time

Run time takes a few weeks, although it is largely depending on the amount of traffic you can drive to the landing page. If the daily traffic is low (i.e., less than 100 unique visitors), then you'll need to run the test for a longer period of time to gather sufficient information.

Evidence

Unique Views
Time Spent on Page
Email Signups

You can calculate the conversion rate by taking the number views divided by actions = conversion rate. Email conversion rates vary widely by industry but on average it's between 2%–5%. For early stage validation we recommend 10%–15% in that you want to be better than average, otherwise why create something new?

Email is a rather weak strength of evidence, in that everyone has email and they give it out freely if even mildly interested. It's not difficult to unsubscribe or send unwanted email to a junk folder.

Capabilities

Design / Product / Technology

Landing pages need to communicate the value clearly and succinctly in the language of the customer. You'll need the ability to do this well, otherwise it has the risk of generating false negatives. If you do not have these abilities yourself, then don't despair because you are in luck. There are many landing page services that have professional-looking templates that allow you to create landing pages using drag-and-drop technology.

Requirements

Traffic

Landing pages need traffic to generate evidence, generally about 100 unique visitors a day. The good news is that there are many ways you can drive traffic to your landing page, including:

- Online ads.
- Social media campaigns.
- Email campaigns.
- Redirecting existing traffic.
- Word of mouth.
- Discussion forums.

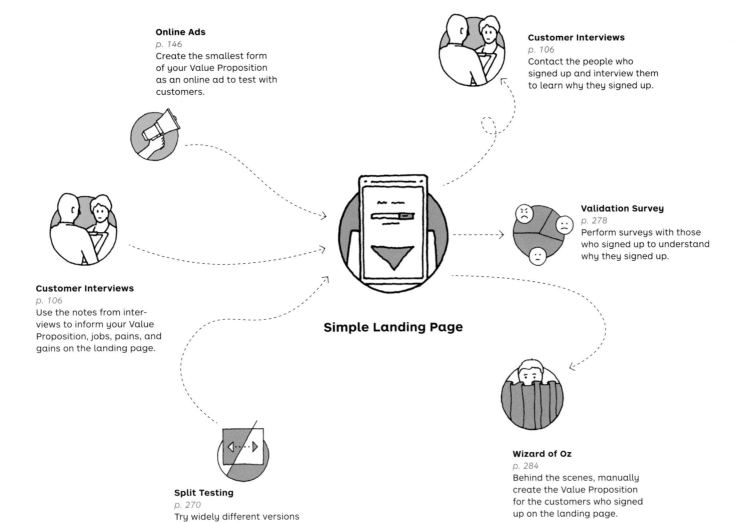

Online Ads
p. 146
Create the smallest form
of your Value Proposition
as an online ad to test with
customers.

Customer Interviews
p. 106
Contact the people who
signed up and interview them
to learn why they signed up.

Customer Interviews
p. 106
Use the notes from inter-
views to inform your Value
Proposition, jobs, pains, and
gains on the landing page.

Validation Survey
p. 278
Perform surveys with those
who signed up to understand
why they signed up.

Simple Landing Page

Split Testing
p. 270
Try widely different versions
of your Value Proposition to
see what resonates best with
customers.

Wizard of Oz
p. 284
Behind the scenes, manually
create the Value Proposition
for the customers who signed
up on the landing page.

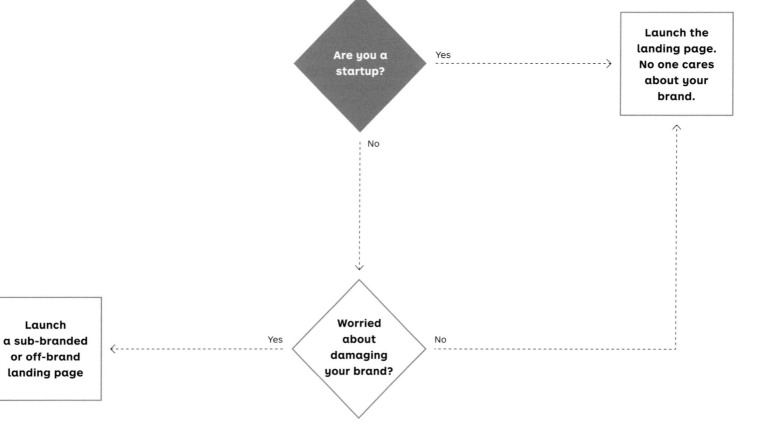

Branding Concerns

Branding the landing page can become a hand-wringing decision if you are part of a larger corporation. Startups have the luxury of testing without drawing attention, based on their brand alone. They can launch a landing page and when people sign up, it's rarely because of the startup's brand. Instead, people sign up because the idea stands on its own merit as a solution that can solve a problem for them.

If corporations keep the landing page on-brand, with the corporate logo front-and-center, it can make things harder for the team. Branding and marketing reviews will usually slow down the process by weeks, if not months. People will visit the page just to check it out because of the branding. It can be difficult to sift through all of the traffic noise to see who is really interested in the Value Proposition.

Create a sub-brand or new company to test the business idea. It allows you to go faster, without the endless meetings around branding and what happens if people sign up. A side effect of this approach is that you won't be able to leverage existing acquisition channels for the brand. This means you'll need to do your own customer acquisition by running ads, talking to people, and using social media to drive traffic.

✔

☐ *Use the words from customer interviews in your headline.*

☐ *Contact the people who signed up and ask if they are available for customer interviews.*

☐ *Use high quality photos and videos.*

☐ *Use a short domain name.*

✖

‒ *Don't include fake testimonials to generate conversions.*

‒ *Don't label products as "sold out" when you've not yet created them.*

‒ *Don't make unrealistic claims for your product.*

‒ *Don't use a negative or harsh tone.*

SIMPLE LANDING PAGE

265

CALL TO ACTION

266

VALIDATION / CALL TO ACTION

Crowdfunding

Funding a project or venture by raising many small amounts of money from a large number of people, typically via the Internet.

 ●●●●●
COST

⚖ ●●○○○
EVIDENCE STRENGTH

🕐 ●●●●○
SETUP TIME

⏱ ●●●●○
RUN TIME

CAPABILITIES *Design / Product / Marketing / Finance*

▦ ✉ ◔

DESIRABILITY · FEASIBILITY · VIABILITY

Crowdfunding is ideal for funding your new business venture with customers who believe in your Value Proposition.

Crowdfunding is not ideal for determining whether your new business venture is feasible.

Prepare

- ☐ Define the dollar amount for your funding target goal. Be pragmatic and specific on how the money will be used for each activity needed to create the product.

- ☐ Choose an existing crowd-funding platform or create your own, custom crowd-funding website.

- ☐ Create your crowdfunding video. It should be high quality and draw the user in to convince them to fund your product.

- ☐ Include a Value Proposition statement below your video in large font, preferably header sized.

- ☐ Place your call to action for funding the product to the right of the video in clear language.

- ☐ Include customer pains, your solution, and the customer gains below the Value Proposition.

- ☐ Include different pledge amounts and desirable perks.

Execute

- ☐ Make your crowdfunding campaign live to the public.

- ☐ Drive traffic to your page.

- ☐ Be active on social media and your campaign page by responding to comments and answering questions as they come in.

Analyze

- ☐ Review how many pledges were received, the amount for each, and if you reached your funding target goal.

- ☐ If you did not achieve your goal, use what you've learned to iterate on the campaign.

- ☐ If you did achieve your goal, then keep actively respond-ing on your progress to backers through social media and email.

- ☐ How did different traffic sources convert? For exam-ple, if a specific social media ad or email campaign causes more customers to pledge, you may want to keep that in mind for cus-tomer acquisition once the product is live and for sale.

Connections

 Your video should tell a story, leading with the greatest hits. Show how your solution solves for the top customer job, pain, and gain for the customer segment in your **customer profile**.

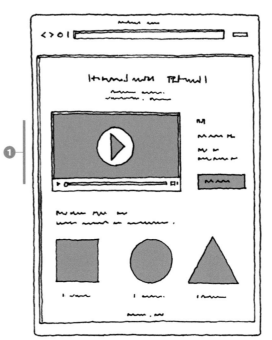

 Pains come from your Customer Profile. Take the top three voted customer pains and include them in the pains description at the bottom left of the crowdfunding campaign page.

 Solution comes from the Value Map product and service. Your potential crowdfunding backers should understand the solution, which is next to the pain on the crowdfunding campaign page.

 Gains come from the Customer Profile. Take the top three voted customer gains and include them in the gains description at the bottom right of the crowdfunding campaign page.

✓

☐ *Account for the commission percentage crowdfunding platforms take as a fee from your campaign.*

☐ *Refund those who contrib-uted if you didn't meet your goal.*

☐ *Be specific and transparent on how the funds you are raising will be used, includ-ing a cost breakdown of the activities.*

✗

- *Include so may perks that you spend all of your time fulfilling them instead of building the product.*

- *Be greedy and raise more than you need for your product build.*

- *Cut corners on the produc-tion quality of your video.*

- *Make unrealistic claims on the benefits of your product.*

● ● ● ● ●

Cost

Crowdfunding costs are typically focused around the video production, marketing, logistics, and length of campaign. Even though there are crowdfunding platforms available, the fidelity needs to be high or you will not garner interest from customers.

 ● ● ● ● ○

Setup Time

Crowdfunding campaigns can take a few weeks to a few months to put together. It's not trivial to produce a compelling, high quality video, create content that conveys the Value Proposition, and structure the pricing tiers and perks for your customers.

 ● ● ● ● ○

Run Time

Run time typically takes 30–60 days for a crowdfunding campaign to run its course. This isn't to say you won't be wildly successful and fund it in less — just be aware that those funded in a few days are the exceptions.

 ● ● ○ ○ ○

Evidence Strength

 ● ● ○ ○ ○

Referrers
# of unique views
# of comments
# of social media shares

Where your visitors are coming from online and how they interact with your campaign.

Views, comments, and shares are all relatively weak evidence but good for qualitative insights.

 ● ● ● ● ●

# of pledges
Pledge amount

How your viewers are converting to pledges. At least 6% of your pledges come from direct traffic. At least 2% of your pledges come from targeted online ads.

Percent funded. Ideally this is 100% and your idea gets funded.

Viewers pledging their money to make your crowdfunding campaign a success is very strong evidence. They are voting with their wallets, not just their words.

Capabilities

Design / Product / Marketing / Finance

Crowdfunding's popularity has created a rise in crowdfunding platforms, which means you don't need an entire development team to create a campaign anymore. You'll still need to create an authentic campaign with interesting perks, while building awareness in the market. Design plays a big role here in that it needs to look professional, otherwise you may get false negatives on your Value Proposition. Finance plays a bigger role, in that you need to correctly spec out your pricing tiers and perks in hopes that you can build a sustainable business from the campaign.

Requirements

Value Proposition and Customer Segment

Before jumping into a crowdfunding campaign, you'll need a clear Value Proposition that you can turn into a high quality video and a target customer segment. Crowdfunding campaigns without videos are few and far between and their success rate is quite low. You'll also want to know how you are targeting the customer, otherwise it'll be very difficult to drive people to it.

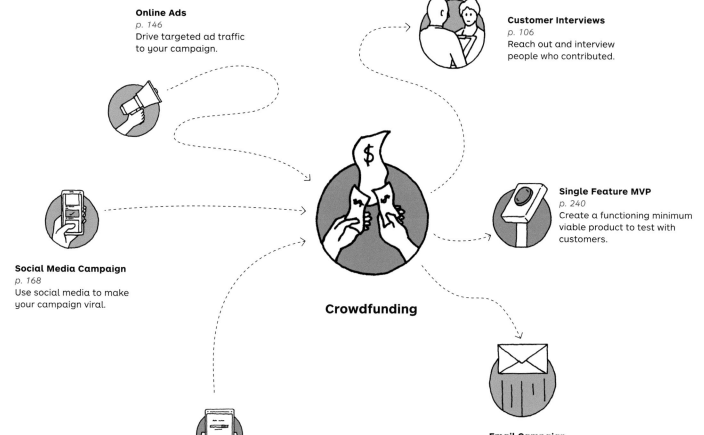

Online Ads
p. 146
Drive targeted ad traffic
to your campaign.

Customer Interviews
p. 106
Reach out and interview
people who contributed.

Social Media Campaign
p. 168
Use social media to make
your campaign viral.

Single Feature MVP
p. 240
Create a functioning minimum
viable product to test with
customers.

Crowdfunding

Simple Landing Page
p. 260
Create a landing page to
drive traffic to your campaign.

Email Campaign
p. 162
Keep contributors in the loop
on what is happening after
the campaign.

CROWDFUNDING

269

CALL TO ACTION

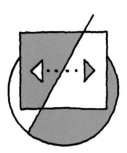

VALIDATION / CALL TO ACTION

Split Test

Split Test is a method of comparing two versions, control A against variant B, and determining which which one performs better.

COST

EVIDENCE STRENGTH

SETUP TIME

RUN TIME

CAPABILITIES *Design / Product / Technology / Data*

DESIRABILITY · FEASIBILITY · VIABILITY

Split Test is ideal for testing different versions of Value Propositions, prices, and features to see what resonates best with customers.

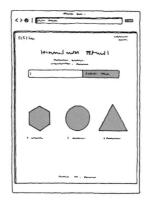

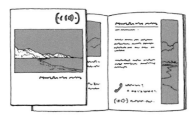

Prepare

☐ Identify the customer behavior you wish to improve (i.e., progressing through a funnel).

☐ Create your Control A.

☐ Baseline your Control A and write it down.

☐ Create your Variant B.

☐ Define the measurable improvement percentage you wish to observe in Variant B.

☐ Identify your customer sample size and percent confidence level.

Prepare

☐ Run your Split Test by randomly driving 50% of your traffic to Control A and 50% of your traffic to Variant B.

Analyze

☐ Review your results once the sample size is met and if it met your confidence level.

☐ Did you meet your confidence level?

- If so, consider replacing Control A with your Variant B as a static element.

- If not, run another Split Test with a different Variant B.

☐ *Use quotes from customer interviews to Split Test your Value Propositions.*

☐ *Contact the people who converted to understand why.*

☐ *Use a Split Test calculator to determine the sample size needed to reach your confidence level.*

☐ *Split Test radically different ideas, especially early on. It'll yield more insights than small incremental tests.*

✗

- *Stop your Split Tests early because you like or dislike the preliminary results.*

- *Forget to keep measuring KPIs that you don't want to go down.*

- *Run too many Split Tests all at once or in conjunction with other experiments.*

- *Give up if your first Split Test doesn't yield amazing results.*

SPLIT TEST

271

CALL TO ACTION

VALIDATION

272

EXPERIMENTS

Cost

Split Tests are relatively cheap and online digital tools allow you to perform them without having to know much about programming. You can copy and paste a script into your page or app, then log into the product and configure the Split Tests. It resembles using a word processor, by dragging, dropping, and typing. Split Tests become more expensive if you are building customized hardware or printing out mailers, since you have to physically make two different versions to test with customers.

Setup Time

The setup time for Split Tests is relatively short, especially with digital products where you can use existing Split Testing tools. Setup time can be a bit longer if you are physically making two different versions.

Run Time

The run time for Split Tests usually spans several days to weeks. You'll want to have statistically significant data to gain insights into which one performed better.

Evidence Strength

Traffic
Control A behavior
Control A Conversion Rate
Conversion rate is the number of people who are routed into the Control A test divided by number of actions. Use previous data if possible to predict what the control conversion rate is for a baseline.

Variant B behavior
Variant B Conversion Rate
Conversion rate is the number of people who are routed into the Variant B divided by number of actions. Define what measurable impact you'd like Variant B to have on the conversion percentage.

Evidence strength is moderate—customers aren't aware they are participating in the Split Test. You'll want to have, at the very least, an 80% confidence level in the results. Ideally you'd want 98% confidence level, but it can vary depending on what you are testing. Use an online Split Test calculator to help guide you through the process.

Capabilities

Design / Product / Technology / Data
You'll need the capabilities required to define what you'll be testing, the expected baseline for Control A, and the needed improvement from Variant B. You'll want to design it visually to fit the overall theme, otherwise you'll receive false negatives. It'll require some degree of technology to integrate if it's software. Lastly, you'll need to be able to analyze the results to help inform your next experiment.

Requirements

Significant Traffic
Split Tests need a significant amount of traffic to generate believable evidence. Your traffic will be randomized to display either Control A or Variant B to the customer. If you have little to no traffic, it'll take entirely too much time to come to a conclusion that one performs better than the other.

Email Campaign
p. 162
Test email subject lines, copy, and images to determine what causes readers to open and click.

Simple Landing Page
p. 260
Test different Value Propositions and call to actions to see what improves conversion.

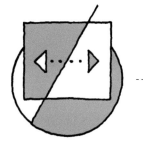

Customer Interviews
p. 106
Interview your customers and find out why they converted.

Customer Interviews
p. 106
Use quotes from your interviews to Split Test what converts better.

Split Test

Online Ads
p. 146
Test different images or copy for your online ad to see what improves click through rate.

Brochure
p. 194
Test different images and Value Propositions to determine what converts best on the contact call to action.

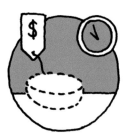

VALIDATION / CALL TO ACTION

Presale

A sale held before an item is made available for purchase. Unlike mock sale, you are processing a financial transaction when it ships.

⬭ ●●●○○
COST

⚖ ●●●●●
EVIDENCE STRENGTH

🕐 ●●○○○
SETUP TIME

⏱ ●●●○○
RUN TIME

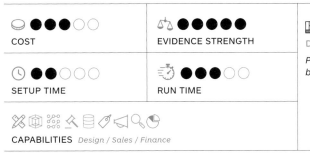

CAPABILITIES *Design / Sales / Finance*

⊞ ▷ ◉

DESIRABILITY · FEASIBILITY · VIABILITY

Presale is ideal for gauging market demand at a smaller scale before you launch to the public.

Prepare

☐ Create a simple landing page.

☐ Insert your price options.

☐ On a price option click, show a "we're not available to the public yet" pop-up with a payment information form. Cards will not be billed until you ship the product.

☐ Integrate and verify web analytics are working correctly.

Execute

☐ Make your page live to the public.

☐ Drive traffic to your page.

Analyze

☐ Review your analytics on how many people:

• viewed your price options.

• clicked on a price option.

• added in their payment information.

• clicked on pre-order to be billed when it ships.

• dropped out of the flow (i.e., web analytics funnel).

• converted on your page, based on traffic source.

☐ Use these findings to gauge viability and refine your Value Proposition and price options.

Connections

• Price options come from your revenue stream in your Business Model Canvas.

Cost

Presales are relatively cheap, but unlike mock sales you have the additional costs of processing the transaction and shipping the product. If you are using a point of sale system, then you may need to purchase hardware or software. In addition, most payment systems take a percentage of your sales (2%–3%) and may charge a monthly fee on top of that.

Setup Time

Setup time for a presale is relatively short. Once you are close to shipping your product, it requires the setup of accepting and processing financial information.

Run Time

Run time for a presale is a few days or weeks. You'll want to target a specific audience with your solution and give them enough time to consider a purchase. Presales aren't usually very long—payment providers may require you to ship product within 20 days of purchase.

Evidence

●●●●●

# of unique views

# of purchases

You can calculate the purchase conversion rate by taking the number people who view the price divided by the number of purchases.

Purchases are strong evidence. Customers are paying for your solution before it is generally available to the public.

●●●●●

# of abandons

Mostly associated with online shopping carts, if people are beginning the purchase process and then leaving, they are abandoning the sale.

You can calculate the abandonment rate by dividing the total number of completed purchases by the number of people who entered the purchase process.

People dropping out of the purchase process is strong evidence, albeit a bad sign. It means something is incorrect with your process, misconfigured, or the purchase price is not appropriate.

Capabilities

Design / Sales / Finance

Conducting a presale will require defining your price options. You'll also need to design the sale in such a way that it is the right fidelity for your target audience. Finally, you'll need sales capability, especially if you are conducting these in person in the physical world.

Requirements

Ability to Fulfill

Presales are different than mock sales: you are collecting and processing payment information, conducting an actual sale. This means you should be close to the final solution or at the very least have a minimum viable product to deliver. Do not rush ahead and conduct several presales without having the ability to fulfill your promise to customers.

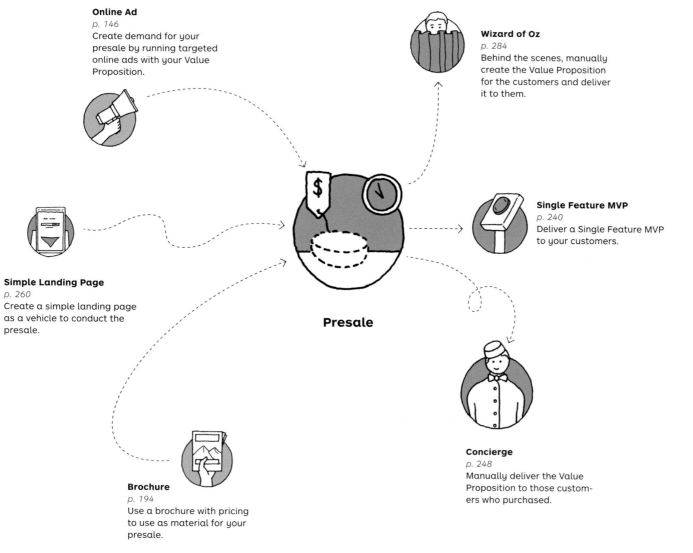

Online Ad
p. 146
Create demand for your
presale by running targeted
online ads with your Value
Proposition.

Wizard of Oz
p. 284
Behind the scenes, manually
create the Value Proposition
for the customers and deliver
it to them.

Single Feature MVP
p. 240
Deliver a Single Feature MVP
to your customers.

Simple Landing Page
p. 260
Create a simple landing page
as a vehicle to conduct the
presale.

Presale

Brochure
p. 194
Use a brochure with pricing
to use as material for your
presale.

Concierge
p. 248
Manually deliver the Value
Proposition to those customers who purchased.

VALIDATION / CALL TO ACTIONE

Validation Survey

A closed-ended questionnaire used in the collection of information
from a sample of customers about a specific topic.

$\ominus$ ●●○○○	Δ ●●○○○○
COST	EVIDENCE STRENGTH
$\bigcirc$ ●●○○○	$\overset{\cdot}{\bigcirc}$ ●●●○○
SETUP TIME	RUN TIME

CAPABILITIES *Product / Marketing / Research*

DESIRABILITY · FEASIBILITY · VIABILITY

*A validation survey is ideal for getting insights into whether
customers will be disappointed if your product went away
or if they'll refer other customers.*

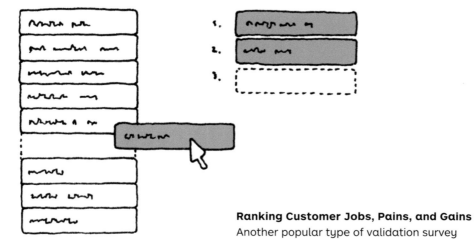

Discovering Missing Customer Jobs, Pains, and Gains

In addition to ranking, you can take inspiration from the discovery survey and include an open-ended question after each ranking, just in case you are missing out on those you didn't think of:

- What job do you wish we would have asked you about that wasn't on this list? Why?
- What pain do you wish we would have asked you about that wasn't on this list? Why?
- What gain do you wish we would have asked you about that wasn't on this list? Why?

Ranking Customer Jobs, Pains, and Gains

Another popular type of validation survey is validating the importance ranking of the jobs, pains, and gains in your Customer Profile in the Value Proposition Canvas. Most teams take their best guess at this ranking in a workshop setting, but need to quickly get feedback from outside the building to see how close they are to the real world. You can easily do this in most survey software today by creating two boxes, one for the list and next to it one for the customer ranking.

Other Types of Validation Surveys

Validation surveys are, in general, very simple with closed-ended feedback responding to a single question. With that in mind, you can apply that to other types of assumptions you wish to validate with your customers such as:

- CSAT (customer satisfaction).
- CES (consumer effort score).
- Brand awareness.

Sean Ellis Test
"How disappointed would you be if you could no longer use this product?"

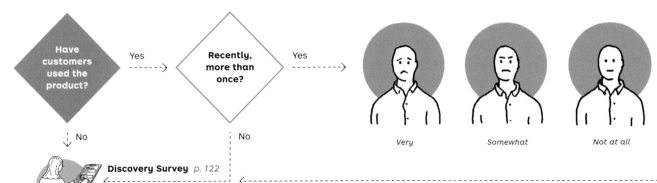

Sean Ellis Test

One type of survey is called the Sean Ellis Test, which is named after it's creator and growth-hacking expert Sean Ellis. His approach is to gauge desirability through scarcity.

The Sean Ellis Test keys in on one important question: *"How disappointed would you be if you could no longer use this product? Very disappointed, somewhat disappointed, or not disappointed?"*

It can be argued that you've not achieved product/market fit until a score of 40% is reached. If customers are apathetic and do not care if your product goes away, then you have a desirability problem. It doesn't make sense to scale before you have fit, otherwise you can waste a lot of money scaling things that no one wants.

Context is important when running a Sean Ellis Test. If you run it as soon as the customer experiences the Value Proposition, it can feel very out of place and return skewed data because they've yet to really experience the product. Who is going to genuinely be disappointed if they've never really used it?

On the flip side, if you show this survey to someone who hasn't used the product in six months, then there's a good chance they're long gone and won't even take the survey at this point.

The recommendation is to show this survey to gauge desirability with customers who have experienced the core of your product at least twice in the past two weeks.

Net Promoter Score (NPS)

*"How likely is it that you would recommend
this product to a friend or colleague?"*

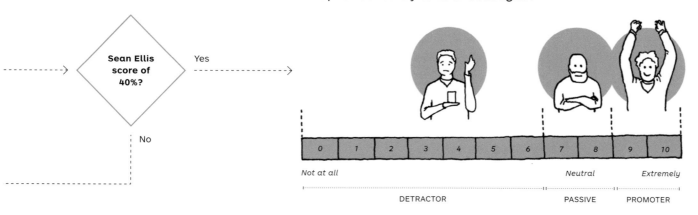

Sean Ellis score of 40%?

Yes

No

Not at all   Neutral   Extremely

DETRACTOR   PASSIVE   PROMOTER

NPS

Net promoter score (NPS) is one of the most common types of surveys and is widely adopted by organizations around the world.

The key question for a NPS survey is:
"How likely is it that you would recommend this product to a friend or colleague? 0 (not at all) to 10 (extremely likely)"

You can calculate NPS score using the following formula:

% PROMOTERS - % DETRACTORS = NPS

Much like the Sean Ellis test, the context of when you show this to your customer matters. They need to have completed something meaningful in your product before they would be willing to recommend it to a friend or colleague. While interesting, it's not enough for customers to want to recommend before they've used it. Likewise, it'll be tough to believe customers who say they'll recommend if they've used it, but wouldn't be disappointed if it went away entirely. Use the NPS after they've answered the Sean Ellis test.

You want to avoid prematurely scaling a business based on hypothetical referrals, from people who'd not be disappointed if your product went away.

Cost

Validation surveys are inexpensive because you should already have a channel to reach them. There are many tools and services today to help you intercept active customers on your website through a pop-up or email, if they trigger a specific action.

Setup Time

Setting up a validation survey is relatively quick and should take you a few hours or a day to configure.

Run Time

If you have sufficient validation survey distribution channels, a survey may only take 1–3 days to get thousands of responses. If you have a difficult time reaching your audience, it may take a few weeks to get enough responses.

Evidence

How disappointed would you be?
% Disappointed.

More than 40% disappointed is an ideal score before you worry about scaling your business. Otherwise, you'll churn out people as fast as you sign them up.

Survey data is rather weak, but hinting that the product could go away will solicit a better response.

○○○○○

How likely would you be to refer?
% Likely to Refer

More than 0% is considered good, although these can vary by industry. You'll want to search online for industry benchmarks.

NPS survey data is weaker than a Sean Ellis test. You are getting answers to a hypothetical referral situation.

Jobs / Pains / Gains ranking
% Accuracy When Compared to Customer Profile

Aim for 80%, since being wrong on this has ripple effects in your entire strategy.

Rather weak strength but an important step before moving to more involved testing.

Capabilities

Product / Marketing / Research

Validation surveys require the ability to carefully craft questions and have the correct tone and structure. Because validation surveys target existing customers, you'll need to be able to identify specific segments and sub-segments to help reduce noise in the data.

Requirements

Quantitative Source Material

Validation surveys are meant to have customers respond to a situation, price, or feature. You'll need to have something for them to respond to so that you can quantitatively measure their responses.

Channel to an Existing Customer

Validation surveys are meant for existing customers, which means you need to confirm you can leverage the existing channel to reach them, whether that is online via the website, by email, or offline via direct mail or a handout.

VALIDATION

EXPERIMENTS

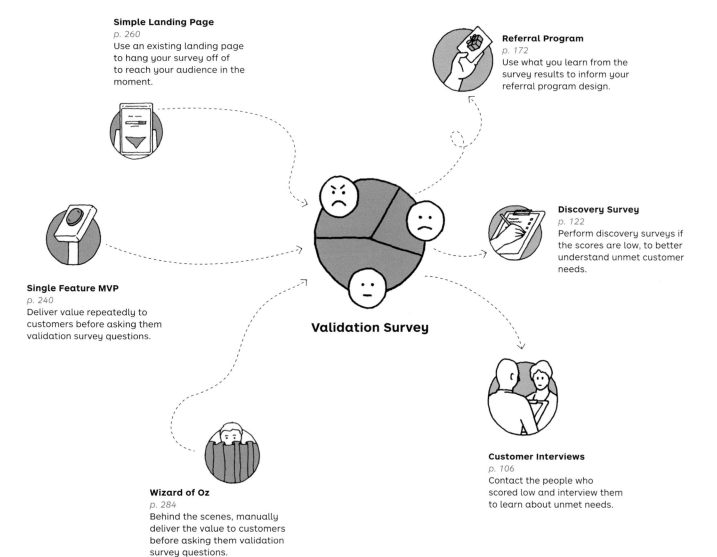

Simple Landing Page
p. 260
Use an existing landing page
to hang your survey off of
to reach your audience in the
moment.

Referral Program
p. 172
Use what you learn from the
survey results to inform your
referral program design.

Single Feature MVP
p. 240
Deliver value repeatedly to
customers before asking them
validation survey questions.

Validation Survey

Discovery Survey
p. 122
Perform discovery surveys if
the scores are low, to better
understand unmet customer
needs.

Wizard of Oz
p. 284
Behind the scenes, manually
deliver the value to customers
before asking them validation
survey questions.

Customer Interviews
p. 106
Contact the people who
scored low and interview them
to learn about unmet needs.

VALIDATION SURVEY

283

CALL TO ACTION

VALIDATION / SIMULATION

Wizard of Oz

Creating a customer experience and delivering value manually, with people instead of solely using technology. The name Wizard of Oz is derived from the movie, where you have a request that is handled by a person. Unlike Concierge, the people involved aren't visible to the customer.

⊖ ●●○○○
COST

⚖ ●●●●●
EVIDENCE STRENGTH

🕐 ●●●○○
SETUP TIME

 ●●●○○
RUN TIME

✂🧊⚙🔨🗄🏷📢🔍📊
CAPABILITIES *Design / Product / Technology / Legal / Marketing*

DESIRABILITY · FEASIBILITY · VIABILITY

Wizard of Oz is ideal for learning manually, firsthand about steps needed to create, capture, and deliver value to a customer.

Wizard of Oz is not ideal for scaling a product or business.

Drawing a Line in the Sand

Wizard of Oz is one way to address the issue of prematurely scaling a solution. We recommend drawing a line in the sand where automation of the manual Wizard of Oz tasks makes sense.

If it takes you 15 minutes to manually create the value for the end customer, ask yourself:

1. How many customer requests could we perform manually each day?
2. What is the cost to deliver each one (cost structure)?
3. What is the most customers will pay (revenue streams)?
4. At what volume is it more cost effective to automate these tasks?

We've witnessed entrepreneurs rush to automate the solution and, in turn, prematurely scale. When you draw a line in the sand to manually deliver the value, then you don't have to scale until that threshold is exceeded. Some entrepreneurs exceed it and and then turn to automation. Others may never hit the threshold. For those who never hit it, we recommend taking a step back and re-evaluating the strategy.

Prepare

☐ Plan the steps of creating the product manually.

☐ Create a board to track all of the orders and steps needed.

☐ Test the steps with someone internally first to make sure it works.

☐ Integrate and verify web analytics are working correctly.

Execute

☐ Receive orders for the Wizard of Oz experiment.

☐ Conduct the Wizard of Oz experiment.

☐ Update your board with the steps for each order. Document how long it took to complete the tasks.

☐ Gather satisfaction feedback from the customers with interviews and surveys.

Analyze

☐ Review your customer satisfaction feedback.

☐ Review your board metrics for:

  • length of time for task completion.

  • where you experienced delays in the process.

  • how many purchased.

☐ Use these findings to improve on your next Wizard of Oz experiment and to help inform where to automate the process.

 ●●○○○

Cost

As long as you keep the Wizard of Oz experiments small and simple, they are cheap to run, mostly because you are doing all of the work manually with little to no technology involved. If you try to scale the experiment or make it overly complex, it'll increase the cost.

 ●●●○○

Setup Time

Setting up a Wizard of Oz experiment takes a bit longer than other rapid prototyping techniques, because you have to manually plan out all of the steps and acquire customers for it.

●●●○○

Run Time

Running a Wizard of Oz experiment can take days to weeks, depending on how complex the process is and how many customers you involve in the experiment. It generally takes longer than other rapid prototyping techniques.

 ●●●●●

Evidence

●●●●●

Customer satisfaction

Customer quotes and feedback on how satisfied they were after receiving the output from your experiment.

Customer satisfaction evidence is strong in this case because you are asking for feedback after the value was delivered to the customer, instead of a hypothetical situation.

●●●●●

# of purchases

Customer purchases from the Wizard of Oz experiment. What are they willing to pay for a manual experience?

Payments are strong evidence, even if you are manually delivering value.

●●●●●

Time it takes to complete the process

Lead time is the total time measured from customer request to when the order was delivered.

Cycle time is the amount of time spent working on the request. It does not include the time the request sits idle before action is taken on it.

The time it takes for you to complete the Wizard of Oz experiment is very strong—it gives you firsthand knowledge of the steps needed to receive a request and deliver value to a customer.

Capabilities

Design / Product / Tech / Legal / Marketing

You'll need all of the capabilities to manually create and deliver the product to the customer. This is very context specific, depending on whether you are delivering a physical or digital product or service to the end customer.

Requirements

Time

The biggest requirement for a Wizard of Oz experiment is time, closely followed by a digital curtain. Like the Concierge experiment, you'll need quite a bit of time to perform the testing but in addition to this, you'll need a curtain to hide the people performing the tasks from the customer. This can take many forms, but the most common is a simple landing page or digital interface where the customer requests and receives the value.

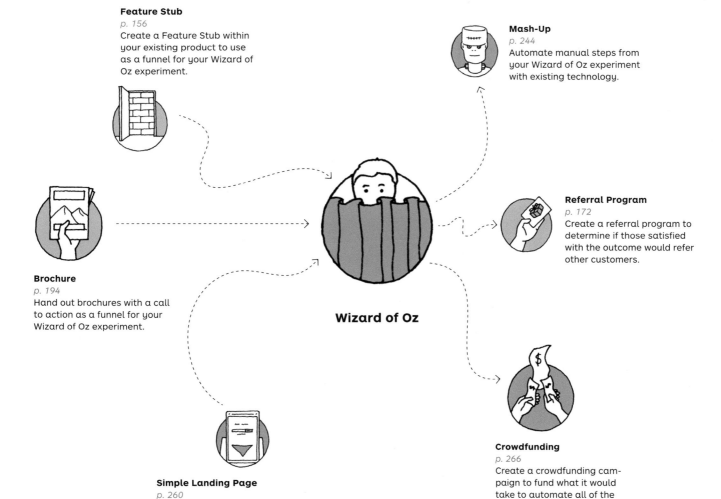

Feature Stub
p. 156
Create a Feature Stub within
your existing product to use
as a funnel for your Wizard of
Oz experiment.

Mash-Up
p. 244
Automate manual steps from
your Wizard of Oz experiment
with existing technology.

Brochure
p. 194
Hand out brochures with a call
to action as a funnel for your
Wizard of Oz experiment.

Referral Program
p. 172
Create a referral program to
determine if those satisfied
with the outcome would refer
other customers.

Wizard of Oz

Simple Landing Page
p. 260
Create a simple landing page
to collect interest in your
Wizard of Oz experiment.

Crowdfunding
p. 266
Create a crowdfunding campaign to fund what it would
take to automate all of the
steps as a scalable product.

WIZARD OF OZ

287

SIMULATION

VALIDATION / SIMULATION

Mock Sale

Presenting a sale for your product without processing any payment information.

COST ●●○○○

EVIDENCE STRENGTH ●●●●○○

SETUP TIME ●●○○○

RUN TIME ●●●○○

CAPABILITIES DESIGN / SALES / FINANCE

DESIRABILITY · FEASIBILITY · VIABILITY

Mock sale is ideal for determining different price points for your product.

ONLINE WITH EMAIL SIGNUP

PREPARE

☐ Create a simple landing page.

☐ Insert your price options.

☐ On price option click, show a "we're not ready yet" pop-up with email signup form.

☐ Integrate and verify web analytics are working correctly.

Execute

☐ Make your page live to the public.

☐ Drive traffic to your page.

Analyze

☐ Review your analytics on how many people:

- viewed your price options.

- clicked on a price option.

- signed up with their email address.

- dropped out of the flow (i.e., web analytics funnel).

- converted on your page, based on traffic source.

☐ Use these findings to gauge viability and refine your Value Proposition and price options.

Connections

- Price options come from your revenue stream in your Business Model Canvas.

OFFLINE RETAIL

PREPARE

☐ Create a high fidelity physical prototype of your product.

☐ Communicate the length and nature of the experiment with store managers and personnel so that employees involved understand what's going on.

Execute

☐ Strategically place the prototype on the desired shelf in the store.

☐ Observe and document who views the product, picks it up, and places it in the basket.

☐ Before or at time of customer purchase, intercept and explain that the product is not yet available.

☐ Get feedback from the customer on whether they want to be contacted when it's available and why they picked it up for purchase compared to other products.

☐ Compensate customer with a gift card for the inconvenience.

Analyze

☐ Review your customer feedback notes.

☐ Review your activity log of how many:

- viewed the product.

- put it in the basket.

- wanted to purchase.

- provided contact information for when the product launches.

☐ Use your findings to improve the Value Proposition and product design.

Cost

Mock sale is relatively cheap: you are price testing your product without building all of it. You'll need a believable level of fidelity for your target audience, so there is some cost in presenting your solution digitally or physically.

Setup Time

Setup time for a mock sale is relatively short, meaning you can create a believable platform for your Value Proposition in a few hours or a few days.

Run Time

Run time for a mock sale is a few days or weeks. You'll want to target a specific audience with your solution and give them enough time to consider a purchase.

Evidence

# of unique views
# of purchase clicks

You can calculate the purchase conversion rate by taking the number of people who view the price divided by the number of purchase clicks.

Purchase clicks are relatively strong, although not as strong as subsequent email and payment submissions.

# of purchase email signups

You can calculate the purchase email conversion rate by taking the number of people who view the price divided by the number of email signups.

Email signups after purchase clicks are relatively strong, although not as strong as payment submissions.

# of purchase payment
Information submitted

You can calculate the purchase payment conversion rate by taking the number of people who view the price divided by the number who filled out payment information.

Payment info submissions are very strong evidence.

Capabilities

Design / Sales / Finance

Conducting a mock sale will require financial modeling skills to inform the price options. You'll also need to design the sale in such a way that it is the right fidelity for your target audience. Finally, you'll need sales capability, especially if you are conducting these in person in the physical world.

Requirements

Pricing Strategy

Mock sale does require some thought and number crunching before you conduct the experiment. This isn't a scenario where you simply ask people how much they'll pay. Customers are notoriously bad at answering that question. Instead, you'll need to be able to present a sale price or multiple prices to have them respond. If you test a ridiculously low price, then you'll receive false positives on something you won't be able to deliver. Therefore, spend time thinking through the cost structure to make the mock sale evidence worthwhile.

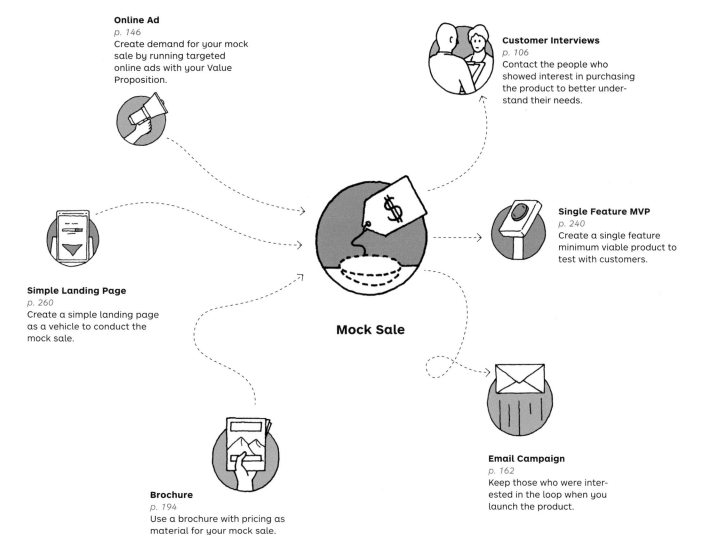

Online Ad
p. 146
Create demand for your mock sale by running targeted online ads with your Value Proposition.

Customer Interviews
p. 106
Contact the people who showed interest in purchasing the product to better understand their needs.

Single Feature MVP
p. 240
Create a single feature minimum viable product to test with customers.

Simple Landing Page
p. 260
Create a simple landing page as a vehicle to conduct the mock sale.

Mock Sale

Brochure
p. 194
Use a brochure with pricing as material for your mock sale.

Email Campaign
p. 162
Keep those who were interested in the loop when you launch the product.

MOCK SALE
They will come, when you build it.
Buffer

When Joel Gascoigne, cofounder of Buffer, started the company from his bedroom nine years ago, he wasn't certain if people would even pay for his social media scheduling service.

At the time, social media managers were still manually logging into multiple social media platforms and posting their content. They used calendars and reminders to tell them the perfect moment to log in and post across time zones. This wasn't ideal, especially when it occurred in the middle of the night.

The Buffer application would solve that problem, beginning with a scheduling service for Twitter, before expanding to additional social media platforms. Joel decided to lightly test the desirability of the Buffer app by adding a "Plans and Pricing" button to his simple landing page. When clicked, it displayed a message about not being ready yet with an email signup to be notified.

After a few people submitted their email, Joel determined there was initial interest but wanted to collect more evidence.

Hypothesis

Joel believed that people would pay a monthly fee to schedule their social media posts on Twitter.

It wasn't enough that people would enter their email without any pricing information. Joel needed to know if it was viable.

Experiment

Price testing different monthly fees to gauge viability.

Joel decided to test viability by adding three different payment tier options to the landing page. Free = $0/month for 1 tweet a day and 5 tweets in your buffer queue. Standard = $5/month for 10 tweets a day and 50 tweets in your buffer queue. Max = $20/month for unlimited tweets a day and unlimited tweets in your buffer queue. These options appeared once people clicked the "Plans and Pricing" button. Once people clicked

an option, an email signup form appeared stating Buffer wasn't quite yet ready for launch. Each option in the page had analytics integrated, so Joel could analyze who was signing up based on the selected price.

Evidence

A $5/month signal.

The evidence showed that the $5/month plan was the clear winner in this initial test. This option generated the most email signups when he compared it to the $0 and $20 options.

Insights

People were interested in paying.

With the data showing the $5/month plan being the most popular, it started to become clear how people valued Buffer. They didn't need to only schedule one tweet a day, because they could simply log in and do that. On the other hand, they didn't need unlimited tweets because social media managers don't want to overwhelm their audience and be perceived as spam. The sweet spot seemed to be 5 tweets per day, where it was enough of a hassle that people would pay a $5/month fee to address.

Actions

Evidence that Buffer should be built.

After generating evidence and insights into the demand of Buffer, Joel decided to build the application. He used this learning to help shape his price points for launch. Joel also kept it lean and manually processed the payments for each customer early on. Today Buffer is used by hundreds of thousands of customers around the world and has a monthly recurring revenue of $1.54 million.

VALIDATION / SIMULATION

Letter of Intent

Short, written contract that is simple to read and not legally binding.

COST	EVIDENCE STRENGTH
⬤○○○○	⬤◉○○○

SETUP TIME	RUN TIME
⬤○○○○	⬤⬤○○○

CAPABILITIES *Product / Technology / Legal / Finance*

DESIRABILITY · FEASIBILITY · VIABILITY

Letter of intent is ideal for evaluating key partners and B2B customer segments.

Letter of intent is not ideal for B2C customer segments.

Basic LOI Sample

[Your Name]

[Title]

[Business Name]

[Business Address]

[Date]

[To Name]

[Title]

[Business Name]

[Business Address]

Dear [Name]

We hereby submit a non-binding letter of intent to [insert terms of partnership here].

Sincerely,

[Your Name]

Prepare

☐ Define your the letter of intent target audience, preferably one that already has knowledge of your business.

☐ Research what legal Letter of Intent format best suits your business. (i.e., B2B customer vs. B2B key partner).

☐ Create your letter of intent template.

Execute

☐ Show the letter of intent to your target audience.

☐ One person on the team conducts the interview.

☐ Another person on the team takes notes on customer quotes, jobs, pains, gains, and body language.

Analyze

☐ Review your notes with the team.

☐ How many were sent, viewed, and signed?

☐ Follow up with those who signed to continue the conversation and push your business idea forward.

Cost

Letter of intent contracts are relatively cheap to produce as they are usually 1 or 2 pages long. You can find free LOI templates online or spend a little money to have a lawyer help you properly craft one.

Setup Time

Setup time for a letter of intent is only a few hours or potentially 1 day if you involve legal help.

Run Time

Run time for a letter of intent is short in that your recipients either accept it or not.

Evidence

●●○○○
# of LOIs sent
# of LOI views
# of LOI signatures
LOI ccceptance rate = # of LOIs sent divided by the # of LOIs signed.

Letter of Intent signatures are not legally binding, but stronger than people merely saying they'll partner or buy.

●○○○○
Customer feedback
Partner feedback
Customer and Partner Quotes
Feedback is weak but generally good for qualitative insights.

Capabilities
Product / Technology / Legal / Finance

To create a letter of intent it helps to have basic legal understanding, even though it's a non-legal document. If using it with partners, you'll need to be able to articulate the key activity or key resource needed in detail. For B2B customers, you'll need to be able to speak clearly about your value proposition and pricing structure.

Requirements
Warm Leads

Unless you have warm leads, meaning there is a basic understanding of your perceived Value Proposition and business, then we don't recommend using a letter of intent. It would be poor form to cold email your LOIs to people, resulting in a dismal conversion rate. Instead, have the LOI ready for scheduled conversations so that you can present it during or shortly after the meeting.

Partner & Supplier Interviews
p. 114
Interview partners and suppliers to better understand their capabilities before creating the LOI.

Customer Interviews
p. 106
Use the notes from your interviews to inform the shape of your LOI.

Letter of Intent

Single Feature MVP
p. 240
Create a Single Feature MVP with your LOI partners or customers.

Presales
p. 274
Conduct a presale of the solution to your customers before it is made available to the public.

Life-sized Prototype
p. 254
Create a life-sized prototype to test with your customer segment.

LETTER OF INTENT
Using LOIs with Landscapers
Thrive Smart Systems

Thrive Smart Systems is a company set on empowering people with the latest in irrigation technology. Their wireless system saves you time and money, providing smarter irrigation.

The cofounders, Seth Bangerter and Grant Rowberry, wanted to know if people would buy their product before they completed product development. Many people, landscapers in particular, expressed so much interest that when they asked them how many they would buy they would respond with "a ton" or "as many as you can give me." While this was exciting to hear, Seth and Grant wanted to get a firm number on how many these customers were willing to purchase.

The Thrive team chose to have interested customers write a letter of intent to purchase. The idea was to allow people to write down, in numbers, precisely what they wanted. Seth and Grant decided to make a template to include vital elements that a letter of intent should have. When a potential customer stated they are willing to buy x amount of Thrive's product, then x amount was to be placed on the letter of intent.

Thrive called this template their letter of intent form.

Hypothesis

Seth and Grant believed that they could generate $25,000 during the test phase through 20 LOIs.

Experiment

Asking customers to write an LOI.

They began to test this hypothesis by asking interested customers to write a Letter of Intent for how many units they were willing to purchase.

After receiving a few, they created a LOI template to pass out to each person that expresses interest in buying the product.

Evidence

Generating over $50k in purchases.

The Thrive team found that with no advertising and by just asking potential customers to fill out a form, they could generate over $50,000 in projected revenue.

Insights

Expectations versus reality.

They also learned that the number of units people say they will purchase is much more than they are willing to put into writing.

Those who said they would buy 1000 units only wrote down that they will buy 300 units. A few who said they would buy 100 only wrote down that they will buy 15–20. From this, Seth and Grant gained insights into how to formalize their purchasing process. Even though the LOI is non-binding, when a potential customer puts pen to paper they have more skin in the game.

Actions

Iterating on the LOI approach.

From the LOI experiments, Seth and Grant refined their LOIs to two different flavors. One being a "pledge of purchase" for those who want to buy the end product. The other flavor being a "testing agreement" for those who want to participate in the beta test.

VALIDATION / SIMULATION

Pop-Up Store

A retail store that is opened temporarily to sell goods, usually a trendy or seasonal product.

⊖ ●●●●○
COST

⚖ ●●○○○
EVIDENCE STRENGTH

🕐 ●●●○○
SETUP TIME

⏱ ●●○○○
RUN TIME

✂🧊⋯⚒🗄🏷📢🔍📊
CAPABILITIES *Design / Product / Legal / Sales / Marketing*

▦ ◔
DESIRABILITY · FEASIBILITY · VIABILITY

A pop-up store is ideal for testing face-to-face interactions with customers to see if they'll really make a purchase.

A pop-up store is not ideal for B2B businesses: consider a booth at a conference instead.

Prepare

- ☐ Find a location.
- ☐ Get the required lease, license, permits, and insurance.
- ☐ Design the experience.
- ☐ Plan the logistics of how it will operate.
- ☐ Promote the dates it'll be open to customers.

Execute

- ☐ Open your pop-up store.
- ☐ Gather evidence you need from customers.
- ☐ Close your pop-up store.

Analyze

- ☐ Review your notes with the team:
  - What did people get excited about?
  - What made them skeptical?
- ☐ Review how many meaning-ful interactions took place:
  - Did you collect any emails from customers?
  - Did you perform any successful mock sales, presales, or actual sales?
- ☐ Use what you've learned to iterate on the experience before running another pop-up store.

POP-UP STORE

301

SIMULATION

Cost

Pop-up stores are generally small, but will still cost more money than low fidelity experiments. Much of the cost is leasing the space and advertising, which can vary depending on the location and access to the store. You can bring costs down if you can find an owner to give you extra space in their existing store for the experiment. Additional costs may include licenses, permits, and insurance required in order to conduct business transactions.

Setup Time

Setup time for a pop-up store can take days or weeks, depending on what locations are available. It'll need to look professional, which requires having the right people and appearance for the store. You'll also need to create demand using ads, unless it is a very high traffic area with your target customers.

Run Time

Run time for a pop-up store is generally short, from a few hours to a few days. The intent here is to learn quickly, synthesize the results, and move on.

Evidence

●●○○○

# of customer visits
# of email signups

Conversion rate on people who visited and provided their email addresses.

Customer Feedback

Customer quotes provided in the feedback to you.

Customer visits, emails, and feedback are rather weak evidence, but good for qualitative insights.

●●●●●

# of presales
# of mock sales
# of sales

Conversion rate on people who are willing to pay or paid for the product.

Sales are strong evidence that customers want your product.

Capabilities

Design / Product / Legal / Sales / Marketing

To set up and run a pop-up store, you'll need legal expertise to determine licensing, permits, lease, and insurance contracts. You'll need online marketing skills to promote the store and sales experience to staff it for customer interaction.

Requirements

Traffic

Pop-up stores thrive on the idea of a niche, limited-time offer for customers. In order to create that demand, you'll need to advertise and create buzz for your shop via:

- online ads.
- social media campaigns.
- email campaigns.
- word of mouth.

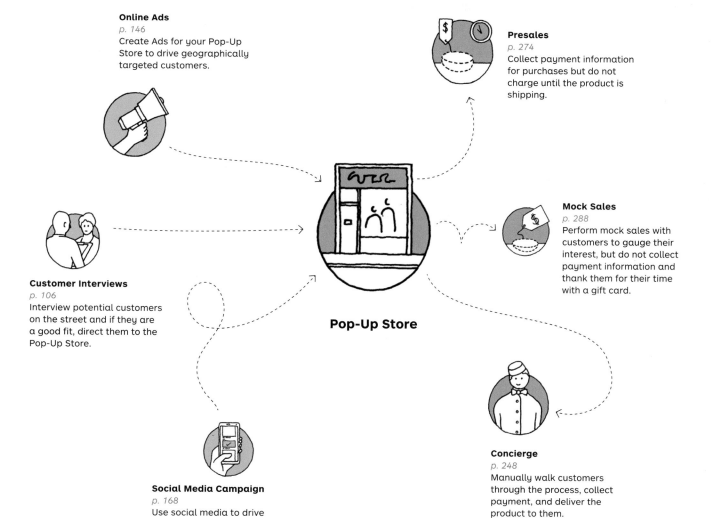

Online Ads
p. 146
Create Ads for your Pop-Up
Store to drive geographically
targeted customers.

Presales
p. 274
Collect payment information
for purchases but do not
charge until the product is
shipping.

Customer Interviews
p. 106
Interview potential customers
on the street and if they are
a good fit, direct them to the
Pop-Up Store.

Mock Sales
p. 288
Perform mock sales with
customers to gauge their
interest, but do not collect
payment information and
thank them for their time
with a gift card.

Pop-Up Store

Social Media Campaign
p. 168
Use social media to drive
people to your Pop-Up Store.

Concierge
p. 248
Manually walk customers
through the process, collect
payment, and deliver the
product to them.

POP-UP STORE

303

SIMULATION

POP-UP STORE
Learning Through Temporary Retail
Topology Eyewear

Topology Eyewear aims to solve the problem of poorly fitting glasses, by making custom-tailored glasses that are sized and styled via an augmented reality app. Customers can take a selfie, see how different glasses look on their faces, and then purchase custom glasses that are specifically sculpted to fit their unique dimensions. As with any new innovation, there are risky hypotheses that need to be tested.

Even though the technology worked, the team needed to test for any barriers to adoption with customers.

Hypothesis

The Topology team believed that many people would identify with the problem of poor glasses fit, and would welcome the high-tech approach as a potential solution.

Experiment

Getting out of the building with a pop-up store.

The team rented a partially empty storefront on San Francisco's Union Street for a Friday and created a temporary company name — Alchemy Eyewear — and commissioned posters and flyers to make it feel exclusive and exciting. Chris Guest, the marketing lead, went out onto the street to cold approach strangers, ask about their eyewear, summarize the pitch, and encourage them to visit the pop-up store. When customers entered the store, Topology staff would first ask them about the problems they experience with their eyewear, taking note of how they describe the problem in their own words. Then they would introduce our solution and note their response and what questions they asked about it. They would then demo the app using a default face model and note their responses and questions. They would then seek their permission to take a face scan so they could try it for themselves. When loaded, they would guide them how to scan themselves and noted and answered their questions. On selecting a chosen design, they would ask if we could get their email address so we could save the design and send it to them.

Evidence

Finding early adopters off of the street.

Despite humble expectations, after 2 hours, they sold 4 pairs of glasses at an average price of about $400.

The conversion rates on email signups were too small to be meaningful in the absolute sense, but they were helpful to see where the biggest drop-off occurred in the the process.

Insights

People knew their glasses didn't fit, but weren't sure why.

Even though the team sold 4 pairs of glasses, it was the qualitative insights that were the most valuable.

The team noticed noticed that people seemed to be "symptom aware" but not "problem aware." That is, when asked if they had a problem with fit, most people would say no. But when asked if their glasses slid down their nose, pinched, created red marks etc, most people would say yes. They understood the symptoms of bad fit, but nobody thought of it as being due to bad fit. This directed marketing messages for years afterwards.

Actions

Using the voice of the customer.

The customer quotes inspired the company purpose and vision, becoming central to the branding.

The team used what they learned to run more pop-up stores to test the Value Proposition, positioning, and marketing, eventually talking to over a thousand customers face to face.

VALIDATION / SIMULATION

Extreme Programming Spike

A simple program to explore potential technical or design solutions.
The term spike is derived from rock climbing and railroads.
It's a necessary task to stop and perform so that you can feasibly
continue to make progress.

○ ●●○○○
COST

⚖ ●●●●●
EVIDENCE STRENGTH

🕐 ●○○○○
SETUP TIME

 ●●○○○
RUN TIME

✂ ⬡ ⦂⦂ ⚒ 🗄 ⊘ ◁ ⚲ ◔
CAPABILITIES *Product / Technology / Data*

⊞ ▷ ◔
DESIRABILITY · FEASIBILITY · VIABILITY

*The Extreme Programming Spike is ideal for quickly evaluating
whether or not your solution is feasible, usually with software.*

*The Extreme Programming Spike is not ideal for scaling
the solution, as it is typically thrown away and re-created
afterwards.*

Prepare

☐ Define your acceptance criteria.

☐ Define your time box for the spike.

☐ Plan your start and end date.

Execute

☐ Write the code to achieve the acceptance criteria.

☐ Strongly consider pairing programming with another person to help navigate the code and create any needed tests.

Analyze

☐ Share what you've found with regards to:

• performance.

• level of complexity.

• outputs.

☐ Determine if the acceptance criteria were successfully met.

☐ Use what you've learned to build, borrow, or buy the necessary solution.

Cost

Cost is relatively cheap and much more inexpensive than building the entire solution—only to find out at the end if it is feasible.

Setup Time

Setup time for an Extreme Programming Spike is usually about one day. This is the time needed to research what methods are available and usually done by someone that already has technical expertise.

Run Time

Run time for an Extreme Programming Spike is typically from 1 day to 2 weeks. It is aggressively time boxed for a reason—you are laser focused on testing feasibility for a specific solution.

Evidence

Acceptance criteria

The acceptance criteria defined for the spike was sufficiently met. Did the code perform the task and generate the output required?

Recommendation

The people working on the spike provide their recommendation on how steep of a learning curve it is to use the software and if it is fit for your purpose in creating the solution.

Spikes generate strong evidence: you are working with code that is representative of the bigger solution.

Capabilities

Product / Technology / Data

You'll need product capabilities to clearly communicate how the solution creates the Value Proposition. This includes answering any questions from the team and customer expectations with regard to speed and quality. Data capabilities are also helpful if there is any visualization or analytics aspect to the spike. The most important capability you'll need is technology and software, since the spike is usually working with code to produce a signal on the next course of action.

Requirements

Acceptance Criteria

Before performing a spike, clearly define the acceptance criteria and time box so that everyone is clear on the goal before getting started. These can turn into never-ending research projects if left unchecked.

**Partner & Supplier
Interviews**
p. 114
Interview partners and suppliers to better understand their capabilities before building it yourself.

Single Feature MVP
p. 240
Create a single feature minimum viable product to test with customers.

Data Sheet
p. 190
Create a data sheet on what specifications the solution should contain.

Boomerang
p. 204
Use competitor solutions and research how they perform and what technology stack they are using.

Extreme
Programming Spike

Min

dset

"The more success you've had in the past, the less critically you examine your own assumptions."

———

Vinod Khosla
Venture capitalist

SECTION 4 — MINDSET

4.1 — AVOID EXPERIMENT PITFALLS

Experiment Pitfalls

The best plans for experimentation don't always come through. We've learned this in working with teams to design, run, and analyze experiments over the years. Part of learning this process is becoming more proficient at quickly running experiments. We have found common pitfalls that you can identify early on and benefit from our mistakes.

Time Trap
Not dedicating enough time.

 X

– You get what you invest. Teams that don't put in enough time to test business ideas won't get great results. Too often, teams underestimate what it takes to conduct multiple experiments and test ideas well.

 ✔

☐ Carve out dedicated time every week to test, learn, and adapt.

☐ Set weekly goals in regard to what you'd like to learn about your hypotheses.

☐ Visualize your work so that it becomes clear when tasks are stalled or blocked.

Analysis Paralysis
Overthinking things that you should just test and adapt.

 X

– Good ideas and concepts are important, but too many teams overthink and waste time, rather than getting out of the building to test and adapt their ideas.

 ✔

☐ Time box your analysis work.

☐ Differentiate between reversible and irreversible decisions. Act fast on the former. Take more time for the latter.

☐ Avoid debates of opinion. Conduct evidence-driven debates followed by decisions.

Incomparable Data/Evidence
Messy data that are not comparable.

 X

– Too many teams are sloppy in defining their exact hypothesis, experiment, and metrics. That leads to data that are not comparable (e.g., not testing with the exact same customer segment or in wildly different contexts).

 ✔

☐ Use the Test Card.

☐ Make test subject, experiment context, and precise metrics explicit.

☐ Make sure everybody involved in running the experiment is part of the design.

Weak Data/Evidence
Only measure what people say, not what they do.

Confirmation Bias
Only believing evidence that agrees with your hypothesis.

Too Few Experiments
Conduct only one experiment for your most important hypothesis.

Failure to Learn and Adapt
When you don't take time to analyze the evidence to generate insights and action.

Outsource Testing
When you outsource what you should be doing and learning yourself.

✖
- Often teams are happy with running surveys and interviews and they fail to go deeper into how people act in real life situations.

✔
- ☐ Don't just believe what people say.
- ☐ Run call-to-action experiments.
- ☐ Generate evidence that gets as close as possible to the real world situation you are trying to test.

✖
- Sometimes teams discard or underplay evidence that conflicts with their hypothesis. They prefer the illusion of being correct in their prediction.

✔
- ☐ Involve others in the data synthesis process to bring in different perspectives.
- ☐ Create competing hypotheses to challenge your beliefs.
- ☐ Conduct multiple experiments for each hypothesis.

✖
- Few teams realize how many experiments they should conduct to validate a hypothesis. They make decisions on important hypotheses based on one experiment with weak evidence.

✔
- ☐ Conduct multiple experimentsfor important hypotheses.
- ☐ Differentiate between weak and strong evidence.
- ☐ Increase the strength of evidence with decreasing uncertainty.

✖
- Some teams get so deep into testing that they forget to keep their eyes on the prize. The goal is not to test and learn. The goal is to decide, based on evidence and insights, to progress from idea to business.

✔
- ☐ Set aside time to synthesize your results, generate insights, and adapt your idea.
- ☐ Always navigate between detailed testing process and big picture idea: which patterns that matter are you observing?
- ☐ Create rituals to keep your eyes on the prize: ask if you're making progress from idea to business.

✖
- Outsourcing testing is rarely a wise idea. Testing is about rapid iterations between testing, learning, and adapting an idea. An agency can't make those rapid decisions for you and you risk wasting time and energy by outsourcing.

✔
- ☐ Shift resources you reserved for an agency to internal team members.
- ☐ Build up a team of professional testers.

"It takes humility to realize
we don't know everything,
not to rest on our laurels,
and to know that we must keep
learning and observing.
If we don't, we can be sure
some startup will be there
to take our place."

———————

Cher Wang
Cofounder HTC

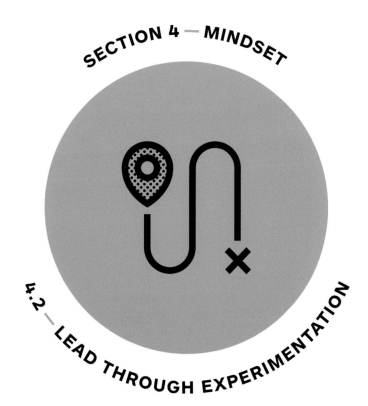

SECTION 4 — MINDSET

4.2 — LEAD THROUGH EXPERIMENTATION

Improving Business Models

Language

Leaders who are improving existing business models need to be aware of their language and tone. Chances are you have evolved into a leader over time because you are an expert with knowledge and experience.

As you lead teams through experimenting on a known business model, be mindful of the fact that overuse of your words can unintentionally disempower the teams. They may feel as though their decision-making authority is taken away, even if you are merely giving your opinion. They'll simply wait for you to assign them experiments, which is not ideal.

Accountability

Accountability often has a negative connotation in today's organizations, but it doesn't need to. Teams do not always need to be "held accountable" to hitting dates and releasing features. While features are important, they are outputs, not outcomes. Remember to focus on business outcomes, not just the features and dates.

Your teams need the opportunity to give an account on how they are experimenting and making progress toward business outcomes. As a leader, it's your job to create an environment for these opportunities to occur.

Facilitation

How you interact with teams while improving business models is also important. As you grow into a leader at higher levels of the organization, you'll realize that facilitation skills are imperative.

We recommend taking courses on facilitation to level up your leadership game. There might be many different options to improve the business and instead of choosing one, use facilitation to select multiple experiments. Have the evidence shape what approach works best for your business.

✔
☐ "We, Us, Our"
☐ "How would you achieve this business outcome?"
☐ "Can you think of 2–3 additional experiments?"

✘
– "I, Me, Mine"
– "Deliver this feature by release date."
– "This is the only experiment we should run."

Allow your intuition to guide you to a conclusion, no matter how imperfect—this is the "strong opinion" part. Then—and this is the "weakly held" part—prove yourself wrong.
— Paul Saffo

Inventing Business Models

Strong Opinions, Weakly Held

Inventing new business models requires experimentation and openness to the idea of being wrong. One way to think about this is from Paul Saffo's "strong opinions, weakly held" approach. It means you start out with a hypothesis, but be open for it to be proven wrong. If you are merely trying to prove that you are right, then you become susceptible to your cognitive biases.

For example, when attending a stakeholder review, teams will be sharing what they tested and where they want to go. If you lead with answers and ignore all of the data that contradict your opinion, it'll be a very frustrating meeting for everyone. It'll essentially unravel the experimentation culture you are trying to build.

✓

- ☐ "What is your learning goal?"
- ☐ "What obstacles can I remove to help you make progress?"
- ☐ "How else might we approach this problem?"
- ☐ "What learning has surprised you so far?"

✗

- – "I don't trust the data."
- – "I still think it's a good idea and we should build it anyway."
- – "You need to talk to 1,000 customers before it means anything."
- – "This has to be a $15 million dollar business by the end of next year."

Steps Leaders Can Take

Create an Enabling Environment: Processes, Metrics, and Culture

Leadership's key role in helping test business ideas is to create the right environment. Give people enough time and resources to test ideas iteratively. Leaders need to abolish business plans and establish appropriate testing processes and metrics that differ from execution processes and metrics. They need to give teams the autonomy to make decisions, move fast, and then get out of the way.

Make Sure Evidence Trumps Opinion: Change Decision-Making

Leaders are used to deciding based on their often deep experience and extensive track record. Yet, in innovation and entrepreneurship, past experience might actually prevent an individual from seeing and adapting to the future. Here evidence from testing trumps opinion. The leader's role is to push a team to make a compelling case for an idea based on evidence, not based on the leader's preferences.

Remove Obstacles and Open Doors: Access to Customers, Brand, IP, and Other Resources

Leaders can remove obstacles when teams that are testing business ideas encounter internal roadblocks, like lack of access to internal expertise or specialized resources. Leaders can open doors to customers when required. It's surprising how few corporate innovation and growth teams have easy access to customers to test new ideas.

Ask Questions Rather Than Provide Answers: Help Teams Grow and Adapt Their Ideas

Leaders need to up their questioning skills to push teams to develop better value propositions and business models that can succeed in the real world. They need to relentlessly inquire about experiments, evidence, insights, and patterns on which teams build Value Propositions and business model ideas.

Create More Leaders

Meet Your Teams One-Half Step Ahead

Leaders need to bring their teams along for the journey, instead of inadvertently leaving them behind. Think of where you eventually want team members to be, then look backward. How will they get here? What steps will they have to take? It's a small cognitive trick but it works. Leaders need a sense of where their teams are today and how to nudge them down that path. Find opportunities to guide them to take that first step, whether it be in scheduled one-on-ones, retrospectives, or in hallway conversations.

Understand Context Before Giving Advice

Leaders need to actively listen and understand the context before giving advice to team members. Practice letting team members speak until they are finished. Once there is a pause in the conversation, ask clarifying questions to make sure you understand the context before giving advice. Don't get too excited and interrupt team members while they are speaking because you've already thought of an answer. You may prematurely provide advice and connected dots where none exist.

Say "I Don't Know."

These three simple words can strike fear into the heart of leaders. "I don't know." We often ask leaders when was the last time they uttered these three words in front of their employees. The answers range from "Why, just yesterday!" to "Never!" It's the latter answer that is concerning. Imagine feeling the pressure of leading an organization and always having the answers. There's a good chance that you don't have them. When building a culture of innovation and entrepreneurship, acting like you have all the answers can be disastrous. Teams will quickly see through the veil once they learn how to run experiments and generate their own evidence. Worse yet, you'll feel like you have undermined your position of leadership by being proven wrong. Instead, we strongly recommend that you practice saying these three words, "I don't know," when you are in a situation where you don't know. It will help your teams begin to understand that you don't have all of the answers, nor should you. Follow it up with "How would you approach this?" or "What do you think we should do?" Saying "I don't know" will help you model the behavior the leaders you create will embrace.

"A bad system will beat
a good person every time."

————

W. Edwards Deming
Professor and author

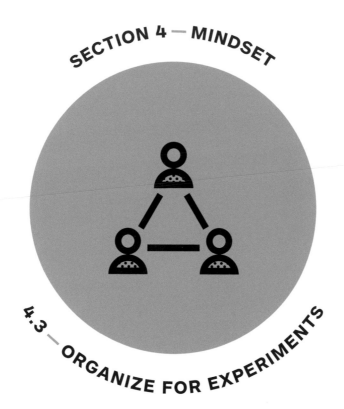

SECTION 4 — MINDSET

4.3 — ORGANIZE FOR EXPERIMENTS

Silos vs. Cross-Functional Teams

Much of how we've structured organizations today is based on the Industrial Era. Back then, you would create a factory to assemble a product, such as an automobile. You'd break the creation of an automobile into tasks, create an assembly line, and have workers complete the same task over and over. This works if you know the solution, since you can analyze your way to efficiently create the solution. Today's corporations are, not coincidentally, modeled the same way. We create projects, break them down into tasks, and assign them across functions. Organizing by function can work if you truly know the problem and the solution—and nothing changes.

We've learned over the last few decades of work that rarely do we know the solution, especially in software. Things change fast. Really fast. So the idea that the solution is known and nothing changes is becoming less and less common in today's market. This is why there has been a shift from traditional, functionally siloed organization models to more agile, cross-functional team approaches. When testing out new business ideas, speed and agility are imperative. cross-functional teams can adapt more quickly than functionally siloed teams. In many organizations, small, dedicated, cross-functional teams can outperform large, siloed project teams.

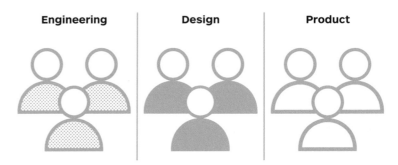

Engineering   Design   Product

Functional Silos

Cross-Functional Teams

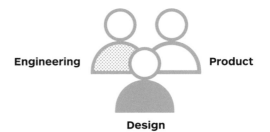

Engineering   Product

Design

Thinking Like
a Venture Capitalist

Another outdated model we observe in organizations pertains to funding. Many organizations still adhere to the big bang, annual funding style of the past. This severely limits the agility of the organization and incentivizes bad behavior. For example, if your department doesn't spend all of its budget, then it is likely your budget for the upcoming fiscal year will be decreased. Therefore, budget is spent not on the most impactful activities, but those that will ensure there will be no money left at the end of the cycle. Annual funding also limits your at-bats, in that instead of taking one big home run swing, you're much better off taking several base hit level swings. This is where organizations can learn from the Venture Capital community. Unfortunately, the level of patience and willingness to give teams space is somewhat limited in organizations, as we illustrate below.

Venture Capital Funding	**Innovation Funding**
8–12 years	1–3 years
20–30 startups	5–10 internal startups
Hands-Off	Hands-On

Innovation Portfolio

In contrast to the annual budgeting, organizations are adopting a more venture capitalist-style approach. This helps leaders invest incrementally in a series of business ideas and double down on the ones that are successful. It greatly increases your at-bats and your chance at finding a unicorn, instead of placing 1–2 large bets.

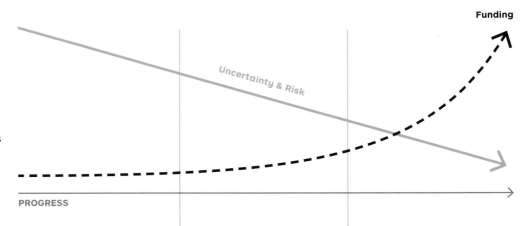

PROGRESS

	Seed	Launch	Growth
Funding	Less than $50,000	$50,000 – $500,000	$500,000+
Team Size	1–3	2–5	5+
Time per Team Member	20–40%	40–80%	100%
Number of Projects	High	Medium	Low
Objectives	Customer understanding, context, and willingness to pay	Proven interest and indications of profitability	Proven model at limited scale
KPIs	• Market size • Customer evidence • Problem/solution fit • Opportunity size	• Value Proposition evidence • Financial evidence • Feasibility evidence	• Product/market fit • Acquisition and retention evidence • Business model fit
Experiment Themes	50–80% 0–10% 10–30%	30–50% 10–40% 20–50%	10–30% 40–50% 20–50%

DESIRABILITY
FEASIBILITY
VIABILITY

Investment Committees

Another important aspect of funding in a venture capitalist-style method is having a small investment committee that consists of leadership to usher the process along. These leaders in the organization need to have decision-making authority when it comes to budget, because they'll be helping the teams navigate from seed, launch, and growth stages. These funding decisions typically take place in the Stakeholder Review Ceremony (see page 80). While we recommend stakeholder reviews to occur every month, the investment decisions usually take place at 3–6 month intervals, depending on your business venture. Here are some guidelines when it comes to creating your investment committee.

Designing the Committee

- *3–5 members:* Keep the committee relatively small in size so that you can make decisions and run fast.

- *External member:* Consider adding an external member or entrepreneur in residence (EIR) who can help bring a fresh perspective to the portfolio.

- *Decision-making authority:* Include members who can make decisions with regard to approval and budget.

- *Entrepreneurial:* While members do not necessarily have to have a history of entrepreneurship, they need to be willing to challenge the status quo. Too many conservative members will prematurely stunt the growth of new innovations.

Create a Working Agreement

Once assembled, create a working agreement for the committee before inviting teams to present their recommendations. As a team, write down and agree upon rules such as:

- *Be on time:* Members have busy schedules, but they have to prioritize the stakeholder review ceremonies, otherwise teams will be left wondering if their initiatives are important.

- *Make decisions in the meeting:* Teams should not leave the review wondering if they can move forward. Decide with the teams present before adjourning.

- *Leave ego at the door:* Have an opinion in the review but be willing to be swayed by evidence. The teams will be bringing what experiments they ran and how to move forward. It is your job to listen, not talk over them.

Foster an Environment

This committee is in part responsible for fostering the team environment we introduced on page 10.

Without your help, the teams will not be able to sustain over time even if they are cross-functional and exhibit the right behaviors.

As a committee, have a plan to revisit how you are helping the team with obstacles centered on:

- Time.
- Multitasking.
- Funding.
- Support.
- Access.
- Direction.

After

word

Glossary

Action
Next step to progress with testing and de-risking a business idea; informed decision to abandon, pivot, iterate, or continue testing.

Affinity sorting
An exercise used to organize ideas and data in which ideas are sorted into groups or themes based on their relationships.

Assumption
A statement or fact that we believe to be true; a statement in which we take something for granted without any evidence to support it.

Assumptions mapping
A team exercise where desirability, viability, and feasibility assumptions are explicitly written down and then decided upon.

Business Model
Rationale of how an organization creates, delivers, and captures value.

B2B
Business to business; exchange of products or services between businesses.

B2C
Business to consumer; exchange of products or services between businesses and consumers.

Business Model Canvas
Strategic management tool to design, test, build, and manage (profitable and scalable) business models.

Call to action (CTA)
Prompts a subject to perform an action; used in an experiment in order to test one or more hypotheses.

Conversion
When a customer interacts with your ad and then takes an action that is valuable to your business.

CSAT
Short for customer satisfaction.

Customer development
Four-step process invented by Steve Blank to reduce risk and uncertainty in entrepreneurship by continuously testing the hypotheses underlying a business model with customers and stakeholders.

Customer gains
Outcomes and benefits customers must have, expect, desire, or dream to achieve.

Customer insight
Minor or major breakthrough in your customer understanding helping you design better value propositions and business models.

Customer pains

Bad outcomes, risks, and obstacles that customers want to avoid, notably because they prevent them from getting a job done (well).

Customer Profile

Business tool that constitutes the right-hand side of the Value Proposition Canvas. Visualizes the jobs, pains, and gains of a customer segment (or stakeholder) for whom you intend to create value.

Daily Standup

A short, daily organizational meeting meant to make the team aware of the project status; derived from the Agile Method.

Desirability

Do your customers want your product or service? Having evidence that customers desire a solution to the problem your value proposition is targeting.

Distributed team

A team that is spread across geographical locations; remote.

Dot voting

Participants vote by placing a "dot" or a sticker next to the options they prefer, using a limited number of stickers (dotmocracy or multi-voting).

Environment map

Strategic foresight tool to map the context in which you design and manage value propositions and business models.

Ethnography

The study of people in everyday life and practice.

Evidence

Data generated from an experiment or collected in the field. Proves or disproves a (business) hypothesis, customer insight, or belief about a value proposition, business model, or the environment.

Experiment

A procedure to validate or invalidate a value proposition or business model hypothesis that produces evidence. A procedure to reduce risk and the uncertainty of a business idea.

Feasibility

Can you build your product or service? Having the resources and infrastructure to build your product or service.

Fidelity

The degree to which the prototype accurately reproduces the product or service. Level of detail and functionality within the prototype.

Fit

When the elements of your Value Map meet relevant jobs, pains, and gains of your customer segment and a substantial number of customers "hire" your value proposition to satisfy those jobs, pains, and gains.

Gain creators

Describes how products and services create gains and help customers achieve the outcomes and benefits they require, expect, desire, or dream of by getting a job done (well).

Hypothesis

A belief drawn from a strategy, business model, or value proposition that needs to be true for your idea to work partially or fully but that hasn't been validated yet.

Iterative approach

The process of repeating a cycle in order to bring a result closer to discovery with every repetition.

Ideation

The process of generating and communicating ideas in a group session.

Jobs to be done

What customers need, want, or desire to get done in their work and in their lives.

KPIs (Key Performance Indicators)
Measurable value that demonstrates how effectively you are achieving your targets for success.

Lean Startup
Approach by Eric Ries based on the Customer Development process to eliminate waste and uncertainty from product development by continuously building, testing, and learning in an iterative fashion.

Learning Card
Strategic learning tool to capture insights from research and experiments.

Metrics
A quantifiable measurement used to track and assess.

Minimum Viable Product (MVP)
A model of a value proposition designed specifically to validate or invalidate one or more hypotheses.

Pain Relievers
Describes how products and services alleviate customer pains by eliminating or reducing bad outcomes, risks, and obstacles that prevent customers from getting a job done (well).

Products and Services
The items that your value proposition is based on that your customers can see in your shop window — metaphorically speaking.

Progress Board
Strategic management tool to manage and monitor the business model and value proposition design process and track progress towards a successful value proposition and business model.

Prototyping (low/high fidelity)
The practice of building quick, inexpensive, and rough study models to learn about the desirability, feasibility, and viability of alternative value propositions and business models.

Solopreneur
Abbreviation for Solo Entrepreneur (building a business on your own).

Stakeholder
Someone with a legitimate interest, can affect or be affected by your business.

Team Map
A visual tool created by Stefano Mastrogiacomo to boost alignment among team members for more effective meetings and conversations.

Test Card
Strategic testing tool to design and structure your research and experiments.

Time Box
A set period of time in which a task must be completed, derived from the Agile Method.

Validate
To confirm that a hypothesis is legitimate, well-grounded, or justifiable.

Value Map
Business tool that constitutes the left-hand side of the Value Proposition Canvas. Makes explicit how your products and services create value by alleviating pains and creating gains.

Value Proposition
Describes the benefits customers can expect from your products and services.

Value Proposition Canvas
Strategic management tool to design, test, build, and manage products and services. Fully integrates with the Business Model Canvas.

Value Proposition Design
The process of designing, testing, building, and managing value propositions over their entire lifecycle.

Viability
Can we make a profit from our product or service? Having evidence that you can generate more revenue than costs from your product or service.

Acknowledgments

This book would have been impossible to create without the love and support of my wife, Elizabeth. She's been my rock throughout the years and continues to provide encouragement for me on this journey. Our kids have been amazing during this writing process, providing me with love and time to focus. So to Catherine, Isabella, and James: I thank you for cheering me on. I'm lucky to be a father to such amazing kids.

I want to thank my coauthor Alex Osterwalder. He provided excellent guidance and insights throughout the entire book. It has been my pleasure and honor to have him be a part of this ambitious endeavor. I'd also like to thank Alan Smith and the entire Strategyzer team for putting in long hours and weekends creating such a beautifully designed book.

Testing Business Ideas is written from the viewpoint that we are standing on the shoulders of giants. To all of those who have influenced my thinking over the years, in small ways and in large, it is only because of you that this book exists. You were brave enough to put your thoughts out there for others to see.

I want to thank all of you who continue to push these ideas forward in practice: Eric Ries, Steve Blank, Jeff Gothelf, Josh Seiden, Giff Constable, Janice Fraser, Jason Fraser, Ash Maurya, Laura Klein, Christina Wodtke, Brant Cooper, Patrick Vlaskovits, Kate Rutter, Tendayi Viki, Barry O'Reilly, Melissa Perri, Jeff Patton, Sam McAfee, Teresa Torres, Marty Cagan, Sean Ellis, Tristan Kromer, Tom Looy, and Kent Beck.

A book can feel like a very large batch waterfall process. We did our best to test our content as we iterated along the way. I want to thank everyone who helped proofread and provided feedback early on. Your insights helped shape the book into what it is today.

— *David J. Bland 2019*

AUTHOR
David J. Bland
Founder, Advisor, Speaker

COAUTHOR
Alex Osterwalder
Founder, Speaker, Business Thinker

DESIGN LEAD
Alan Smith
Founder, Explorer, Designer

336

David J. Bland is an advisor, author and founder who lives in the San Francisco Bay Area. In 2015, he created Precoil to help companies find product market fit using lean startup, design thinking and business model innovation. He has helped validate new products and services at companies all around the world. Prior to advising, David spent over 10 years of his career scaling technology startups. He continues to give back to the startup community by teaching at several startup accelerators in Silicon Valley.

@davidjbland
precoil.com

In 2015 Alex won the strategy award by Thinkers50, called the "Oscars of Management Thinking" by the FT, and currently ranks #7 among the leading business thinkers of the world.

He is a frequent keynote speaker at Fortune 500 companies and has held guest lectures in top universities around the world, including Wharton, Stanford, Berkeley, IESE, MIT, KAUST, and IMD. Alex works regularly with senior executives from leading companies such as Bayer, Bosch, WL Gore, and Fortune 500 companies such as Mastercard on projects related to strategy and innovation.

@AlexOsterwalder
strategyzer.com/blog

Alan uses his curiousity and creativity to ask questions and turn the answers into simple, visual, practical tools. He believes that the right tools give people confidence to aim high and build big meaningful things.

He cofounded Strategyzer with Alex Osterwalder, where he works with an inspired team on product. Strategyzer's books, tools, and services are used by leading companies around the world.

strategyzer.com

DESIGN LEAD

Trish Papadakos

Designer, Photographer, Creator

Trish holds a Masters in Design from Central St. Martins in London and a Bachelor of Design from the York Sheridan Joint Program in Toronto.

She has taught design at her alma mater, worked with award-winning agencies, launched several businesses, and is collaborating for the fourth time with the Strategyzer team.

@trishpapadakos

ADDITIONAL DESIGN

Chris White

Editorial Designer

Alan and Trish would like to thank Chris for hopping on and providing significant extra muscle near the finish line to help make this project a success.

ILLUSTRATION

Owen Pomery

Narrative illustration

Deep thanks to Owen for his patience and willingness to iterate to communicate the right ideas.

owenpomery.com

ICON DESIGN

b Farias

Contributor

Icons: team, light bulb, report abuse, flask, visible, gear, telescope, checkbox, cross bones, destination, paper note, dashboard, like, clipboard, charty pie, chemistry book, map pin, trophy, and graduate hat by b farias from the Noun Project.

thenounproject.com/bfarias

Strategyzer uses the best of technology and coaching to support your transformation and growth challenges.

Discover what we can do for you at Strategyzer.com

TRANSFORMATION
Create Change
*Skill building at the Strategyzer
Cloud Academy course library.*

Build value for customers, value for
your business, testing your ideas,
and an in-depth experiment library.

GROWTH
Create Growth
*Systematize and scale your
growth efforts.*

Growth strategy, innovation
readyness assessment, innovation
funnel design, sprints, and metrics.

Index

D

F

345

T